WALFRID

AND

The Bould Bhoys!

Celtic's Founding Fathers, First Season & Early Stars

LIAM KELLY | DAVID POTTER | MATT CORR

THE CELTIC STAR

Walfrid & the Bould Bhoys
by Liam Kelly, David Potter & Matt Corr

Published by The Celtic Star in cooperation
with Matt Corr Media.

First Published in the UK in 2020 by The Celtic Star.

ISBN 978-1-8380207-1-2

A catalogue for this book is available from
the British Library and the Irish Library in Dublin.

Cover & page design and typesetting by Stephen Cameron.

Publisher - David Faulds: email editor@thecelticstar.co.uk

Printed by CPI Group (UK) Ltd, Croydon CR0 4YY

CONTENTS

Acknowledgements

A few words of thanks from your authors...

To all those involved in the labour of love which has produced Walfrid & The Bould Bhoys

David Faulds for creating the project design and team and for writing the foreword

The Celtic Star and Matt Corr Media for editorial and publishing input

Stephen Cameron for his book design expertise

Niall J for his work on the Dan Drake article

CPI Group (UK) Ltd for binding and print services

To those wonderful Celts whose research creates such invaluable reference sources, such as The Celtic Wiki

To our families, for your continued patience and support whilst we live our dreams

And to all the Celtic supporters across the globe...

...where do we start?

There can be no other football club in the world whose history is devoured, shared, cherished then handed down through the generations of the Celtic family, so that our children and grandchildren can recall and recite the great names and events of the past, with the same knowledge and passion as for those they witnessed in the flesh.

Without that appetite, that thirst for Celtic knowledge, there is no point to carrying out the many hours of research.

There would be no book.

We hope you enjoy the fruits of that research, as you take a trip back to the early days of the magical thing that is the Celtic Football Club.

Visit - https://thecelticstar.com
Shop - https://thecelticstarbookstore.co.uk

Foreword

Walfrid & The Bould Bhoys

is the second book published by The Celtic Star in 2020.

Matt Corr's 'INVINCIBLE' set the bar very high. It really was the perfect way to re-tell the story of the most remarkable season in Celtic's history since Jock Stein's side cleared up in 1966-67. Those two seasons will always be remembered but perhaps the most important season in Celtic's long, impressive and unbroken history was the very first one. Brendan Sweeney, in his definitive 'Celtic, The Early Years,' provided a remarkable insight into the formation of a football club in the East End of Glasgow and proved that there is a tremendous appetite among the Celtic support for the history of the club. At The Celtic Star, we always strive to, perhaps more than any other site, re-tell the stories of the past that have all combined to make our club so unique, so special and so incredible.

And in assembling this book, Walfrid & The Bould Bhoys, The Celtic Star's own formidable team sheet was brought into action, spanning three separate generations of Celtic supporters. All three co-authors are published authors in their own right.

The 'young team' is represented by Liam Kelly, who published 'Our Stories & Our Songs' in 2015 and followed that up last year with 'Take Me to Your Paradise.' In Walfrid & The Bould Bhoys, Liam's focus is on a set of individuals who collectively deserve to be known as The Celtic Founding Fathers. Brother Walfrid is, of course, the best known among this group but there are many other men who played a crucial role and without their input, there might not have been a Celtic for us to adore.

Matt Corr, the author of 'INVINCIBLE', represents the middle-aged Celtic support and is a popular member of the Stadium Tours team at Celtic Park. In Walfrid & The Bould Bhoys, Matt takes us month-by-month through the first year of Celtic, from the clubs first-ever match to Celtic's first trophy win, 12 months that shaped Celtic at a time when we were the 'new club' in Glasgow. How times have changed.

Then there's the fascinating contribution from Dan Drake, a Celtic supporter who attended Celtic's first-ever match, and 132 years after the final whistle was featured on The Celtic Star, on 28 May 2020. Niall J, another of the team on The Celtic Star, transcribed an interview with Dan that first appeared in The Celtic View in 1972 and provides this book with a marvellous 'stepping stone' from the present back to 1972 and, from there, back through a lifetime of supporting the club to the very first kick of a ball for a team calling itself Celtic Football Club.

The third author is the respected club historian and veteran Celtic supporter David Potter, who has been a contributor on The Celtic Star since the site started. David has written scores of wonderfully informative Celtic books and these will be valued for generations of supporters to come. In Walfrid & The Bould Bhoys, David concentrates his attention on the early Celtic heroes. The players who the supporters adored in those early years, players that Dan Drake would have worshipped as a boy, a teenager then a young adult.

A word about The Celtic Wiki, the reference site for all things Celtic that is so invaluable to so many supporters in general, and Celtic writers in particular. I doubt there is a resource such as this at any club in world football and it has been created by Celtic Supporters, for Celtic Supporters and driven by one thing and one thing only, the love of Celtic.

Overleaf is the extract from that piece by Niall J, which appeared on The Celtic Star on 28 May 2020, fittingly, on the anniversary of Celtic's first-ever game.

It is a wonderful, first-hand insight to the very early days of Celtic Football Club, and, therefore, will provide the perfect appetiser for the chapters that follow from Liam Kelly, Matt Corr and David Potter, in Walfrid & The Bould Bhoys.

Hail Hail!

David Faulds
Editor, The Celtic Star

9

DAN DRAKE: AN EYE-WITNESS ACCOUNT OF CELTIC'S FIRST GAME

Having read David Potter's fine article on Joe Baillie and the 1951 cup-winning team, I was left feeling rather melancholic. In particular, the part where David stated:

"There must now, one fears, be very few 'survivors' of that 1951 Scottish Cup final – one of them is the great Celtic historian Tom Campbell – but the players have now all gone, as indeed have most of the 134,000 crowd."

After reading David's article, I started looking at Celtic's first-ever game, 132 years ago today. Initially, I was just looking for a match report, when I came across this brilliant article on the Celtic Wiki, from a supporter who was at that very first game, a 5-2 win over Rangers, or Rangers Swifts, depending on where you read it or who you choose to believe. The supporter's name was Dan Drake, and he was 94 years old when The Celtic View interviewed him in 1972.

According to Frank Rafters in his book 'Uniquely Celtic', Dan was one of six children. Born in 1878, unlike his siblings who were all born in Glasgow, Dan is recorded as being born in England, though no exact details of location are given. The 1891 census has him living in Anderston, though the particular area where he lived is no more, having been replaced by motorway. Dan is recorded as living in Maryhill in the next couple of decades and the 1911 census - after Celtic had won six consecutive league titles - has Dan recorded as working as a tailor, while living with his mother and sister following the death of his father.

Mr Drake was a 10-year-old boy when his Dad took him and his brother to that historic game. Here is what he had to say in that brilliant interview. Thank you once again to the brilliant Celtic Wiki site, where one can find the Celtic View clippings of the original interview.

10

The article below was published in The Celtic View in the summer of 1972, under the heading;

'Our very first game and the man who saw it.'

Dan Drake is an alert and fit-looking man of 94 who can remember the first Celtic games of 1888 and enjoys talking about them.

Mr Drake was a boy of 10 when his father took him and his brother to see Celtic play their first game as a club.

"My father didn't know the first thing about football," Mr Drake said, "but my brother and I were keen, and my father took us to see the Celts to encourage our interest in the sport."

Sitting in a room of the Home run by the Little Sisters of the Poor at Roystonhill in Glasgow, Mr Drake, who must be one of Celtic's oldest supporters, warmed to his favourite subject.

He said:

"You used to go down Dalmarnock Street to the old Celtic ground (Barr's Lemonade occupy the site now behind Janefield Cemetery) and although it wasn't very big, it held several thousand spectators quite comfortably. As a matter of fact, although the park had a small stand, many of the more able fans climbed on to the cemetery boundary wall for a better view of the matches."

"At the time, the site of the present Celtic Park was a large piece of waste ground with a huge crater in the middle which was about 30 or forty feet deep."

"In those days there was no Scottish League competition. The programme, apart from cup ties, was filled up with game against famous English sides like the Corinthians, [Birmingham] Mitchell's St George, Bolton Wanderers and Burnley."

"Celtic were founded to provide charity, but no-one can really appreciate just how successful they were in those very hard times. They also gave an interest to the down-trodden Irish community in Glasgow, who were able to identify themselves with the uphill fight of the club."

11

Speaking of the players in that first game, Mr Drake said they came from all over the country, but they combined as though they had played football together for years.

In the first game, Celtic beat Rangers 5-2 before a crowd of about 2,000 spectators. But it was as he spoke of great individuals that Mr Drake really got into his stride.

He said:

"Peter Dowds was about the best half-back I ever saw play, but my upstanding memory of a Celtic half-back line was that of Willie Maley, James Kelly and Paddy Gallagher (not to be confused with Patsy Gallagher). That was the half-back line in the Celtic team of 1892 that won the Scottish Cup, Glasgow Cup, [Glasgow] Charity Cup and finished runners up in the Scottish League Championship, which had just started the previous year."

"Other outstanding players I remember included Willie Groves, who was a great ball player and James McLaren, a left-half from Hibernian known as 'the General'. Mickey McKeown, Neilly McCallum and Johnny Madden were other great players I remember. Talking of Johnny Madden, he went to Prague at the beginning of the century and became a national figure as a result of his wonderful coaching of footballers."

"The great thing about the Celtic teams was their ability to play football on the ground. They combined so well in their passing that people who disliked them said they needed a carpet to play football."

"One problem Celtic had in the beginning was finding a really good goalkeeper, but that was solved with the arrival of Dan McArthur. He was on the small side but his timing and agility more than made up for his lack of height. Although most people consider John Thomson to have been the greatest Celtic goalkeeper of all time, I think Thomson and McArthur were so outstanding you couldn't say one was better than the other."

"The best full-back partnership was that of Jerry Reynolds and Dan Doyle, though strangely enough they were very different types of players. Reynolds could head a ball as far as most players could kick it, and Doyle could kick a long ball with deadly accuracy. Doyle used to be a torment to opposition players when taking free kicks. He could hit the ball right into the opponents' penalty area from his own half of the field, but if anyone moved, as he ran to hit the ball, he just stopped dead and started his run all over again. This seemed to have an unsettling effect on defences."

"I also remember with joy the great left-wing partnership of Sandy McMahon and Johnny Campbell, who each seemed instinctively to know what the other was going to do. Celtic had, in fact, signed the Benburb left-wing of Barney Crossan and Campbell but Crossan couldn't oust McMahon from the inside left spot. In the middle nineties, however, Crossan won a Scottish Cup medal with the now-defunct St Bernards, whom he had joined from Celtic."

According to Mr Drake, Celtic's other outstanding quality was their tremendous fighting spirit, a quality which has remained with the club since their early difficult days. One great example of this, he remembers, was in a Glasgow Cup final against Rangers at [First] Cathkin Park. Celtic lost Willie Maley and Sandy McMahon through injury, but the team rolled up their sleeves and won by two goals to nil.

Mr Drake hasn't seen Celtic now for about two years, but he thinks the club's success is attributable to three main qualities. Good football, the will to win, and discipline on and off the park.

"What Willie Maley did for half a century," he said, "has been carried on by Jimmy McGrory and Jock Stein and, judging by the players they've got at present, Mr Stein can go on adding successes to those he has already won."

"Considering all the things that have happened in Celtic's history, I think the greatest triumph of all has just been completed - winning seven League Championships in succession."

"I don't think I'll see that feat equalled in my lifetime," concluded Mr Drake, with a suspicion of a smile. *[The Celtic View article ends]*

Dan Drake passed away in 1976 at the age of 97. Alongside attending that first-ever match, he witnessed Celtic lift the European Cup, as well as seeing the completion of that first 9-in-a-row, and everything in between.

It would, of course, have been fascinating to listen to his stories, but having Mr Drake's thoughts on attending that first game as a wide-eyed 10-year-old, and his description of the players who entertained the early Celtic support, is a wonderful record to have.

When Celtic won 9-in-a-row for the second time, I wondered just what my grandfather would have made of it all. When Rangers won their nine titles, he said:

"Who remembers the second man to climb Everest?"

I liked that. What would he and Dan Drake think about Celtic going for a record-breaking 10 consecutive titles, I wonder? Something tells me there would be comparisons made to teams from the past. It would be wonderful to hear their thoughts.

At least we have Dan Drake's interview from 1972.

What a fine record to have.

Niall J
The Celtic Star

Section 1:

CELTIC'S FOUNDING FATHERS

By Liam Kelly

Most Celtic supporters could tell you that the club was founded for charitable purposes and that an Irishman named Brother Walfrid was involved in forming the club. The fact that a statue of the great Marist stands outside Celtic Park today only confirms that understanding. However, sadly, many are not aware that there were at least 20 other individuals involved in establishing Celtic Football Club, whilst many more donated funds as original subscribers in response to the following circular:

The main objective of the Celtic Football Club is to supply the East End conferences of the St Vincent De Paul Society with funds for the maintenance of the Dinner Tables of our needy children in the missions of St. Mary's, Sacred Heart and St. Michael's. Many cases of sheer poverty are left unaided through lack of means. It is therefore with this principle object that we have set afloat the Celtic, and we invite you as one of our ever-ready friends to assist in putting our new park in proper working order the coming football season.

Unquestionably, Brother Walfrid was the key behind the club's formation. However, it is often overlooked that Celtic would not exist without the assistance of at least 20 other men. Those founding fathers have largely been forgotten, yet they too shaped the history, culture and identity of the Celts. Without their entrepreneurship, religious and political memberships, or professional contacts, the club would not exist today as we know it.

To identify a founding father is not an exact science. Of course, such a person must have been involved with the Celtic project prior to the establishment of the club and must have been part of the group of individuals responsible for setting it afloat.

These individuals, who were Roman Catholic to a man and almost entirely of Irish origin, brought their own values, skillsets and endeavour to make the club what it was and what it has grown to be.

In a time when the Irish community and people of the Catholic faith faced many challenges and outright poverty in Glasgow, these men defied the odds. They succeeded in business, education, and entrepreneurship. They immersed themselves in the church, politics and charity. There were lawyers, clergymen, pawnbrokers, politicians, teachers, academics, charity leaders, trade union organisers, Irish Republican revolutionaries, publicans, engineers, and musicians.

Some consider the likes of Willie and Tom Maley, Stephen J Henry and Timothy Walls to be founding fathers. However, in my opinion at least, there is not sufficient evidence of them playing an active role in forming the club, despite their early presence on Celtic committees. All would play their part in due course.

I have identified those covered in this section of the book as unambiguous founding fathers.

Together, the following 21 people shared a common vision.

This is their story.

Chapter 1:

PAT WELSH: THE TAILOR WHO SUITED THE CELTS

The story of Patrick Welsh is one of both intrigue and importance, in terms of the history of Celtic. Welsh was born in the town of Killargue, County Leitrim, in 1848. He grew up to become a Fenian activist, and it was his political action that eventually entwined him with the club.

The tale has its beginnings in the 1867 Fenian Uprising. The Fenian Brotherhood had been founded by Irish immigrants in the USA, less than a decade after the great famine. Its ranks were bolstered by the emergence of the American Civil War, in which thousands of Irishmen had taken part, fighting on both sides of the Union/Confederate divide. The experiences that had been gained in the battlefield encouraged a swell of volunteers to enlist with the Fenian movement, the organisation's name deriving from the 'Fianna' – a legendary band of warriors in the realm of Gaelic mythology. The Brotherhood's leadership wasted no time in attempting to strike a blow for Irish freedom, when, in 1866, they carried out a series of unsuccessful raids in Canada (then under British rule). The aim of the raids was to seize the transportation network of the country, with the ambition that this would force the British to exchange Ireland's independence for possession of their Province of Canada.

The Irish Republican Brotherhood (Irish-based counterpart of the Fenian Brotherhood, known as the IRB) soon decided to mount a militant insurrection of their own. The decision was taken following considerable unrest within the Nationalist community, which had largely been instigated by the suppression of The Irish People newspaper: the voice of the IRB.

17

The Rising of early 1867 was initially stifled, due to a combination of poor planning and British infiltration. However, the latter stages of the year saw resurgent efforts, in the form of a dynamite campaign and a series of raids.

A youthful Patrick Welsh participated in this effort, which, although ultimately unsuccessful in a military sense, led to the establishment of the Amnesty Association, of which he later became Vice-President. The Association was a group set up by Isaac Butt, with the aim of gaining release from prison for the men of the Fenian Rising.

For his part in the rebellion, Welsh found himself on the run from the authorities in the latter stages of the year. One evening, he hid from security forces in Dublin at the docks in the vicinity of Pigeon House Fort, on the banks of the River Liffey. Welsh was hiding with the hope of boarding a ship bound for Scotland, however, he looked to his horror as he found himself being confronted by a British soldier wielding a rifle.

The soldier, who was on patrol with the North British Fusiliers Regiment, barked at Welsh: "Halt he who goes there?" Welsh instantly detected an Irish accent and pleaded, Irishman to Irishman, that he had no sinister intentions and only longed for a life of peace in Glasgow. The soldier, a County Clare man from Ennis, understood the plea, as he himself had previously left home to join the army in England. Thus, at considerable risk to himself, he led Welsh to the appropriate ship. Before parting, the pair exchanged names. The name of the soldier: Thomas Maley.

Once in Glasgow, Pat Welsh served an apprenticeship as a tailor, before becoming a master in the trade, owning a renowned business on Buchanan Street. The Irishman immersed himself in the local community and built some sound relationships within his local parish of St Mary's.

Enjoying his fruitful new life, the runaway Fenian maintained appreciation for the soldier who had granted his freedom. Indeed, the pair always kept in touch, and after Thomas Maley had completed 21 years of active service with the British Army, he informed Welsh that he had started to view the prospect of life in Glasgow as a notion much more appealing than attempting to raise a young family where he had been stationed, in an Ireland that was still suffering from the effects of the famine.

Approaching his discharge from the army in 1869, on the invitation of Welsh, Thomas Maley and his young family headed to Glasgow, where his Canadian-born wife's parents hailed from. Welsh was glad to be of assistance to the Maley clan, and agreed to see to their housing in St Mary's parish until such a time that Thomas found new employment. Thomas soon found a job, appointed Drill Instructor of the 3rd Renfrewshire Rifle Volunteers at Thornliebank.

The former Sergeant's sons, Tom and Willie (the latter being born in an army barracks in Newry prior to their move), embedded themselves into city life. Both had a keen interest in sport, becoming respected footballers, whilst Willie also earned the title of the 100 Yard Scottish Sprinting champion.

The aforementioned events proved to be of great import, when Pat Welsh was among the committee that founded Celtic Football Club in late 1887. During a preliminary meeting between the founding fathers, the name of Tom Maley was raised as a possible player that Celtic could attract the signature of. Welsh had vouched for the family and assured the committee that he would be an ideal fit for the club. Therefore, the decision was taken for Welsh to visit the Maley household in Cathcart, where Thomas (senior) had been transferred, with the accompaniment of fellow founders Brother Walfrid and John Glass.

It is thought that the Celtic delegation only held intention of securing the signature of Tom when they knocked the door, however, Tom was not at home. The Celtic trio then began to speak with Willie and asked that he would ensure that his brother contact them with a response to their proposition of him signing for the club. As the Celtic delegation left the premises, Walfrid turned to Willie and said: "Why don't you come along too?"

Although not of the same ability as his brother, who had featured on occasion for Hibernian, Willie had played for Third Lanark (3rd LRV) reserves. Once his modesty and doubts over a future in the game were shunned, Willie agreed to put pen to paper for Celtic Football Club immediately. Upon hearing of the visit, his brother Tom contacted the Celtic founders and agreed to join him at Celtic Park. It would prove to be the beginning of an enduring 52-year love affair between the Maleys and the Celts.

Pat Welsh himself went on to become Celtic's Match Secretary, which, perhaps ironically, was also a position that Willie Maley took up, the latter having been invited to do so due to his qualification as a chartered accountant.

Welsh also made his mark beyond the direct Hoops domain. He was a much-loved parishioner in St Mary's who was a member of a number of groups that held close ties with the club, including The League of the Cross, the local conference of the Saint Vincent De Paul Society, the Home Government branch of the Irish National League, and he was the leading organiser of the Connaught Reunion in Glasgow.

The following extract is taken from Patrick Welsh's obituary, which appeared in The Glasgow Observer on 12 August 1899:

'The funeral, which was a public one, took place on Sunday to Dalbeth. The cortege was a very large one, all the societies of the parish accompanying the remains to the cemetery.'

Chapter 2:

WILLIAM MCKILLOP: IRELAND'S GLASGOW MP

The results of the recent Irish election see a party with a radical stance on the constitutional question winning a majority of the vote for the first time in decades. Sinn Fein's largest victory in Ireland was in the 1918 election, when the party championed the cause of Irish Republicanism and sought total independence from Britain. Prior to that shift in the Irish political paradigm, largely brought about through the aftermath of the 1916 Easter Uprising and the conscription crisis of 1918, the contemporary cause of the day was Irish Home Rule. The Irish Parliamentary Party (IPP) advocated the Home Rule cause most vigorously and, indeed, its central objectives were legislative independence for Ireland and land reform.

These two objectives were also prevalent at Parkhead, in the years surrounding the club's foundation. One of the founding fathers, and the first person to ever kick a ball at Celtic Park, Dr John Conway, spoke at a reception held in St Mary's Church Hall to celebrate Hibernian's Scottish Cup triumph in 1887.

Conway was talking about establishing a football club for the Irish community in Glasgow, when he said: "Glasgow Irishmen, we can emulate the Hibernians example not only in social but in political matters as well, so that the goal of every Irishman's ambition – legislative independence of his country – will soon be attained."

Not only did Celtic come to fruition later that year, but the club would appoint the great land reformer, Michael Davitt, as its Patron. Michael Davitt was a convicted member of the Irish Republican Brotherhood, who co-founded the Irish National Land League and served as an MP for the Irish Parliamentary Party. As club Patron, Davitt was invited to lay the first sod of turf at the new Celtic Park in 1892.

The turf was imported from Donegal and was ceremoniously laid at the club's third annual sports day event, an event at which MP Timothy Daniel Sullivan also sang the famous Irish rebel song that he had penned about the Manchester Martyrs – God Save Ireland.

The focus of this chapter is on William McKillop MP, who had the most obvious political role of Celtic's founding committee, being a member of parliament, with ideals which tie into the prominence of Irish Nationalism (Sinn Fein's recent election victory).

William McKillop was born in Dalry, Ayrshire, in 1860. His parents, Daniel and Matilda, had emigrated from Glenarm in County Antrim, along with his brother John (fellow Celtic founding father), and seven other siblings in the mid-1850s. Sticking to the Celtic connection, John was a labourer at an iron works as a teenager in 1871, whilst William, six years his younger, was a cotton picker in a factory.

Fast forward a decade and the family had moved to the Gorbals, giving William and John an opportunity to commence a business venture as licensed grocers in the city. The business was a success, enabling William to buy the Royal Restaurant on West Nile Street and the pair to open the highly popular Grosvenor Hotel in 1899.

Despite being of Irish origin, the brothers won the catering contract for the Glasgow Exhibitions of 1901 and 1911, becoming two of the most famous businessmen in the city. William, like so many Celtic founding fathers, was key to the survival of the club in the early years. He had been on the club's first committee and was then elected Vice-President at the 1891 Annual General Meeting (AGM), ousting Belfast-born Francis McErlean after two years in the position. William also hosted a celebratory supper for the Glasgow Cup-winners in March 1891, when fellow founding father John Glass, to whom Willie Maley claims, "Celtic owe their existence," presented him with Celtic's first major trophy. Greater still, William McKillop was elected Honorary President of the club between 1893 and 1897.

While John McKillop looked after the pair's business, William immersed himself in Irish politics, and as Honorary President of Celtic, he received huge praise from Michael Davitt for his efforts in raising money for the Irish Parliamentary Fund. As a leaseholder and guarantor at Celtic, William was of the more business-minded club members and was, thus, a strong supporter of the limited liability proposal.

A heated exchange took place at the 1895 AGM, as the battle for the soul of Celtic was raging. The debate centred on the issue of club debts, measured against charitable donations, and William is thought to have responded to a request for charity by describing the question as "clap-trap."

After a long association with the Home Government branch of the Irish National League in Glasgow, William McKillop was asked by newly-elected party leader, John Redmond, to stand for the Irish Parliamentary Party as a candidate for North Sligo in 1900. It is thought that the request was made due to McKillop's financial prosperity, considering that MPs did not get paid in this era and thus needed to support themselves. Despite residing in Scotland, William obliged and was duly elected, unopposed, to the House of Commons as an Irish Nationalist MP. He held the seat for six years, when, for reasons unknown, he swapped seats and was elected MP for South Armagh. This South Armagh seat was returned unopposed, and was a seat that he held until 1909. Meanwhile, the successful politician had also become Treasurer of the Irish Parliamentary Party!

Due to the fact that so many people only seem to recognise Brother Walfrid as founding Celtic Football Club, William McKillop is perhaps best-known today for the still-famous McKillop Cup, which he donated to the Armagh Gaelic Athletic Association in March 1906. Indeed, the Armagh County Committee of the GAA accepted his offer to present a cup and set of medals for competition among Gaelic Football clubs in the county. The cup was made in Scotland and was described in the Dundalk Democrat, in 1907, as "a very valuable one" and "a triumph of the silversmith's art." Made of solid silver and weighing over 82 oz, the cup is over two feet high! The William McKillop Cup was first presented to the winners of the 1906–07 League, and, since 1931, it has been awarded to the county's Senior Championship winners. The

William McKillop Cup was retired by the Armagh GAA in 1995, after being replaced with the Gerry Fagan Cup, though it is still well known in GAA circles today.

Aside from his political, business and sporting interests, William McKillop married a Miss Fisher, who tragically died in 1892, after just a couple of years of marriage. He was not to re-marry until 1908, when he wed Rose Dalton, sister-in-law of Willie Redmond. Willie was an Irish Nationalist MP too, in his case from New South Wales, and was the brother of the IPP leader, John Redmond. Rose gave birth to the couple's only child, Margaret Mary, in May 1909, but by this time William McKillop was suffering from an illness which would eventually lead to his death three months later at the age of 49. Rose then took her daughter to Australia, where Willie Redmond lived and Margaret, or Peggy as she was later known, went on to become a pioneer in Australian aviation!

William McKillop's passing sent not only his family, Celtic Football Club and Armagh GAA into mourning, but it was also a loss felt by the entirety of Irish Nationalism, a cause to which he had dedicated his whole life.

His obituary in the oldest Nationalist newspaper in Dublin, The Freeman's Journal, was the epitome of this point. The publication described him as "a staunch Irish nationalist who took a lively interest in the Irish movement in Glasgow and was a leading member of the Home Government Branch, to which he always gave splendid financial support."

His funeral took place in Glasgow, and over 100 carriages made up the cortege as it headed from St Andrew's Cathedral to Dalbeth Cemetery. William is buried with his brother John.

Chapter 3:

JOHN GLASS: "THE MAN TO WHOM CELTIC OWES THEIR EXISTENCE"

Just as William McKillop's political life connected him to current affairs, the story of John Glass is equally relevant to recent news, as the Celtic View reported, in early 2020, that a painting of Glass has now been fully restored and is able to be viewed as part of the stadium tour at Celtic Park.

The painting was offered to the club by Mrs Coulter, the granddaughter of John Glass, in November 1946. It was then that Mrs Coulter wrote a letter to club manager, Jimmy McGrory, who put the matter before the board. In reply, McGrory broke the news that although the club was interested in the piece, they felt it was probably too big to be positioned in either the hall or the boardroom at Celtic Park, but that they would like a second look at the painting. Having reflected, the club thought better of it and decided to accept the gift.

The news of its restoration and return to display at Paradise is something that should please all with an enthusiasm for the club's history. After all, in Willie Maley's book, 'The Story of The Celtic,' John Glass is accredited as "the man to whom Celtic FC owes its very existence." Indeed, without diminishing the roles of other founding fathers, it could well be argued that Brother Walfrid was the main man responsible for founding Celtic Football Club, whilst Glass was the man who established it.

It was Glass who, together with Brother Walfrid and Patrick Welsh, brought Maley to the club, as referenced in the previous chapter, which focused on Welsh. Yet, Glass' role in the Celtic story carries much more significance than that.

John Glass was born in 1851, at the Broomielaw, in one of the poorest slums in Glasgow. He hailed from proud Donegal stock, his parents having fled Ireland to escape the devastation of An Gorta Mor, often referred to as 'the famine.' A glazier by trade, John took up employment as general manager of his brother's (Peter) successful wood merchant and builder's business in the Gallowgate. The business employed many of the city's Irish population, which inspired Glass to meet regularly with Dr John Conway and Brother Walfrid, to discuss ways of tackling the poverty that surrounded them, particularly within the Irish community.

As a strong and stocky individual, Glass is said to have possessed a presence and sense of authority which was impossible to ignore. These qualities were invaluable when he became Celtic's first President, Brother Walfrid's right-hand man and, ultimately, the man who made things happen for the club. He worked day and night to ensure that Celtic had a stadium and team good enough to prosper, and so devoted to the Celtic cause was Glass that he never missed a single committee meeting from the club's inception in 1887 to his death in 1906!

In Brendan Sweeney's book, 'Celtic: The Early Years,' Glass is described as "THE politician around the table at the time of Celtic's formation." This comment stems from the fact that Glass held many prominent roles within Glasgow's Irish Catholic community. He led the Catholic Union Committee - a body set up to contest local school board elections - he was also the President and Secretary of the St Mary's League of the Cross and the Treasurer of the Home Government Branch of the Irish National League, with whom he campaigned tirelessly for Irish Home Rule.

John Glass used his contacts in the building trade to obtain materials and enlist volunteers to assist Patrick Gaffney with his task of building the first Celtic Park in 1888. Such was his charisma and persuasion, that he was the man, more than any other, who convinced various players, particularly from Hibernian, to join the club.

The quote previously alluded to, from Willie Maley's book, explains this point well:

John Glass is the man to whom the club owes its existence, as he never shirked from that time till the day of his death to further the project which to him appealed as his life work. He was a great Irishman, ever ready to stand up for his rights and, later, did much politically for the cause so dear to him. These were not the days of written agreements, and John Glass' word was always as good as any bond. For years, he thought of nothing but Celtic. It was thanks to Glass that the organisation fulfilled the object which the first committee set out to make good; to prove that Irishmen could build a club as good as anyone.

Glass gave the players who joined Celtic a stable job, which was something that the likes of Hibernian were reluctant to do. For many of the early Celtic greats, Glass gave them proprietorship of public houses, a source of payment in the days before professionalism in Scottish football. Of this notion, Glass was a pioneer in Scotland. He had observed the development of professionalism in English football, and correctly predicted that Scotland would follow suit. Hibernian took a different approach, attempting to preserve the amateur game and stick to their 'Catholic-only' signing policy. Celtic, under the influence of Glass, adapted and made the aforementioned unofficial forms of payment through his businesses and contacts. The club also signed an Orangeman to play in goal during its second season, showing its inclusive credentials very early on.

The importance of Celtic's progression was key. Celtic was one of an estimated 40 Irish football clubs in Scotland at the time. Most failed to survive, including at least two other clubs that were also named Celtic! The foresight and financial support of people like John Glass enabled Celtic to maintain its competition with the establishment clubs of the time, such as Queen's Park, who treated Irish-influenced clubs with much disdain and, indeed, refused to sign players of Irish Catholic extraction. Thus, the involvement of those like John Glass, after the founding of the club, was essential in terms of allowing the initial ideas of the likes of Brother Walfrid to come to fruition.

His finest hour in the battle for the club's survival was when he persuaded James Kelly to join Celtic on 28 May 1888. That same day, Kelly scored in Celtic's first-ever match, a 5-2 victory against Rangers at the original Celtic Park! James Kelly was an exceptional talent who had been capped for Scotland, and his capture was a star signing, ensuring that an early interest was generated in Celtic Football Club. Enticing a player of this calibre to a fledgling Irish club was not easy, particularly when faced with stiff competition from more established clubs of the type such as Hibernian.

Glass and his committee made it a priority that the most important aspect was the team on the pitch and the legendary Kelly was granted the honour of being Celtic's first captain. It was famously said that, had Celtic not signed James Kelly, then it could have ended up a case of "No Kelly, No Keltic!"

Speaking of the club name, there is a theory that Glass may have been involved in the choosing of 'Celtic'. Glass and an Ulster Protestant named John Ferguson, who moved to Scotland and campaigned for Irish Home Rule, organised several political rallies at which Michael Davitt (Celtic's Patron) addressed the Highland crofters. The theory goes that the name 'Celtic' may have originated from this popular political influence of the day, and that Brother Walfrid and John Glass may have seen this name as a suitable way to celebrate Ireland and Scotland. This is purely speculation though, and others suggest there is no evidence of Celtic having anything other than an Irish Catholic identity in its formative year.

One point of contention on John Glass is his involvement in the events surrounding the club's cessation of donations to the Poor Children's Dinner Table, and its move towards professionalism. Whilst Glass is said to have called those in favour of prioritising charity "Soup kitchen cranks," and "Dinner table sore heads," it should also be noted that the club were in debt and Glass stated that once the debts were cleared then the club would be "Only too willing to do whatever it could to assist the charities mentioned."

Those on the opposing side of the argument referenced the fact that the club's board of directors, after becoming a limited company, consisted of six wine and spirit merchants and a builder's merchant (John Glass), by naming the board "Six publicans – only one Glass."

John Glass died on 2 June 1906. His legacy lives on in the sense that without him, there would be no Celtic, and for that reason it is criminal that his story is not better known. He is laid to rest at Dalbeth Cemetery in Glasgow's East End.

His greatest quote should, in my opinion, be on the walls of Celtic Park as a permanent tribute.

After all, it is more relevant now than ever before:

"Let them scoff and jeer. Celtic will yet win to their proper position by their merits and those who scoff today will one day have to applaud!"

Chapter 4:

BROTHER DOROTHEUS: WALFRID'S RIGHT-HAND MAN

One of the two Marist Brothers behind Celtic's formation, Brother Dorotheus was Brother Walfrid's friend and confrere.

Born Henry Currie in Dundee in 1855, Dorotheus trained as a pupil teacher under the Marist Brothers for three years at St. Mary's Forebank, in his home city, before heading for pastures new in July 1874, when he joined the Dumfries Novitiate. Making his Vow of Obedience two years later, Dorotheus then taught at St. Joseph's College in Dumfries for just shy of 12 months.

Having plied his trade in Dundee and Dumfries, Dorotheus was transferred to Glasgow, where he began teaching at St Mungo's. Only in the post a short while, his qualities shone through, and Brother Dorotheus was promptly appointed as the headmaster of St Mary's Catholic School on Abercromby Street in the Calton.

Whilst Dorotheus was the head of St Mary's, Brother Walfrid was sent to the same school as a teacher. Brother Dorotheus spotted the undoubted talents of the Sligo man, some 15 years his senior, and encouraged him in all of his external charitable endeavours. The pair became great friends, particularly when Brother Walfrid was given his own school to manage, with the opening of the new Sacred Heart in the Glengarry area of Bridgeton.

Walfrid continued to work closely with his confrere, Brother Dorotheus. Taking over a disused blacksmith's in the school yard, Dorotheus set up the Penny Dinner Scheme for pupils at St. Mary's, Walfrid having done likewise for Sacred Heart. As the year progressed, the scheme's success grew to such an extent that it became challenging to continue to satisfy the increasing demand, and so other initiatives would require to be explored to sustain benefit for the children.

Football would provide that solution.

In May 1886, Brother Walfrid held what is believed to be one of his first major footballing fundraisers, when Dundee Harp faced Clyde at Barrowfield Park. The hosting of these friendly matches at Barrowfield, Clyde's home on French Street, off Dalmarnock Road, initially involved local teams established by Walfrid and future founding father, John Glass. After this, the biggest Scottish clubs of the day took part, with the matches sometimes being held at Glengarry Park in Bridgeton. Teams such as James Kelly's Renton pitting their wits against national Cup holders Hibernian, an event which drew a crowd of 12,000, would build on the early success of the Penny Dinner Scheme initiatives within the local community and would sow the seeds which would lead to the eventual establishment of Celtic Football Club.

Walfrid was the organiser, the one with the ideas behind the creation of the Poor Children's Dinner & Breakfast Tables and, as it transpired, in terms of founding football clubs, however, Brother Dorotheus followed him every step of the way, acting as an assistant and carrying through the ideas with his great friend.

So, whilst Brother Walfrid is to this day synonymous with Celtic, in many ways Dorotheus is a forgotten man. Undoubtedly, he played 'second fiddle' to Walfrid, however, his assistance to him deserves much greater recognition. He was ever-present at all the key moments in the precursor to the establishment of Celtic.

Dorotheus was present at the meetings to discuss founding a football club for the assistance of three local parishes, with his and Walfrid's charity being the primary beneficiaries. Though he was a non-committee member among the founding fathers of the club, he was appointed as one of two auditors on Celtic's first published accounts in 1889.

After leaving St Mary's, Brother Dorotheus went on to become headmaster at St Alphonsus. In 1892, he was transferred to Ireland, where he became a headmaster of schools in Sligo, Athlone and

Swinford until 1911. He appears to return to Scotland at that point, living in Largs for nine years, before returning to the Emerald Isle again.

Brother Dorotheus passed away on 18 September 1934, one week shy of his 79th birthday. He is buried in a family plot in Athlone with his father, who had gone to stay with him prior to his own death. Sadly, the grave does not bear his name.

Chapter 5:

HUGH DARROCH: CELTIC'S FIRST TREASURER

Hugh Darroch was the original treasurer of Celtic Football Club and one of the key founding committee members. He was born in Glasgow in 1859, to Irish parents from County Antrim. His father, also named Hugh, passed away in a mining accident before his second birthday, following which the family downsized, moving to London Road, Bridgeton, where his mother opened a clothes shop.

By the time Hugh Darroch left education, he was a manager in a very successful pawnbrokers, which prompted him to move out to a property on the Gallowgate, within St Mary's parish. He also took over his mother's shop on Bain Street at this time, turning it into one of the most successful in the city.

A central part of the St Mary's parish, Darroch became involved with the St Vincent De Paul Society, assisting the local conference of the organisation, which brought him into contact with the likes of Brothers Walfrid and Dorotheus. Hugh was a popular figure in the community, excelling as a member of the Catholic Literary Society, and his popularity rolled over to the founding fathers of Celtic Football Club, of which he was one. It was thus no surprise when he was elected as Celtic's first Treasurer, upon the establishment of the club.

Darroch was busy helping Celtic get off the ground, yet at this time he married Mary Walls, a widowed woman, on Boxing Day 1888. He had a son with Mary, whom they named Hugh, in line with family tradition. Dr Joseph Scanlan, a prominent Celtic club member, was Darroch's best man and would later marry Mary's younger sister, Sarah Walls.

Shortly after the marriage, Hugh and his young family moved into

Monteith Row, overlooking Glasgow Green. This address was once one of the most sought after in Glasgow, but by this time, most of the wealthy residents had moved to the west of the city and the area was populated by respectable, working-class people, many of whom were of Irish extraction. Living along the row, was fellow Celtic founder, William McKillop, and original subscriber to Celtic, Francis Henry, who was also the older brother of one of the club's committee members, Stephen J Henry.

Tragically, Hugh Darroch was diagnosed with malignant cancer on his neck, four years later. During his illness, he maintained his Treasurer duties with Celtic, sharing the role with John H McLaughlin and James McKay. Sadly, he would become the first of the founding fathers to pass away, at home on 11 September 1891, aged just 32, leaving his wife widowed for a second time. Prior to his death, Hugh had been looked after by fellow founding father Dr John Conway, the first man to ever kick a ball at Celtic Park.

His obituary, in the Glasgow Observer, confirms that he died as a result of the disease and that he was interned at Dalbeth Cemetery, after a requiem mass at St Alphonsus. The obituary also outlines his involvement and love for Celtic:

Football was his favourite game.

He was among the first promoters of the Celtic Club, and on its institution, he was elected Treasurer.

In his death, the club loses a zealous and devoted supporter.

At their game on Saturday – out of respect for deceased – the club's team wore craps bands on their arms.

Hugh was the first person in tribute to whom Celtic players ever wore black armbands. The flags at Celtic Park also flew at half-mast, as the funeral cortege passed the stadium on its way to Old Dalbeth.

A report in the Weekly Freeman's Journal, on 14 September 1891, revealed what happened at the funeral of the great Celt:

A Requiem Mass was sung by Father Trawley, in St. Alphonsus' Church on Monday, for the repose of the soul of Mr. Hugh Darroch, a gentleman engaged in the pawnbroking business in the East End of this city, and who died at the early age of thirty-two years the previous Friday.

The remains of the deceased, encased in a brass-mounted coffin, lay on a catafalque in front of the high altar. The sanctuary was draped in black cloth, and on the coffin were several floral wreaths, including one from Mr. Darroch's late employees and from the Celtic Football Club.

During the mass, Monsignor Munro was present in church, as were also Messrs. Francis Henry, Glasgow School Board; E. Williamson, and J. Quigley, P.L.G.; Dr Conway, Dr Scanlan, S.J. Henry, Glasgow Catholic Literary Society; Brothers Walfrid and Christopher, of the Marist Order; John Heass and J.H. McLaughlin, Celtic Football Club; and McCairns, solicitor.

At the conclusion of the Mass, the funeral party proceeded in ten mourning coaches to Dalbeth Cemetery, where the interment took place.

Mr. Darroch, who had friends everywhere, and an enemy nowhere, was connected with St. Mary's Conference of the St Vincent de Paul Society. The first treasurer of the Celtic Football Club, he was one of its chief promoters. He appears to have been highly popular in the football world, and one writer remarks that the Celtic Club will miss Mr. Darroch's sound practical advice. Another writer in an athletic paper writes that in him, the poor ever found a friend to succour and help them.

Chapter 6:

DR JOHN CONWAY: THE FIRST TO EVER KICK A BALL AT CELTIC PARK

Thousands of people have kicked a ball at Celtic Park – players, celebrities, fans, opposition teams etc. It's an honour for many, but only one man can say he was the first to do so, and that man is Dr John Conway.

John Conway was born in Glasgow in 1859. He was the son of a Glasgow Irish pawnbroker (John Conway Senior), and grew up in a very dedicated Roman Catholic household. Indeed, Conway's father was the first Catholic representative on the Parochial Board in Glasgow, whilst Conway (Junior) was educated at St Mungo's Catholic School, where a certain Brother Walfrid was his tutor. Excelling as a school pupil, Conway went on to study at St Aloysius College, before enlisting with Glasgow University as a student of medicine. Such educational exploits should be not be understated, for very few Catholics studied in this field at the time, as most were not accepted.

Upon graduation, Conway was admitted to the Royal College of Surgeons in London, however, he decided against the opportunity in the English capital, in favour of assisting the poor in his native Glasgow, where poverty and infant mortality rates were among the most horrific in Europe. Conway opened a medical practice on Abercromby Street in the Calton, part of the city's East End, which was the worst afflicted area. His role as a doctor in this region brought him back into contact with one of his old mentors, Brother Walfrid. Walfrid was by now the headmaster at Sacred Heart School in Bridgeton and Conway assisted pupils at the educational institution, by acting as an unofficial medical adviser at Walfrid's request.

Beyond the realm of medical practices, John Conway was a prominent member of the St Vincent De Paul Society within St Alphonsus, the most local parish to Monteith Row, beside Glasgow Green, where he and his wife lived. The doctor also took up positions within the Catholic Union, the Catholic Benefit Society, the Catholic Literary Society and the O'Connell branch of the Irish National Foresters. All of these organisations were frequented by multiple men who would go on to found Celtic. Meanwhile, Conway further utilised his medical expertise in the community after Celtic's establishment, when he became the honorary physician to the Whitevale Children's Refuge in 1890, at the age of just 30.

John Conway was absolutely pivotal to the creation of Celtic Football Club. As a doctor, practising on local Glasgow Irish people, he courted enormous respect in the local community. His devotion to Catholicism and medical welfare ensured that he was a keen supporter of the Temperance Movement, something that would later prove to be of great import in the fledgling days of the club, as his presence brought respect to Celtic's name and maintained the club's close links with the very pro-Temperance organisations – The League of the Cross and Catholic Young Men's Society – whilst a big oxymoron was being carried out by founding fathers such as John Glass, who utilised the licensing trade as a means of attracting players to Celtic!

Despite the importance of his credibility for the reputation of the club, it could be argued that John Conway's most influential moment, in terms of Celtic history, occurred on 12 February 1887, when Hibernian defeated Dumbarton by two goals to one to win the Scottish Cup. After the match, a jubilant reception was held in St. Mary's Church Hall. It may appear surprising that the Leith outfit decided against returning to the capital, however, the adulation with which Hibernian were greeted in Glasgow was more than a match for the support that they'd become accustomed to from the Irish communities of Edinburgh. Among the admirers were leading Glasgow Irishmen, such as Brother Walfrid and John Glass, who would, of course, play immense roles in the founding of Celtic Football Club. Dr John Conway led the victory speeches. He remarked that "All Irishmen are delighted at Hibernian's victory today," and, crucially, that he "strongly urges" his fellow

Glasgow Irishmen to "emulate their example, not only in social but in political matters as well, so that the goal of every Irishman's ambition – legislative independence of his country – will soon be attained."

It is reported in the Glasgow Observer, which Conway promoted and published, that John McFadden, Hibernian's Secretary, responded with some final words before raising his hand in valediction. He thanked his Glasgow-based compatriots for their "warming hospitality," and claimed that "imitation is the sincerest flattery." The reception then concluded with a heartfelt rendition of God Save Ireland, the unofficial anthem for Irish Nationalists at that time.

As the soiree departed, John McFadden is reported to have privately encouraged the Glasgow men to "go and do likewise," (i.e. set up a football team for the Irish community in Glasgow). Dr Conway later said to his parishioners: "As it has become proverbial that imitation is the sincerest flattery, I think we could not please them [Hibernian] better than by following their example." Given that there was a far greater Irish population in Glasgow than in Edinburgh, it made sense to accept the gauntlet that had been thrown down, especially considering that successful football initiatives held within the city for The Poor Children's Dinner and Breakfast Tables were still fresh in the memory.

Some months later, Celtic were officially constituted in that same St Mary's Church Hall. Conway was present at the meeting and was made Celtic's first Honorary President. His greatest and most famous honour came six months after the club's inauguration, when the first Celtic Park was opened on 8 May 1888. The grand opening signified the launch of Celtic, with Hibernian invited to play against Cowlairs. Dr Conway took to the field and became the first person ever to kick a ball at Celtic Park, something that will have been much more memorable for the Honorary President than the rest of the match, which resulted in a 0-0 draw.

Dr John Conway took his role with Celtic Football Club very seriously. He represented the Celts at multiple public events and spoke at a function for Celtic Club members and guests at Waterloo Street, Glasgow, on St Patrick's Day of 1890. His speech that night highlighted his pride in the fact that Celtic had paid off their £1500 outstanding costs for putting together the playing surface at Paradise, and that the club had still managed to donate approximately £400 to charity so far that season.

As great and as glowing as the report by Conway had been, change was on the horizon. A battle for the soul of Celtic was on, as professionalism and business priority loomed large. Without going into the dispute in detail, which would require a book of its own, a split emerged within the Celtic committee. On one hand, people such as John Glass and John H McLaughlin viewed the professionalism route as not only preferable but necessary to the future stability of the club. On the other, the likes of Walfrid and Dr Conway felt that the club should not disobey its raison d'etre, which envisaged that all profits should be donated to charitable causes.

The matter came to a head prior to the 1890/91 AGM and wasn't helped by the fact that two committee men had been paid without the consent of all members. Additionally, Conway was very unhappy at the fact that John Glass put forth the notion that Willie Maley should be paid for splitting his roles between playing for the club and acting as its secretary. This infuriated Conway, as season 1890/91 had gone completely against the script of the previous campaign, when he gave his appreciative speech. Instead, £445 had been donated to charity (£220 of which went to The Poor Children's Dinner and Breakfast Tables), however, the club had a total income of over £4400.

Conway's strong principles led to him being voted out of his role as Honorary President, his position being filled by Joseph Nelis, whilst the doctor also failed to oust John Glass from the overall presidency. The fall-out left a bitter taste, resulting in Dr Conway cutting all ties with Celtic.

As it transpired, John Conway didn't live to see the club turn professional, as he suddenly died on 24 January 1894, aged just 35. The cause of death was noted as apopolexy, which is an antiquated term for a cerebal haemorrhage, that often invokes a stroke. It is an utter disgrace, in my opinion, that nobody at Celtic made any reference to Conway's passing and that the only word on his death was given by the Glasgow Observer newspaper, who stated:

It was greatly owing to his [Conway's] exertions that the Celtic Football Club was started and, in acknowledgement of his efforts in that direction, the members appointed him honorary president for three years.

The doctor was laid to rest in Dalbeth Cemetery. There is no known report of the funeral and, thus, it is unclear as to who, if any, from his time at Celtic attended, though it is likely that Brother Walfrid would have been present if he could have travelled from London, where he had been transferred by then.

Chapter 7:

MICHAEL CAIRNS: CONWAY'S COMPANION

Michael Cairns is one of the many founding fathers of Celtic Football Club who has gone under the radar. Born in Glasgow, to Irish parents, in 1857, Cairns was educated alongside Dr John Conway at St Mungo's school in Townhead. During his schooldays, Michael lost both his parents and was forced to live with relatives in Renfrewshire. His name soon courted respect among the Irish surrounding his new home, for his father was a master tailor and had owned an efficient business in the trade.

Much like fellow founding father, Dr Conway, Cairns was tutored by Brother Walfrid during his time at St Mungo's, before he went on to Glasgow University. There, he studied law, and, upon graduation, he became one of the first Catholics in the city to qualify as a solicitor, passing the Final Law Agents examination. Michael quickly found employment in the industry, serving an apprenticeship with Murdoch & Stewart in Glasgow. He quickly outgrew their offices, and began to work as an assistant for the writer AR Ferguson, who was based in Neilston, Renfrewshire, and as an agent for the Clydesdale Bank. Beyond these roles, Cairns undertook a position as agent for the Neilston branch of the West Renfrewshire Liberal Association.

Whilst based in Neilston, Cairns juggled his time between working and joining a number of community projects. He was an active member of St Thomas parish and, in January 1888, he put on an evening of Irish entertainment for locals in a nearby school hall. Among the performers on the evening were Fr Charles O'Malley and Tom Maley. The latter would, of course, go on to become Celtic's first signing.

One year later, Michael Cairns ventured into the legal business on his own. He returned to Glasgow to do so, and his wide circle of friends from various community organisations enabled him to develop a successful business in its early years. This was an impressive achievement for a man of 32.

Making use of his return to Glasgow, Cairns became involved in local politics, standing as a candidate for the Tenth Ward in the municipal elections. It was at this time, in 1889, that Cairns was elected onto the first-ever Celtic Football Club committee, however, he had been involved with the club from the outset.

It is thought that the key motivating factor in Cairns helping to launch the Celtic project, besides being a football enthusiast, was his very close friendship with Dr John Conway. Conway was, of course, a fellow founding father of the club and a man who had been educated by Walfrid at St Mungo's, before also graduating at Glasgow University, however, it was through the Catholic Literary Society that the pair became great friends. Conway was an avid public speaker and often spoke on behalf of the organisation, yet Cairns once took it upon himself to propose a toast in tribute to "Ireland's a nation," during an eloquent speech that he put together for the Catholic Literary Society's St Patrick's Day social gathering. As a side point, it was noted that one of the most popular features of those St Patrick's celebrations that evening was the artistic programmed provided by the Rangers FC Musical Association!

The fact that his dear friend Conway, and former tutor Walfrid, were both involved in preliminary meetings regarding the establishment of Celtic encouraged Michael Cairns to get involved. Like so many from the early years, his business acumen and prevalence within local Irish/Catholic organisations gave faith to the club's leadership to get it off the ground and make it successful. He was one of three lawyers among the founding fathers, and this gave invaluable assistance to Celtic, when complemented by the hard work of those such as John Glass and the charitable endeavour of Brother Walfrid.

Sadly, Michael Cairns fell gravely ill in early 1892. He was looked after by his close friend and doctor, John Conway. Nevertheless, there was no saving the young Celt, and he tragically passed away on 18

February 1892, at his home in Apsley Place, Glasgow, aged just 35, thus becoming the second founding father to die. Michael was buried in the Conway family plot at Dalbeth Cemetery, a mark of the relationship between the pair.

The Glasgow Observer paid the following short tribute to Michael upon his passing:

He never forgot his race or religion, and as a Catholic and an Irishman, he was always on the alert, in his own quiet way, to spread the light.

Chapter 8:

JOHN O'HARA: THE DERRY DIRECTOR

Many of the founding fathers were born in Glasgow from Irish stock, however, some were actually born on the Emerald Isle itself. John O'Hara was one such man.

Born in Faughanvale parish, Greysteel, County Derry, in 1847, O'Hara fled Ireland with his family to escape the famine at a young age. The clan settled in Bannockburn, near Stirling, however, by the mid-1860s, John had moved to the east end of Glasgow, taking residence on Millroad Street in the Calton. The move came about when O'Hara was offered a job with a shoemaker in the city. The job was vital to take, for he was a young man who had an upcoming wedding to pay for. Indeed, he was to marry an Irish-born girl, Sarah McDonald, at St Alphonsus Church.

O'Hara took the welfare of his peers very seriously, and rose to prominence as a branch organiser of the Boot and Shoe Operative's Union. He also served as secretary of the Operative Shoemaker's Society. Following a feud between the artisan shoemakers and the finishers in 1873, O'Hara formed the National Union of Boot and Shoe Riveters and Finishers. This breakaway union grew to have over 4,000 members and 35 branches. In addition, John O'Hara spoke on behalf of the Glasgow branch of the first conference of the National Union of Boot and Shoe Operatives at Northampton in 1874. One year later, the union established a funeral fund and an offer of sick pay at a rate of ten shillings per week.

By 1881, O'Hara had bought a house on 77 East Rose Street, adjacent to St Mary's Church Hall. A key member of St Mary's Parish, living so close to the local church, John became secretary of the Local Catholic Union Committee. This role meant that he was invited to be part of the soiree that feted the Hibernian team at St Mary's Church Hall when they won the Scottish Cup in February 1887. Most Celtic founding fathers were present that day, and he would have been privy to the words of Dr John Conway and Hibernian Chairman, John McFadden, at the event, which were key in developing the embryonic idea of Celtic.

O'Hara was present from the outset of Celtic. A founding father of the club and a member of the club's first committee, he was tasked with being the collector of subscriptions when they were requested, in January 1888, to construct a stadium and sort out a playing surface. His contacts and professional work in so many secretarial roles then enabled him to be elected as the first club secretary.

As a man who dedicated much of his life to fairness through his work with trade unions, O'Hara acted out of character with Celtic in some ways. His dedication to the club was such that he was second only to John Glass in terms of securing players for the club, doing so by underhand means in those days of amateurism. Indeed, it is reported that he once got involved in an altercation with Mick McKeown concerning money, and that O'Hara was punched during the debacle! John was also reprimanded by the SFA for the illegal tapping up of the Celtic legend, Dan Doyle, from Everton in August 1891. Doyle had already agreed terms with Everton, yet prior to a Celtic versus Cowlairs match, on 10 August 1891, the Scottish Sun wrote of the following incident:

On entering the Cowlairs enclosure, a jubilant Mr O'Hara buttonholed me and, with a mischievous twinkle in his eye, quietly whispered, "I'm sorry you're too late for the names of the teams but perhaps you can distinguish the men for yourself."

There was something in his manner I did not quite understand, but glancing over his shoulder, I was astonished to see the Everton cracks, Doyle and Brady.

John O'Hara remained in the position of secretary for Celtic until the 1891 AGM. It was then that he resigned from the role, not long after a public slagging match, when himself and John H McLaughlin argued with James Quillan, who formed a breakaway Irish club named Glasgow Hibernian together with some other disillusioned members of the Celtic committee. Upon stepping down from the position, O'Hara warned those present at the AGM of the abuse and difficulties that come with the job, insisting that he would not continue for any money. He was replaced by John H McLaughlin.

O'Hara remained involved with Celtic as a committee member, however, after stepping back from his key role, he invested more time into personal affairs. He had changed occupation to become a life insurance agent and had moved residence once more to a property in Moore Street, Dennistoun, with his wife and eight of their nine children. In addition to a change in employed work, O'Hara also ventured into the wine and liquor trade and took over a pub at 140 London Road. He also had his own blend of Scotch whisky, called the Royal Shield. These projects grew his wealth to an astronomical level, by the standards of the time, yet he invested his money further by acquiring the licenses of the Clyde Vaults on Nuneaton Street - very close to the current Celtic Park - and Norfolk Street.

Though he owned a house on 351 Gallowgate, for his visits to Glasgow to oversee his work, O'Hara had moved his family up the social ladder and into the upper-class area of Rothesay on the Isle of Bute, where he purchased an estate for his primary address.

Despite his business interest and sizable family, John O'Hara stepped up his role at Celtic Football Club again, when he was voted onto the board of directors as the club became a limited company in 1897. He held 100 shares, before expanding that holding to 300! His passion for Celtic shone through further, when he represented the club on both the Glasgow and Scottish Football Association boards.

Having given 18 years of service to Celtic, John O'Hara died of cardiac failure whilst at his secondary home on the Gallowgate, on 29 May 1905. Upon his death, the majority of his shares passed to John Glass.

Chapter 9:

DANIEL MOLLOY: THE FOUNDER ON THE FIDDLE

Daniel Molloy was born in Bridgeton to second generation Irish parents in 1862. His Irish-born grandparents had settled in the area in the 1820s, where they were employed as handloom weavers.

It is unclear as to where Molloy was educated, however, one could speculate that he would have attended his most local Catholic school, Sacred Heart, upon its opening in 1874. Sacred Heart was a school where Brother Walfrid taught, and Molloy could have come into contact with him here. Regardless, Daniel would have met many Celtic founding fathers through his social exploits as a member of the Irish National Foresters, the Irish National League and the League of the Cross (St Mary's parish). As evidenced by these memberships, Irish politics and Catholicism was important to Daniel at a young age, something which encompassed the lives of almost all of the men who founded Celtic.

Daniel Molloy was a very popular person. He was an ever-present at social events and used to play the fiddle at gatherings after Celtic matches, whilst John H McLaughlin would play the piano and the legendary Neil McCallum would sing Irish political songs.

By 1887, Molloy was working as an ironmonger's traveller, or 'sales representative' as we may call it today. He lived on Adelphi Street, Bridgeton, with his wife and two young children. At this time, of course, Celtic were founded, and Daniel was involved in the establishment of the club from its inception. He was also present at the opening of the original Celtic Park, when Hibernian played Cowlairs in May1888. After the match, a reception was held at the George Hotel, in George Square, Glasgow. Molloy was present at the function and entertained those in attendance by performing songs such as 'God Save Ireland' and 'Wearing of the Green' on the fiddle.

Daniel Molloy was one of the youngest members of the original Celtic committee, which was put in place in 1888. He was a likeable, upbeat and jovial character, which ensured he was re-elected in 1889. One year later, he would step down, as he emigrated with his family to America. The Molloy's settled in New York after arriving at Philadelphia. The famine memorial in the city demonstrates that many other Irish citizens, or those of Irish extraction, also arrived in Philadelphia by boat, to seek a brighter future, right up until the early 1900s.

When in New York, Daniel's wife gave birth to two daughters, yet sufficient employment to sustain the larger family was difficult to come by, hence the Molloy clan had no choice but to return home to Scotland five years later. Indeed, in October 1895, the Molloy family sailed on the City of Rome ship from New York to Glasgow. When back on home soil, Daniel returned to Celtic, as a matter of priority. He was a keen supporter of the club, and was involved in assisting the committee in an unofficial capacity. Then, in June 1896, he made a serious attempt to be re-elected onto the club's committee at the AGM. Unfortunately, he very narrowly failed to do so, however, he remained a popular man at the club.

Like so many of the founding fathers, Daniel Molloy was very ambitious. Thus, it comes as no surprise that he moved to Rutherglen and went into the wine and spirit trade. As a comical character and entertainer, he was well suited to being a publican, and his business was steady. Meanwhile, he maintained his association with Celtic and its directors, as evidenced by the fact that he named John Glass, John H McLaughlin and Joseph Shaughnessy as trustees in his will.

As seems to be far too commonplace when writing about these great Celtic men, Daniel Molloy suddenly passed away, on 9 December 1899, at the age of 37. His death, caused by hepatitis, came as a great shock to his friends and family. He was laid to rest at Dalbeth Cemetery.

Following his funeral, a comical story emerged, which was originally printed in the Herald newspaper on 22 May 1888. It told of Molloy's dabbling in the wine and spirit trade, before he became a publican on his return to Scotland. The anecdote went that there was a court case in Hamilton Sheriff Court, for an offence that took place in Wishaw, where Daniel Molloy sold two gallons and a quart of beer to a woman on a Sunday. He was heavily fined, as it was a second offence!

Daniel left behind his widow, Elizabeth, and four daughters, who later moved to live in Girvan, in Ayrshire.

Chapter 10:

JOSEPH SHAUGHNESSY: LEGAL, POLITICAL & FAITHFUL

Joseph Shaughnessy had a huge impact on the outwardly political identity of Celtic in the early years. Born in Bridgeton in 1850, to Irish parents, Shaughnessy grew up being well-educated on the ideology of Irish Republicanism. At six months old, his family moved to Rutherglen, and he began school life being educated by the Marist Brothers at St Mungo's Academy and the Jesuits at St Aloysius College.

Excelling academically, Joseph went on to Glasgow University, where he obtained a law apprenticeship at the age of 21. Whilst in the role, Shaughnessy met and wed a young Catholic girl from Fort Augustus named Mary McDonald. The pair married in Glenmorrison but moved into their own home in Rutherglen. Despite these events in his personal life, there was no let-up on the educational front, as Joseph graduated as a student of law in 1877.

Shaughnessy wasted no time in utilising his qualifications. He swiftly opened a legal practice on Hope Street, in Glasgow. He developed a reputation which saw him become the legal adviser to the largest accident assurance society in the world, and he attracted the attention of Scottish trade union leaders, who contacted him to take part in a number of high-profile cases.

Indeed, Shaughnessy was heavily involved with ensuring the welfare of local mining communities in Rutherglen, whilst he also represented a number of miners imprisoned following the Blantyre Riots of April 1887. As a result, Joseph Shaughnessy was appointed as agent for the Scottish National Miners Federation, a position which saw him elected on to the Rutherglen Burgh Council for the next 18 years.

A man of great social conscience, it wasn't just local causes that enthused Joseph. Make no mistake, like many of the founding fathers, Shaughnessy viewed himself as an Irishman living on Scottish soil. He was acutely aware of the reasons behind his parents move to Glasgow, and he was a keen supporter of Irish Republicanism.

The personal and professional had already intertwined, prior to his involvement with local miners, when he defended 10 members of the Irish Republican Brotherhood, who were on trial under the accusation of bombing the gasometers at Glasgow's Tradeston district, in January 1883. Try as he might, Shaughnessy could not get the Republicans off the hook, with five being sentenced to penal servitude for life, whilst the other five suffered the same fate for seven years.

Joseph Shaughnessy's dedication to the working-class, and to the notion of Irish freedom, was further evidenced by the organisations that he enlisted with. He was secretary of the Rutherglen Liberals and a respected member of the Home Government branch of the Irish National League (INL). Although the INL focused on Irish land and political reform, Glasgow's INL branch also spread the message of Michael Davitt's land rights campaign, which he had spoken about not only in Ireland, but in the Scottish Highlands too.

Davitt's right-hand man, John Ferguson, who was an Ulster Protestant, took the view that the Irish could unite with their Celtic cousins in the Highlands over common injustices, in terms of land rights and landlord evictions. It was a position that Glasgow's INL branch drove forth, thanks greatly to Joseph Shaughnessy rallying political support for the Highlander's plight.

Though a staunch Irishman, Shaughnessy's position may also have been influenced by his in-laws, whose hometown of Fort Augustus was very close to Glengarry. The family were originally shepherds and crofters, and the area of their residence had been a stronghold of Scottish Catholicism since the McDonald and McDonnell clans were driven south, ahead of the Reformation.

Joseph Shaughnessy had met many future founders of Celtic Football Club through his professional work, and those political memberships of Irish organisations. Beyond those domains, he was also a deeply-religious man, who was a member of the local conference of the St Vincent De Paul Society. This brought him into contact with yet more future founding fathers, one of whom, Joseph Nelis, he combined with to establish the St Aloysius Association.

It came as no surprise when Shaughnessy was invited to be part of the Celtic project from the beginning. One of three lawyers among the founding fathers, his legal advice and renowned contacts within local powers would have been key to setting Celtic afloat. Thereafter, he assisted with any of the club's legal concerns, whilst at Celtic's first AGM at Bridgeton Mechanics Hall, on 21 June 1889, Shaughnessy proposed that Michael Davitt be named the club's first Honorary Patron.

Davitt was a great Irish Patriot, a founder of the Land League and tireless campaigner for Celtic land reform. He was also a convicted member of the Irish Republican Brotherhood, who had served several years in English prisons for his battles to free Ireland, which led to charges of gun-running, among other accusations. Celtic took forward the suggestion and duly appointed Davitt to the position.

Make no mistake, this was akin to having a Gerry Adams-type figure as a public ambassador of the club. The move really symbolised what Celtic stood for in those early days, something that was further endorsed when Michael Davitt was invited to lay the first sod of shamrock-smothered turf, freshly imported from Donegal, at the new Celtic Park in 1892.

Such bold moves show the esteem in which Joseph Shaughnessy was held at Celtic, highlighted once more at the club's 1891 AGM, when he was elected to succeed Dr John Conway as Honorary President. The legal and political aspects had shown the importance of Shaughnessy to the Celtic project, whilst his faith had ensured that he covered every dimension of the club's identity. However, Joseph was more than that to Celtic Football Club. Indeed, in December 1892, he outlined plans for floodlighting to be installed at the new Celtic Park, albeit the trial of this notion was an utter disaster. Nevertheless, Shaughnessy showed his worth again within a few months, as he was one the club's major guarantors and is listed as a leaseholder of the new stadium.

Joseph and his eldest son, John, took a big interest in the Celtic Cycling Club, which was established as a means of additional funding in the early years of the club. So good was the track, perimetering the pitch, that the club would host the World Cycling Championships in 1897, the first time that they were hosted in the UK. John was often found umpiring the cycle events at the ground, whilst Willie Maley handed out the prizes in Scotland versus Ireland track races.

The renovations necessary to facilitate the World Cycling Championships would have a huge impact on the whole direction of the club and on its turning professional. Those in favour of the club becoming a limited company banked on Shaughnessy's enthusiasm for the sport to sway him in their direction. However, he had already raised the suggestion when discussions first started surrounding the notion, at the 1893 AGM.

Shaughnessy donated vast sums of his own money to finance the club, and felt that limited liability would enable the club to stand on its own two feet. Four years later, in February 1897, the matter was coming to a head. There was a clear divide among the committee, however, Shaughnessy said that he would resign from his position with the club, and no longer be a guarantor of its debt, if limited liability did not happen. Of course, the change did take place later that year and, despite not taking a seat on the newly-formed board, Shaughnessy put forward the suggestion that Willie Maley be appointed Secretary of the new Celtic limited company. The idea was seconded by James Curtis and duly went ahead.

Joseph Shaughnessy remained a huge Celtic supporter until his sudden death in 1906. On the day of his funeral, all shops in Rutherglen were closed and the flag on the Town Hall was flown at half-mast. He was laid to rest at Dalbeth Cemetery in Glasgow, where the Celtic Graves Society restored his headstone and held a commemoration for him in January 2018.

Shaughnessy's oldest son, John, who was also a solicitor, was voted onto the Celtic board in 1911. This was not the last of the family's association with the club though, for the Celtic director James Farrell joined the Shaughnessy law firm, remaining with them until the 1980s.

Chapter 11:

JAMES CURTIS: A PUPIL OF THE CELTIC TRADITION

James Curtis was born in Glasgow to Irish parents in 1846. His father, William,, and mother Ann, settled on Sister Street in the Calton. They sent James to school at St Mungo's, where he became yet another of the founding fathers to be educated by Brother Walfrid.

After completing his education, James Curtis qualified as a teacher himself. His family had moved deeper into the Calton, now residing on Abercromby Street, Curtis finding employment with the local parish school, St Mary's, in the mid-1880s. St Mary's was headed by Brother Dorotheus at that time, right-hand man of Brother Walfrid and the co-founder of the Poor Children's Dinner and Breakfast Tables. He operated the Penny Dinner Scheme from the school, whilst Walfrid did likewise at Sacred Heart in Bridgeton, where he had been transferred to take over as headmaster.

Despite going on to move to 3 Comelypark Place, James Curtis remained an integral party of the St Mary's parish, where he continued to teach under Brother Dorotheus' guidance. By April 1887, he had become the Chairman of St Mary's Young Men's Society. The Society was based in the local church hall, and was created to promote Irish culture, such as poetry, dancing and history. Through this organisation and his role as a teacher, Curtis was invited to attend the celebratory soiree for Hibernian FC, held at St Mary's Church Hall in February 1887 to mark the club's Scottish Cup triumph. An indelible impression was clearly left on him that day, for he personally sent a telegram to Hibernian secretary John McFadden, offering congratulations on behalf of the Young Men's Society.

In late 1887, Brother Dorotheus was among the founding fathers of Celtic. As his protege, it was no surprise that James Curtis was involved with the club from the beginning too. He may not have been one of the foremost founders, in terms of setting Celtic afloat, but he played an important functional role as match secretary of the first-ever Celtic reserve team.

Under his stewardship, Celtic reserves were very successful in the early years. Indeed, in 1890/91, the team won both trophies for which they competed and lifted the Scottish Second XI Cup, by defeating St Mirren Strollers 13-1 in the final!

In 1892, Curtis was tasked with an unusual first-team role. Scottish football had not yet gone professional and, thus, did not receive compensation for the loss of their prized assets. Sandy McMahon was one such asset, who had been persuaded by Celtic legend Neil McCallum to head to Nottingham for high wages. A vigilante committee was set up in Johnstone to deal with English agents, who would often force Celtic players into a car to travel south where they would then try to persuade them to sign. However, on this occasion it was not the Johnstone Vigilante Committee who set to work; it was a posse sent by Celtic to retrieve McMahon, and James Curtis was part of that group.

After covert success, James Curtis returned to reserve team duty and was named Celtic's representative on the Second Eleven Association board in May 1893. At the AGM, one year later, he composed and read out the club's annual report to the committee members present at Bridgeton Mechanics Hall. In the report, he claimed that the season which had just finished had been the most successful in the club's short history and that the annual sports days held by the club were the best in Scotland. In addition, Curtis remarked that the new Celtic Park, built in 1892, was now so superb that it was worthy of its Paradise nickname. Interestingly, Curtis closed the report by giving a nod to the club's foundations, stating the obvious in that Celtic had been founded for charitable purposes. However, he remarked that, when the liabilities are cleared, there will not be a club in Scotland who will assist the needy as much as the Celts. Perhaps this was a subtle hint of support for the club becoming a limited company, given that the debate on professionalism had been underway for some time at this point.

By late 1895, James Curtis had stood down from his role with the reserves, handing the baton to Johnny Coleman. Coleman was a cycling enthusiast, who ran a local bicycle shop and was present at many of the sport's events at Celtic Park in the early years of the club. In December of that year, Coleman's role with the reserves took on greater responsibility, as the Scottish Reserve League was formed on the suggestion of Rangers. Celtic's second-string went unbeaten throughout that debut league campaign, finishing joint-top with Hearts. Consequentially, James Curtis was granted £25 from Celtic at the subsequent AGM in 1896, in tribute to his services for the club, as it was widely felt that the success of the reserve team had stemmed from his work in the years prior. Indeed, Curtis' time working with those coming through the ranks of the fledgling Celts paid dividends, as some of the early greats, such as Dowds, McArthur and Divers, broke through to the first team on his watch.

James Curtis still remained involved with the Celtic committee after stepping back. He lived locally, attended first team matches and seconded Joseph Shaughnessy's motion for Willie Maley to be named secretary of the club once it had become a limited company in 1897.

In terms of his personal life, Curtis got married in St Mungo's on 12 July 1899. His wife gave birth soon after the wedding, and the pair named their son William Dorotheus Curtis. The name was in tribute to both James' father (William Curtis) and his old Marist mentor, Brother Dorotheus. The family emigrated to Canada, in the late 1910s, yet James remained in Glasgow on his own. He continued to teach at St Mary's school until declining health forced him to retire in 1921, at which point he moved to Canada to reunite with the rest of his family. By the middle of the decade, James was on the move once more. This time he sought a new home in Melbourne, where some of his family members had gone.

James lived out his remaining days in Australia, before passing away in 1933, at the age of 87. He thus had the distinction of being one of the only founding fathers to live a long life.

Chapter 12:

JOSEPH NELIS: ALTRUISTIC ATTRACTION

Joseph Michael Nelis is not a name that is very familiar with many Celtic supporters. Hopefully, this chapter rectifies matters, for he was a highly influential figure, in terms of the club's founding and its core value of charity.

Born in Bridgeton in 1853, Joseph Nelis was the son of an Irishman, John Nelis, who was an egg and butter merchant and had a business which had been well-established in the Bridgegate area since the 1830s. Joseph's education took place locally, at St Mungo's and then St Aloysius College. Upon leaving school, he followed his father into the provisions industry, within which the pair began to sell Irish eggs and butter on the advice of Joseph's Irish-born mother, who knew that this variety of the product was very popular in the city at that time.

Joseph's career took a different path when he found love. Indeed, he married a local woman named Sidney Collins in 1874. Sidney's father, Patrick, was an Irish immigrant, who owned a pawnshop in Rutherglen. That same year, Joseph Nelis left the world of egg and butter trading to become a pawnbroker himself. As with all the Celtic founding fathers, Nelis was ambitious and, unsurprisingly, opened his own pawnbroker's shop on Nuneaton Street, near the current Celtic Park, in 1877.

As a local Catholic businessman with great social conscience, Nelis was a member of the Parochial Board for Bridgeton in 1884 and was elected as a Manager of the Poor by the Barony Parish, one year later. From these positions, Nelis became one of the earliest members to join the Catholic Union of Glasgow. His enlistment with the Union combined religion with politics and put him in touch with a few like-minded professional Catholics operating in the city, not least Dr John Conway and Joseph Shaughnessy. The trio formed a good relationship and duly founded the St Aloysius Association together. The Association was designed to give the minuscule Catholic professional class in Glasgow some representation.

Nelis had some involvement with Celtic from the beginning. Knowing that he was close to Celtic figures, such as Conway and Shaughnessy, along with his charitable proclivity as Manager of the Poor, it comes as no surprise that the launch of a local Irish football club with aims of supporting various missions located in the East End was attractive to him. The entire Nelis family lived together at Newhall Terrace (now Greenhead Street), overlooking Glasgow Green, at the time of Celtic's founding. Thus, despite his business prowess, he was still very much locally based and would have been acutely aware of the poverty that the Irish diaspora faced within his immediate surroundings.

The qualities Nelis could bring to a group of men seeking to establish a successful charitable football club are there for all to see and are similar to the other founding fathers in many aspects. The key thing that made him stand out was his membership of the Parochial Board though, as these men controlled everything in terms of building - or what we now call planning permission - in their region. The Boards were distant predecessors to modern local councils and were replaced with elected parish councils in 1894. Consequentially, it is safe to say that Nelis was an important figure in 1887, supporting the Celtic project enthusiastically, just a step back from the absolute forerunners of the club, such as Brother Walfrid, John Glass et al.

Joseph Nelis appears as a member of the first Celtic committee in 1890, yet not in one of the seven key positions. However, he would replace Dr John Conway as Honorary Club President one year later. It should be noted that many clubs with an Irish identity existed in Scotland at this time, up to 40, in fact. Most failed, all faced discrimination and each, aside of Hibernian, struggled to win outright support ahead of their competitors. One area where Celtic differentiated themselves was in terms of sourcing external funding, whilst concurrently securing community support. The club did this by organising sporting events, such as pedestrianism, track cycling races and an annual sports day. Joseph Nelis served as a steward at all of these events and, indeed, at functions put on by the Celts, where other founding fathers, such as Joseph Shaughnessy and John H McLaughlin, would perform Irish music and sing rebel songs of the era to a Church hall full of local supporters and footballers, who were provided with soup and sandwiches!

Testament to the regard in which Joseph Nelis was held at the club, he was the Celtic representative nominated to collect the Glasgow Charity Cup, upon their triumph in the competition in 1892. The trophy was formally presented in an afternoon ceremony at the Council chambers in George Square. Ordinarily, the Lord Provost would make the presentation, yet, for whatever reason, he was absent, and Bailie Paton presided on his behalf, whilst a number of other councillors were present. Paton's speech produced a great smile on Nelis' face, as he began by announcing that the cup had raised £12,000 for local charities since its inception and had raised £1,000 in that year alone. The presentation report published in the local press shows a list of all the donations. It reveals that 58 charities were the beneficiaries of the money, including a £15 donation made to the Poor Children's Dinner and Breakfast Tables, to which Celtic Football Club had been instituted. Nelis collected the trophy, the club's third piece of silverware that season. He addressed those present by expressing his pride at the success, before remarking that it was ironic and appropriate that the Charity Cup should be won by his Celtic, a club whose very reason for existence was charity.

As Celtic grew, Nelis' involvement grew with it. He was named as one of the leaseholders of the new Celtic Park, when the club first secured a 10 year rent of the disused brickyard, adjacent to Janefield Street, from James Hozier (or the Lord Newlands as he later became titled). Once the construction was complete, the club opened the new stadium on Saturday, 13 August 1892, with Celtic's third of what would prove to be annual sports days. Joseph Nelis was present for the laying of the first sod of turf by Michael Davitt that afternoon.

A quote from the 1932/33 Celtic handbook reflected on the day:

The old trouble landlord brought about a change of field, and it was in keeping with it, too, that a seeming impossible site was converted into a splendid enclosure. A case of leaving the graveyard to enter the paradise. A happy title did that pressman strike.

The lessons learnt and the experience gained on the old monument to the loyalty and fidelity of the pioneers of the club - did they not give their labour to construct it - were not lost. The splendid pedestrian and cycling tracks, which surround the playing area on which champions the world over showed their paces, added another title: 'The home of sport.'

It was an auspicious occasion and great day when the late Irish Republican, Michael Davitt, laid a fresh centre sod of turf from Donegal with a handsome silver spade presented to him by the club.

It wasn't all joyful for Nelis at Celtic during this time though. Indeed, the AGM of 1892 had already brought about whispers of limited liability. The debate hadn't really turned bitter by this point, but it was cause for some discontent and friction among the committee. Joseph Shaughnessy was the man who put forward the motion on that occasion. Joseph Nelis strongly disagreed, for he was a man incredibly committed to charity work. The minutes of the meeting suggest that Nelis felt the club had progressed every year and thus, in his eyes, this was sufficient to demonstrate that the club could still be a success in its amateur format. He was concerned that limited liability could lead to profit for the businessmen behind the scenes, despite the fact he was one of those himself, and that it would destroy the identity of the club because it was established primarily for charitable purposes. Such a principled man was Nelis, that he offered to donate £500 of his own money to secure the club and maintain its charitable outlook.

The tide was turning against those in favour of preserving the original ideals of Celtic. Brother Walfrid had been transferred to London, and the major players, such as John Glass, were strongly in favour of Celtic going Ltd. Once on a secure footing, Glass said that the club would only be too willing to donate to charity again, yet, despite this claim, Nelis departed the club when it became apparent that limited liability was inevitable.

Outside of Celtic, Joseph Nelis was still very much business-orientated. He retired from pawnbroking in May 1897, going under the radar somewhat. It is possible that he spent time caring for his wife in this period, as she died in Helensburgh in 1900. Meanwhile, there were unconfirmed rumours that he had dabbled in the liquor trade.

In the census of 1901, Nelis is listed as a publican. Celtic's founding fathers, early star players and committee members boasted a huge number of successful publicans, leading to that famous quote "six publicans only one Glass." Perhaps this was an inspiriting factor behind the decision. By this point, Joseph had moved out to Partick, and was living on Minard Road. It is unclear as to how long he worked in the industry, as reports on his death in 1943 suggest that he was a retired education authority clerk.

Having lived to the age of 90, and only succumbing to death during the middle of the Second World War, Joseph Nelis was the oldest survivor of Celtic's founding fathers. Aside of Willie Maley, he was also the longest-serving member of the first committeemen. Fitting it was then, when Maley gave mention to him in his book, The Story of the Celtic, which was published in 1938. Maley was writing about Celtic's Golden Jubilee dinner in Glasgow, on 16 June 1938, when he outlined his own words, written in the third person:

Mr Maley expressed regret at the absence through illness of the last surviving member of the first Committee, Mr. Joe Nelis. They had with them, however, two of their oldest enthusiasts, Dr. Scanlan and Mrs. Arthur Murphy, who had been with them from the very beginning.

Chapter 13:

FRANCIS MCERLEAN: BELFAST BHOY TO FOUNDING FATHER

The connections between Celtic Football Club and the city of Belfast are innumerable. It could be argued that the club has no greater link with any other city throughout Ireland. Equally, Celtic has a higher volume of historical attachments to Antrim, than any other county on the emerald isle.

Francis McErlean was one of those connections. Born in Belfast, County Antrim, in 1845, he moved to Glasgow in his 20s. His migration likely came as a result of the economic devastation which followed the famine. Francis embedded himself into life in the Dear Green Place, and married Bridget Gallagher, a local girl of Irish descent, in 1869. Bridget was the daughter of Charles Gallagher, who was a pawnbroker in the East End. Soon after the wedding, the pair moved to Belfast, where Francis was a wholesaler of spirits, which he supplied to local taverns. They settled in Ireland and had three daughters, born between the years of 1872 and 1882.

Although the family immersed themselves in Belfast life, the McErleans moved back to Glasgow in the mid-1880s. Francis followed in his father-in-law's footsteps, when he rented a property at 735 Great Eastern Road (the Gallowgate) and opened a pawnbroker's shop in the upper flat. Disaster struck on 5 March 1888, when a defective chimney caused a fire which severely damaged the shop. Fortunately, Francis was insured, and was able to claim £600 for his losses.

A parishioner of St Michael's, Parkhead, McErlean was a key member of an important parish in terms of the discussions that took place between several East End parishes and an embryonic committee of men who would found Celtic in 1887. It is beyond doubt that he became involved with the budding Celtic project during this time, unambiguously making Francis a founding father of the club.

In June 1889, James Quillan led a breakaway from the club at Celtic's very first AGM. Those who abandoned the Celtic project to form a rival Irish club in the city at this time were known as Quillanites. Quillan had been the Vice-President, and his position was filled by Francis McErlean. Being an Irish Catholic businessman, and a major player in the St Michael's parish, Francis fit the bill, in terms of aligning with Celtic's values and having the connections necessary to help the club succeed.

McErlean sold tickets to club events from his shop, to reach a wider support base. Naturally, as a Belfast native, he also accompanied the Celtic delegation on the club's tour of Ireland in 1896. During a match against Belfast Distillery, Francis alerted Willie Maley to the talents of the Irish club's half-back, Patrick Farrell. Maley took heed of the advice and brought Farrell to the club ahead of the new season. A debut appearance wasn't handed to the Irish defender until 9 January 1897, when Celtic infamously lost 4-2 to Arthurlie in the Scottish Cup. The result is still regarded as the most embarrassing in Celtic history. Farrell had only been selected to make up the numbers, as Celtic only had seven first teamers available, due to player strikes, injuries and suspensions. Suffice to say that he returned to James Curtis' reserve team and never made another senior appearance for Celtic, before leaving for Woolwich Arsenal in May 1897.

Outside of the football and business arenas, McErlean dedicated a lot of time to his faith and family. He was appointed Treasurer of the Father Beyaert Presentation Fund Committee, which was established to ensure that the Catholic people of St Michael's parish were able to present a suitable leaving gift for their local priest, who was to be transferred to Kirkintilloch. Not only was Father Beyaert a priest, but he was one of the earliest Celtic supporters, whose name can be found on the list of subscribers who donated money when the founders of Celtic pleaded for assistance in order to set the club afloat. He gave the Celts 20 gratefully received shillings.

In January 1891, Francis McErlean's eldest daughter, Bridget (named after his wife), married the Celtic captain, James Kelly. Kelly was an absolute legend in Scottish football. He was an internationalist, and so pivotal to attracting crowds that the famous saying of the day was "No Kelly, No Keltic!" Needless to say, the wedding took place at St Michael's Roman Catholic Church, with Father Beyeart conducting the ceremony.

Three months after welcoming James Kelly to the family, the McErlean clan (including James Kelly) resided together in Burgher Street at Parkhead Cross. This location meant that the men of the house only had to walk a couple of hundred yards to their beloved Celtic Park. It was an interesting time for the household, in terms of their respective positions at Celtic. Indeed, at the AGM that June, Francis McErlean was not re-elected as Vice President. However, he could take comfort in the silver lining of his son-in-law being voted onto the committee. The fact that an MP, in the form of William McKillop, was the man to oust him from his own position may also have curtailed too much disappointment, as few individuals would bring as much to the table as a man of that stature.

Francis was voted onto the committee again at the 1896 AGM, yet when the club became a limited company a year later, he did not take the opportunity of purchasing additional shares. It is evident that he moved back to Ireland, with his wife and children, at this point.

Francis McErlean remained on home soil until his death at Portglenone, County Derry, aged 61, in February 1906.

Chapter 14:

DAVID MEIKLEHAM: THE RARE FOUNDING FATHER WITHOUT IRISH ANCESTRY

David Meikleham was born in Rothesay in 1852. He was an anomaly among the Celtic founding fathers, in that he was born into a Catholic family without any Irish ancestry. Almost every other member of Celtic's first committee identified as Irish, whether through being born in Eire, or as a descendant of those who had been.

Before his 10th birthday, David and his family had moved to Glasgow, settling on Broad Street in the Calton. At the age of 19, he moved with his parents to Hunter Street, along the road from an old Army barracks in the Gallowgate. David's father, William, opened a shoe repair shop nearby, and David began working in it as a shoemaker. This would have brought him into contact with another future founding father of Celtic, John O'Hara, who was the leader of the Shoemaker's Union.

In his personal life, David Meikleham married Robina McLaughlin at St Alphonsus Catholic Church in 1873. The couple had 13 children (six boys and seven girls), and lived together on Shuttle Street, which was located just off High Street in Glasgow's city centre.

David soon decided to go it alone in the business world, building up his own shoemaker's shop to the point whereby he employed seven members of staff, in 1881. Five years later, he took his large family back to the Calton, purchasing a house on William Street (now Templeton Street) and integrating into the local parish where he had married. The parish was dominated by Irish people and their descendant community, however, the Catholic Church in Scotland had pushed for the integration of the small number of Scottish Catholics and welcomed them to join their congregations to avoid the total Gaelicisation of the church. Meikleham did just that, becoming popular in the community and enlisting as a member of the local Catholic Union in 1887. His role with the Union increased quickly, as he was tasked with representing St Alphonsus parish on the Central Committee of the organisation.

Aside of joining the Catholic Union, Meikleham also became a member of the Caledonian Catholic Association in Glasgow. He was somewhat of an enigma, in that he was a Catholic, solely proud of his native Caledonia and a middle-class individual, yet he had gladly worked with many Irishmen through his different memberships and parish involvements. On the flip side, Meikleham was a longstanding member of Queen's Park FC, the establishment team of the day. The Spiders were not fond of signing Catholic players, they were largely anti-Irish and very much middle-class. It is somewhat of an oxymoron that David would maintain links with that club for so long, whilst simultaneously supporting so many Catholic causes. Nevertheless, Queen's Park were one of the most successful teams in world football at the time, so he certainly had the sporting understanding to go with his middle-class business status and prestigious aura.

Boasting several qualities that would be useful to Celtic, especially being a Scottish middle-class individual with sympathy for the Catholic plight in Glasgow, David Meikleham joined the Celtic project at a very early stage. He was involved in the preliminary meetings to discuss the establishment of the club and appeared as a member of the club's first committee.

His role became more important in 1892, when Celtic moved to their new stadium. Meikleham was named as one of four leaseholders and remained such until the landlord was convinced to sell the site to Celtic on a permanent basis in 1897. He was also part of the group that went to Nottingham to retrieve Neil McCallum and Sandy McMahon, who were taken south by English agents without the offer of compensation being made to Celtic. Along with Meikleham, the group consisted of John Glass, James Curtis and Sandy McMahon's brother!

McCallum was retrieved easily, however, Nottingham Forest kept McMahon on the move. Fortunately, David Meikleham found him on a random street and grabbed hold of him, before jostling him into a taxi!

Cue a Wild West-style chase as the pair made way for the local train station, with Forest officials in pursuit.

Unfortunately for the English club, McMahon was taken to Manchester, where the rest of the Celtic delegation met him. He was then placed on an additional train, which arrived in Glasgow without detection. This was Meikleham's greatest-ever contribution to Celtic, as in those pre-professional days, the clubs did not get transfer fees for the loss of star players. The result of losing Sandy McMahon permanently would have been damaging to Celtic's success, and would have depleted the attendances at matches. Thanks to Meikleham's eagle eyes, the 'Duke' McMahon would go on to play for Celtic on over 217 occasions, becoming one of the early legendary figures in the club's history.

In 1893, David Meikleham had a dispute with some staff at his business, who subsequently went on strike. Not only was this an ironic position, given that David was a Union member, but it also meant that he was investigated by the Boot and Shoe Operatives Union, which was ran by John O'Hara, with whom he had helped to establish Celtic Football Club.

In a letter to the Glasgow Herald newspaper, printed on 21 February 1893, Meikleham stated:

I notice from the report of the Glasgow United Trade Council in your last issue, that that body has been in correspondence with the Home Secretary regarding a strike which I had with men in my employment, or as stated in your report, in connection with the action of a certain reformatory and industrial school in doing work for a shoemaker who has a dispute with his men, the shoemaker being myself.

Now I wish to state exactly the position of matters, which is as follows:-

On 30th November last, I spoke to my foreman regarding two of my men who I had reason to believe were not doing their fair share of work. There is no piece-work in my employment, the wages being what are called set weekly wages. Shortly after I had spoken to my foreman, and on the same day, one of those men came to me and asked if I was going to reduce his wages. I said no, I had no intention of reducing his wages, nor those of any of the men, but that I hoped he would do a little more work. This man immediately thereafter reported to the other men in my employment that I was going to reduce my men's wages. This is not correct. I did not intimate a reduction of my men's wages, nor did I intend to make any reduction of wages. And I spoke to the men individually and collectively and told them so. However, for some reason best known to the men, they struck work and said they would not do any further work for me unless I would tell them how much work each is required to do. I told the men that up to that moment we had never had any dispute about wages, and it was rather an extraordinary thing if, on complaining to my foreman about a couple of my men, who I thought were not doing what I considered was a fair amount of work, that should be a pretext for all the other men striking work. To put myself right with the men's association, on 2nd December I wrote their secretary, Mr Park, the following letter.

(the letter outlines the above points, almost word for word)

Now I believe that at a meeting of the Boot and Shoe Operatives Union, which was held on the Thursday after the receipt of my letter, the matter of the so-called strike in my shop was discussed, but although the secretary had my letter as above quoted before him, with a request therein that he should read the same, the secretary, for some reason or other best known to himself, declined to do so.

I have never had a strike among my employees; I have never intimated a reduction of wages; my workmen are all on set wages. I am still paying my men in the same way as I was before the strike and I should like therefore to know what reason the Glasgow United Trades Council have to interfere where there was no reduction of wages intimated on my part and no advances of wages asked by my workmen.

I may mention that I pay my men according to merit and that the average wages of men in my employment is 27s per week. It is true some of the better men, who, in my opinion, are much more skilful than others, get a little more – say from 30s to 32s per week – but I consider that the men who get these higher wages, from 30s to 32s per week, are better worth their money than men in receipt of from

24s to 26s per week, and I am perfectly willing to pay the minimum wage to all competent workmen.

I am not aware that any trades' union can contest me paying one man more than another man, provided I give all my men a fair day's pay for a fair day's work in the recognised pay in the trade. I may state that it would be impossible for me to fix any particular quantity of work that each man in any employment should do, there being so many different classes of work that a man may have to do in one day, and thus is well known to my men. I have no objection, and never had any, to pay the minimum wage of 27s per week to competent workmen, and this the men who were lately in my employment know perfectly well.

D. MEIKLEHAM

Following the strike by his staff, Meikleham struggled to fulfil jobs and, in order to relieve the backlog of work, he turned to a Celtic committeeman and player, Tom Maley. At that time, Maley was the superintendent at Slatefield Industrial school, where shoemaking was one of the trades taught to pupils. Generously, Maley agreed to help a fellow Celt out, an act which incensed Meikleham's staff. The men on strike felt that their action had been undermined by Meikleham's shifting of production, and thus wrote a complaint to their union, who in turn contacted the Glasgow United Trades Council once more. Thereafter, the issue was handed up the chain to the Secretary of State again, who immediately demanded that Tom Maley stopped assisting an employer who was in dispute with his workforce.

It is unclear as to how the issue was finally resolved, albeit Meikleham's name appears in the list of Scotch Bankrupts in the 24 November 1900 edition of the Glasgow Herald, suggesting he lost staff members and custom as a result of the feud.

The bankrupt note reads:

Carrying on business as slipper manufacturer at 146 London Street, Glasgow. Creditors to meet in the Faculty Hall, St George's Place,

Glasgow, 3rd December at twelve o'clock.

Chas Byrne, writer, 122 Wellington Street, Glasgow agent.

During the seven-year intervening period between the strike and his bankruptcy, Meikleham maintained his work with Celtic. He could be found stewarding at the club's annual sports days with the rest of the committeemen, whilst he also took a keen interest in the Celtic Cycle Club. By 1895, he was duly nominated to be Vice-President of the Celts, but he lost out to John H McLaughlin on that occasion; his nomination having been refused by Tom Maley!

A year later, on 28 November 1896, Meikleham was at the centre of another strike dispute. This time, the strike was being held by three Celtic players; the legendary Barney Battles, Peter Meehan and John Divers. The Celtic committee described the trio as "malcontents," and said that they would "never kick a ball for the club again." In addition, Celtic later contacted the governing body to request that the dissenters be suspended. In more immediate terms, the team was playing Hibernian at Celtic Park that day and Meikleham was needed in action.

The match was delayed by 15 minutes, when the three men refused to take to the field, their strike coming in the wake of recent criticism from the press. The trio said that they would play if Celtic barred the pressmen from the media box, however, Celtic were not willing to do so and thus manager, Willie Maley, and Barney Crossan, who had not played in over a year, filled two of the three positions as the Bhoys took to the field with 10 men.

Meikleham was immediately tasked with heading to Hampden Park, doing so by horse-drawn carriage. The Celtic Reserves were playing against a Queen's Park second string at the national stadium, and David's job was to get Tom Dunbar from the Celtic team and return him to Paradise as quick as possible! Extraordinarily, Meikleham managed to get Dunbar back to Parkhead in time to play the second half for the first XI, and the match finished 1-1.

Little over six months later, the 1897 AGM brought an end to amateurism, and Celtic became a limited company. Despite his middle-class business life, Meikleham left the club at this stage, seeking no further involvement with Celtic once the ideal of charity was no longer primary. This suggests that, like many of the founding fathers, he kept his business life separate from Celtic, which was a charitable, sporting and perhaps Catholic pursuit for him.

After leaving Celtic and declaring himself bankrupt, Meikleham bounced back by going into business in the telephone industry, which was in the pioneering stages at the time. From there, he became a sales manager at a local Post Office, a position he held until his retirement.

David Meikleham lived to the ripe old age of 87, passing away in May 1938, one month before Celtic's Golden Jubilee Dinner. He was laid to rest in Dalbeth Cemetery, his grave located just yards from that of fellow founding father, John Glass.

Chapter 15:

JOSEPH MCGROARY: CELTIC'S PUZZLING SON OF DONEGAL

Joseph F McGroary was born in Glasgow, on 25 February 1865. He was one of 13 children and his parents hailed from Mountcharles, in Donegal. As with many other founding fathers, Joseph was taught by the Marists at St Mungo's Academy, and at St Aloysius College under the tutorship of the Jesuits. Whilst at St Aloysius, McGroary studied alongside Celtic founding father, John H McLaughlin, and appeared in shows with him.

Upon leaving education, McGroary met another Celtic founding father, in the form of Joseph Shaughnessy, with whom he commenced a law apprenticeship in 1880. Midway through learning the trade, Joseph attended Glasgow University for a couple of terms, before returning to Shaughnessy's Hope Street practice as a fully qualified lawyer in May 1887.

Life as a pupil was not easy for McGroary. Indeed, his family returned to Mountcharles when he was just 12 years old, leaving Joseph and his father behind in Glasgow. The reason for this is not known, however, he remained a frequent visitor to Donegal and met the love of his life, Catherine Cannon from Drumkeelan, on a trip to Ulster. The pair married in Mountcharles on 12 August 1888, then lived together in Joseph's Glasgow home, before having six children.

Unlike the other founding members of the club, McGroary did not live in the East End of Glasgow, nor did he have any immediate connection with that part of the city. Instead, he was a prominent member of St Joseph's parish, on North Woodside Road. Nevertheless, when a conglomeration of Glasgow Irishmen, including his boss Joseph

Shaughnessy, were holding preliminary meetings to establish a football club for the benefit of the local impoverished Irish community, Joseph became involved. He would also have been drawn to the project through his meetings with other founding fathers, whom he had met through his membership with the Irish National League and as a representative for St Aloysius within the Glasgow Catholic Union.

After the famous meeting on 7 November 1887, in which a new Irish Catholic football club was officially constituted, Joseph McGroary was elected onto the first Celtic committee. Newspaper reports of the time confirm that he was present at the opening of Celtic Park, alongside his boss, on 8 May 1888. He witnessed many of the club's early events and is among the committee members famously pictured with the star-studded Celtic squad who played Blackburn Rovers in October 1889.

McGroary does not appear as a member of the club's committee after that first season, until the AGM held on Tuesday, 4 June 1895. The AGM took place in Annfield Halls on Gallowgate, where the Bellgrove Hotel stands today. That meeting saw McGroary re-elected, and he wasted no time in voicing his opinions, addressing those present and remarking that he felt the West End of Glasgow should also get a portion of any money distributed to charity, as the club was supported by people in all areas of Glasgow, not just those within the three chosen parishes in the east of the city.

It was during this period that Joseph came to the fore in discussions surrounding Celtic's future as a charity or a limited company. At a meeting in late 1895, McGroary stated that the club had spent nearly £5,000 on the ground during the years 1891 to 1894, and that they were going to spend a further £800 to enlarge Celtic Park. John H McLaughlin contested those comments, claiming that the figures given were entirely erroneous. Regardless, it was clear from an early stage that he was against the business route, pointing out that the club had made great progress every year. When costs started to rise, he is reported as saying that despite having a bigger balance in years gone by, there was no doubt that Celtic was rapidly progressing. He then read out a number of the past balance sheets of the club, in an attempt to convince his peers that there was no need to change the status of Celtic.

Before the issue reached its peak, McGroary took part in a number of other aspects of the club. In February 1896, he attended the annual Celtic Brake Club reunion. Meanwhile, in September that same year, Joseph was among the official Celtic delegation sent to represent the club at the Irish Race Convention, a national event organised to campaign for Irish Home Rule. He was also representing the Thomas Davis branch of the Irish National League that day.

Eventually, the infamous battle for the soul of the club would need to rear its ugly head once more. Most who wished to preserve Celtic's charitable ideals deserted the club upon defeat, however, McGroary was willing to, albeit begrudgingly, accept the new direction of the club.

A meeting was arranged in St Mary's Church Hall on 18 February 1897, its purpose being to discuss the proposal to make a new cement cycle track at Celtic Park, as the renovations would be required to meet the standards necessary for Paradise to host the World Track Cycling Championships later that year. Believe it or not, the funds required to construct the renovations led to discussion surrounding limited liability and played a huge part in the ultimate direction of Celtic. The outcome of the debate was that a sub-committee should be appointed to attend another meeting on the following Thursday, with the purpose of putting a plan in place to turn the club into a limited company. Among those appointed were John Glass, Willie Maley, Tom Maley, Joseph Shaughnessy, John H McLaughlin, Michael Hughes, Michael Dunbar, James McKay, Frank Havlin and a certain Joseph McGroary.

By 1900, trouble with the courts had caught up with McGroary. He was sued by Alexander Porteous for "salary as his clerk, and for sums alleged to have been advanced by pursuer in connection with certain betting transactions," according to the report in the Glasgow Herald on 2 November 1897.

The case had begun in January of that year and had gone on for some time. The newspapers of the time highlight the pleadings of the case as it developed, although there is no definitive outcome shown. However, one can deduce the case did damage to McGroary, who emigrated to the USA in this period, leaving behind his wife and children, who returned to Donegal.

The betting scandal may have led to McGroary being struck off and forced to leave, or perhaps he chose to escape the stress of Glasgow with all that was surrounding him. Whatever the reason, he settled in Brooklyn, lodging in a family's house and working as a packer in New York. Whilst living in the Big Apple, McGroary's niece, Mary Harley, was shot dead by the Black & Tans during a raid in Mountcharles in February 1921. Shortly after the murder, Joseph received a graphic letter from his daughter, Gertrude McGroary, who detailed everything about the vicious attack as she had witnessed it. She also sent a similar letter to her uncle, John McGuire, who was living in Glasgow. She had hoped that her family could then contact the local press with this information, to highlight the plight of the Irish and bring global attention to the brutality of the British occupation of Ireland.

Eight years later, on 22 February 1929, Joseph's son appears in the Brooklyn Standard newspaper, with a report suggesting that he was in trouble with local police whilst visiting his father. A puzzling family, the McGroary clan was reunited shortly after this incident, when Joseph returned to Mountcharles and moved in with his wife and children once more. Joseph saw out his remaining days with the family in South Donegal, where he died on 28 February 1937. He is buried in Frosses graveyard with a headstone marked Ogilvey McGroary.

A ceremony was held at Joseph McGroary's graveside by the Celtic Graves Society in 2013.

Chapter 16:

JOHN CHARLES MACDONALD: THE IRISH ENGINEER OF CELTIC

John Charles MacDonald was born in Ireland in 1858. At the age of five, he moved to Glasgow with his parents, and the family settled in the Irish ghetto that was High Street. Soon after adapting to life in Scotland, the MacDonald's moved to an Irish boarding house in Springburn, where John's father, Bernard, found work as a labourer, in the nearby St Rollox locomotive works.

John was educated locally, and by the time he left school at the age of 14, he joined his father working as a labourer. It was very much all hands to the pump in the MacDonald household, who worked tirelessly to get by. That was until John defied the odds by managing to secure an apprenticeship as an engineer in the city. An Irish Catholic being awarded such a thing within the engineering trade was as a rare as a solar eclipse in those days. John qualified as a mechanical engineer some time later and remained living with his parents, assisting the family with their income.

John MacDonald and his uncle, also named John, were founding members of the Catholic Literary Society in Glasgow and, through the organisation, the pair met future Celtic founders, Dr John Conway, Hugh Darroch and Joseph McGroary. The younger John was also a member of the League of the Cross, St John's branch, located on Portugal Street, in the Gorbals. As such, he developed a number of contacts relevant to the founding of Celtic, who invited him to join the project ahead of the club's inception.

Not only was John Charles MacDonald one of the first people involved with starting Celtic, but he was also a keen supporter of Powderhall professional foot-running, which led to Willie Maley describing him, in his 'The Story of the Celtic' book, as one of only two founding fathers who had any sporting knowledge whatsoever.

MacDonald was in the crowd at the grand opening of Celtic Park in May 1888, when Hibernian played out a 0-0 draw against Cowlairs. At a post-match reception, held in the Royal Hotel in George Square, MacDonald and O'Hara were the two committeemen who were told that they were tasked with securing the signature of James Kelly, ahead of Celtic's first match. Kelly was one of the best players in world football, who played for the unofficial 'world club champions' of the time, Renton. The pair travelled to the West Dunbartonshire town but failed to persuade Kelly to join, before John Glass' silver tongue and heavy wallet did the trick. Nevertheless, it shows the esteem in which MacDonald and, indeed, O'Hara were regarded among the Celtic founding fathers, to be tasked with such a job, given that the famous saying of the time was "No Kelly, No Keltic!"

In contrast to Maley's comments, there were a few known cycling enthusiasts among the founding fathers of the club. However, few had as rounded sporting knowledge as MacDonald, and it was thus unsurprising that he acted as an umpire at regular Celtic sports events.

John MacDonald appears on the first Celtic committee on which he served for several years. Just prior to the club becoming a limited company, he left Scotland, due to finding better paid engineering work in Manchester, then latterly in Leeds. His stay in England was brief, as he returned to Scotland to marry in 1901, but not in Glasgow. Instead, MacDonald had settled in Aberdeen, where again the work he did offered better pay.

As a keen sportsman, his interest in football did not waver, and MacDonald became involved with Aberdeen FC, a few years after the club's formation in 1904. He kept in touch with his friends at Celtic, and thoroughly enjoyed meeting his Irish compatriots when the Hoops came north to fulfil fixtures at Pittodrie.

John Charles MacDonald's last involvement with Celtic came on New Year's Day 1910, when he attended Paradise as a guest of the club's directors. Disappointingly, the Hoops couldn't give him a suitable send-off with victory, however, he did witness a 1-1 draw against Rangers that wet afternoon, in a match that was played in front of 47,000 people.

John Charles MacDonald passed away in his adopted Granite City, Aberdeen in 1929, aged 71.

Chapter 17:

JAMES MCKAY: THE MAN WHO GAVE THE GIFT OF PARADISE

James McKay was another pioneer of Celtic, who was born in the Calton in 1853. His mother was Irish and his father Scottish, with the traditional identity of Celtic Football Club being further extenuated as the family lived on Abercromby Street, just yards from St Mary's Church.

James' grandfather was originally from the Highlands and was part of that first wave of Scots Roman Catholics who moved to a Catholic enclave in the Glengarry area of Bridgeton at the end of the 18th century. James' father, who was also named James, owned a barber's shop on the Gallowgate, just next to the Bellgrove Hotel and James junior went the same way by learning to cut hair and joining the family business.

He married Margaret Malley in St Mary's Chapel in 1884. The couple had four daughters and three sons together and, in a great coincidence, the wedding gave McKay a brother-in-law named Willie Malley. The eagle-eyed among the readership will notice that this wasn't the legendary Celtic figure, Willie Maley, whose surname adopted a single L, however, it was pronounced in the same way.

McKay was a founding father of Celtic, having been involved with the club from the beginning. This was most likely due to his connections at the local church and within St Mary's parish, where so many other men behind the establishment of Celtic spent their time. A member of the original committee, James became an office-bearer in 1892, when, at that year's AGM, he was elected as club Treasurer. The election made perfect sense and was somewhat of a natural progression for James, as he had assisted each of the previous men in the post, Hugh Darroch, John H McLaughlin and Tom Maley.

The position of Treasurer remained James McKay's until 1897, however, he is most famously and, indeed, fondly remembered for his role in the construction of the new Celtic Park. The move was forced by the original landlord's rather ubiquitous demands to raise the rent from £50 to £450 per annum. Such a huge change came as a result of the landowner spotting Celtic's rising fortune, and whilst the new stadium may have been a necessary reaction, the committee wanted it to reflect the club's growth, success and ambition.

Once constructed, the new Celtic Park was widely regarded as the top sporting venue in Scotland. The fact that the ground hosted so many enormous events, such as the first World Track Cycling Championships and Speedway meetings ever seen in the UK, stand testament to this. So good was the new stadium that the local press described it as "moving from the graveyard to Paradise," a nickname that Celtic Park holds to this day. Yet none of this would have been possible, if not for several individuals, from builders to contributors and the overseer /project manager, James McKay. Appointed master-of-works, McKay supervised the laying of the structure. It was not an easy task, considering that £4,000 was spent. In his wisdom, McKay spent much of the funds on converting the disused quarry into a playing surface and erecting a new pavilion, whilst a saving was made when the stands from the original Celtic Park were lifted and put in place at Paradise.

On the opening of the stadium, James McKay helped to sell season tickets for seven shillings and sixpence, ahead of the new season. He was appointed as oversman for the stadium in 1895, thus putting him in charge of the various upgrades to the ground. He is also the person credited with making the initial suggestion to install the double track around the pitch, which brought the club much-needed profit through cycling, speedway and pedestrianism contests in the early years.

The mid 1890s saw the debate over limited liability and charity commence, however, even in the midst of this argument, James McKay was singled out for an honorarium of £100. Shortly after receiving this money, McKay was part of the delegation sent to represent Celtic at the 1896 Irish Race Convention in Dublin.

The following April, after a sub-committee was established to meet in regard to preparing the club's conversion to a limited company, James sat on Celtic's provisional board. When the change in status finally went ahead, at the 1897 AGM, McKay was no longer considered one of the club's key men and he did not take up a seat on the board. He did remain a keen Celtic supporter and club member, getting involved with the powers-that-be at Parkhead again when it emerged that a deal for cheaper season tickets, which he brokered with Celtic Brake Club representatives as club Treasurer, was no longer being honoured by Celtic. McKay spoke up on the Brake Clubs' behalf, but Celtic refused to budge, and he let the matter go shortly after.

James McKay died in August 1924. The following fantastic article, summarising his life, appeared in the Glasgow Observer that week:

Celtic Pioneer Passes

CALTON LINK BROKEN

The death of Mr. James McKay, which occurred on Thursday at 189 Abercromby Street, Calton, broke another link in the chain of East End events extending from last century.

Mr. McKay was born in Stevenson Street in 1853. His father, too, was born in the Calton.

Father and son carried on a hairdresser's business at 546 Gallowgate in the good old days, when a shave cost a halfpenny, and Dr Scanlan, an old friend of the family declares that the two were very popular, and indeed, the only barbers he was acquainted with at that time who could make money at their trade.

In June of 1884 James McKay married Margaret Malley, a power loom weaver of 11 Greenvale Street. They were wed by Rev Donald Carmichael in St. Mary's Church.

Shortly afterwards, he became identified with the Celtic Football Club, founded in 1887. He and the late Hugh Darroch were, for many years, joint treasurers of the club.

In 1905, his mother died and Mr. McKay succeeded to her business, that of chandler and tobacconist in Abercromby Street. There he carried on until the death of his wife, five years ago, when the shock rendered him unfit for any active work.

A family of four daughters and three sons survive. All the ladies are in Glasgow. One son is in Detroit, one in Dublin and the other carries on the business in Abercromby Street.

To them and to Mr. McKay's many other sorrowing relatives and friends, we extend our sincere sympathy.

Chapter 18:

JAMES QUILLAN: THE FOUNDER WHO DEFECTED AND FORMED A RIVAL IRISH CLUB

James Quillan's Celtic story is quite astonishing. In one sense we must thank him for all he did to give us the club we love, in another sense we must curse him for seeking to destroy the club we love and lastly, we must forgive him for returning to the club we love!

It all began in 1856, when Quillan was born in Glasgow to Irish parents. Like many from his background, James was the son of a labourer, Peter Quillan, whilst he married within the Irish descendant community, wedding his neighbour, Roseanne Moore, in April 1874. The pair were 18 years of age at the time and Roseanne was the daughter of an Irish master confectioner named John Moore. The ceremony took place at the nearby St Andrew's Chapel on Great Clyde Street, a parish that was frequented by many Irish Catholics.

Keen to provide his wife with the best possible life, James Quillan rented premises on High Street, in the centre of Glasgow, where he operated as a barrel dealer, selling solid oak casks. His initial success enabled him to move to a larger property, which he titled East End Cooperage. The premises took up an entire side of Wilkie Street and would remain one of his bases for the next 17 years.

Beyond the Wilkie Street HQ, Quillan opened for business on East Nelson Street (now known as Millerston Street), before expanding further onto Janefield Street. His Janefield Street premises sat in the shadow of Paradise, situated behind the site of the Jock Stein Stand at the current stadium. Boasting a 380ft frontage, Quillan named the site Caledonian Cooperage.

His successes go further than simply expanding his business property portfolio. Indeed, by 1881, James Quillan was a master cooper who owned the largest cooperage in Britain, with over 180,000 casks passing through it per year!

Inevitably, such a major player in the business world would soon become a prominent part of his community circles. As a Catholic of Irish descent, who was by then living in the Calton, Quillan became a leading member of St Mary's parish and an extremely committed personality within the Home Government Branch of the Irish National League. He is described as being always ready with purse or voice in support of the old cause, and at the forefront of the Irish battle at a time when it was not fashionable to be so.

Newspaper reports of the time suggest that he was present at the victorious reception in St Mary's Church Hall for Hibernian FC, following their Scottish Cup triumph in February 1887. He was then part of the Home Government Branch of the Irish National League members, who were invited to present the Hibernian players with their winner's medals three weeks later.

Quillan was involved with the Celtic project prior to the club being founded. Following the club's fundraising circular in January 1888, he donated 20 shillings as an original subscriber to Celtic and was duly elected to be the club's first Vice President. His presence on the Celtic committee, as an office-bearer and founding father, was a great coup for the ambitions of the fledgling Celts. Not only was he a wealthy and influential man, he epitomised the identity and values of Celtic Football Club, in that he was a Catholic, an activist supporting Irish freedom and a charitable individual. Those values were something the founding fathers never hid and are not anything to be ashamed of, for they are part of the Celtic DNA, whilst not excluding others from outwith these traditions.

Within a year, things had changed quite considerably...

These days, people may have heard the term 'malcontents' being used to describe the rebel shareholders of the 1990s. However, the term was originally used to describe those who would later become 'Quillanites', after the first Celtic AGM, a century earlier.

Celtic's first AGM was held in Bridgeton Mechanics Hall, on 18 June 1889. The hall was bursting at the seams, with most members having much to be pleased about. Celtic had scored 217 goals in the 63 matches that the club had played during its debut season. The team also had a trophy to show for their efforts, alongside the impressive record of reaching the Scottish Cup Final. Impressive though the footballing achievements were, the warmest applause was reserved for Honorary President Dr John Conway's announcement that Celtic had raised £421 16s and 9d for charitable causes. To put that figure into perspective, the sum raised was the equivalent of £25,000 in today's money.

News of discontent among the custodians of Celtic had entered the public domain though, on 24 May 1889, when The Scottish Sport reported that "a group of malcontents from the Celtic Club had met in a public house in Bridgeton." The newspaper also alleged that this so-called meeting had "two matters under consideration," those being the present committee's mismanagement and the advisability of those present taking charge of the club, begging the question, "Should they sever the connection with the Celts and form their own club?"

One of the self-proclaimed 'so-called malcontents' wasted no time in responding to the newspaper. In an anonymous letter, he described the claims of this meeting as "purely fabricated" and "spiteful."

In contrast to this response, another newspaper by the name of The Scottish Referee, wrote:

While being neither desirous nor able to discuss the affairs of Celtic, we cannot refrain from putting on record our opinion that the scandals which have been too frequently raised about the club, and out of which other people have been making capital, tend to show up the management in very bad light.

That dissatisfaction exists and has existed for some time among certain members of the Celtic is proved by the fact that, a short time ago, arrangements were all but completed for the formation of another Hibernian club in the east end of the city. A ground had been secured and over £500 had been raised in order to give the new organisation a fair start, when it was resolved to abandon the idea, temporarily, and await certain developments in the Celtic camp.

These developments are expected in the next three weeks, when we will discover the settlement to the question as to whether we are to have a new club in Glasgow next season.

Should the new club be formed, its objects will be the public distribution of aid to charitable institutions, to widen the resources of the working class and to popularise the game generally.

The prime objective of the club – the public distribution of aid to charitable institutions - strikes at being a hit at Celtic. That club holds the position it does towards charity and, as we have always held, have made known their dealings with various funds to which they contribute. If Celtic showed the distribution in a public rather than private way, the present dissatisfaction may never have come.

The annual general meeting of the Celtic will take place in a fortnight, when there will be, no doubt, some fun over the election of office-bearers. Almost all last season's officials will be put up again and there are several prominent outsiders anxious for the posts, the competition is likely to be keen. Some of the players are, we believe, so strongly in favour of re-election of John Glass to the President's chair that they have, in private, declared that they will leave the club should he be ousted. This says much for Mr Glass' popularity in the playing section. Among the members he has not so many friends and no doubt he will have to fight for the honour.

It soon transpired that the malcontents were led by James Quillan, and he outlined his grievances with the Celtic committee in the letters page of The Glasgow Evening News, on 28 May 1889.

SIR – As there have been various rumours circulated in regard to the working of this club, will you kindly grant me space for the following remarks;

– On the 2nd May, a meeting of the club was held to appoint auditors and adopt rules. I moved that old members should be admitted on

payment of 5s, which was seconded by Mr Howie, and carried by 59 against 42 votes. By the rule as read, this majority (including myself) understood that new members were to be admitted on payment of 7s, 6d. On seeing the new rules when published, we were surprised to find that instead of 7s, 6d, the sum of 12s, 6d was stipulated.

I protested – and my protest was duly noted – against members who had joined the club previous to 1st September 1888 being excluded from the meeting in direct violation of rules 10 and 24.

On the 9th July 1888, a meeting was alleged to have been held, notice of which was not given to me, although I then held and still hold the office of Vice President, at which another violation of the rules occurred, a resolution being passed making the entry money 10s instead of 5s.

Without acting in any way, the part "the captious critic," it seems to me that 12 out of 24 rules have been disregarded. As a sincere well-wisher of the club, and in its best interests looking to the good it has accomplished, and in the hope that a bright and useful future is still in store for it, I take this opportunity of laying those facts before its many friends.

James Quillan – Vice President, Celtic FC

To produce such a letter regarding internal club matters was a very unorthodox and exceedingly unpopular move. Therefore, it is of little surprise that the Chairman of the club, John H McLaughlin, responded in kind, to set the record straight:

SIR – I read with great pain, but with no surprise, the extraordinary effusion our Vice President treats your readers to in your issue of last night. As the person directly responsible for drafting and printing the rules, perhaps you will allow me space to reply to his misrepresentations. I will refrain from commenting on the indecency of an official in his position, who so loudly proclaims himself "a sincere well-wisher of the club," dragging into print matters which ought never to have been discussed outside of the club but will confine myself to a bare statement of the facts.

The rule which Mr Quillan calls in question reads as follows:

"The annual subscription shall be 5s. New members, besides their subscription, shall pay an entry money of 7s, 6d."

Now this rule was read over at the meeting on 2nd May no less than five times, and was, moreover, discussed clause by clause, and this last clause adopted unanimously. If Mr Quillan didn't understand the rule at the time, it can only be attributed to his inability – which was quite apparent – to grasp the terms "entry money" and "subscription"- a difference he has since seemingly mastered. Through the rest of his rambling letter, I do not care to follow him. His alleged grievances have been discussed at many committee meetings, and he has again and again been proved to be totally and hopelessly wrong.

Arguments and facts, however, seem to be thrown away on him, and I shall, therefore, not recapitulate what has been explained to him a dozen times over; but for the benefit of those of the Celtic members who do not know Mr Quillan, and might therefore be inclined to attach some weight to his vapourings; allow me to state – firstly that the alleged meeting on 9th July was the usual weekly meeting of the committee, and that if Mr Quillan was absent from it, it was entirely his own fault; and secondly, that that meeting did not pass a resolution to make the entry money 10s, but simply resolved that no new members should be admitted on account of the precarious condition the club then stood in, and this was done on the advice of our late agent, a fact which Mr Quillan is perfectly well aware.

What he means when he says that 12 out of 24 rules have been disregarded, I don't know – probably he does not himself – and until he explains it, I shall take the liberty of regarding it as unintelligible nonsense; a fitting ending indeed for a tirade of misstatements, which, in common with the other ebullitions of himself and his friends in print lately, I can only designate as electioneering dodges of the club, or a desire to advertise himself, and to pose as "the poor man's friend," (a role he seems to have a special liking for), that has inspired his precious epistle.

John H McLaughlin - Glasgow, 29th May 1889

McLaughlin's strong rebuttal triggered a lengthy public argument between the pair, which other committee members waded into. The debate, which revealed much about Quillan's motives at the time, raged in similar vein to the letters shown above, until the eve of the AGM. This despite the fact that McLaughlin had withdrawn from discussing matters in public on 7th June and opted to wait until the AGM to air his thoughts through the appropriate platform.

Throughout the exchanges, it became deducible that Quillan's decision to delay the malcontents from setting up Glasgow Hibernian was a tactical one, allowing himself time to build greater support for the motion ahead of the Celtic AGM. His motive for leading the malcontents away from the club in the first place, seemed to be primarily based around management and bureaucracy issues. However, there could also be reason to believe that, beyond the matter of rule changes affecting the working-class, some of the malcontents may have simply disliked people such as John H McLaughlin being able to shape the ideals of Celtic. This theory stems from 3 June 1889, when Hugh Murphy partook in the public mudslinging, and aimed a few choice remarks at McLaughlin.

Hugh Murphy was heavily involved with the Irish National League and had been a good friend of James Quillan, thanks to their shared enthusiasm for Irish Nationalism. John H McLaughlin, however, centred himself around religious groups, and tended not to indulge in Irish political matters to quite the same degree.

The following is quoted from a letter that Murphy wrote to McLaughlin via the press:

SIR – although a long-time admirer of the Celtic Club since its inauguration, I may state that the last letter of Mr McLaughlin staggered me. Having copied as much American slang as his fertile brain contains, he makes an attack upon an Irishman who through weal and woe has stuck to "Ireland's a nation."

I may tell him that Mr Quillan has had in the past – and, indeed, at the present time – more honourable positions assigned to him than any position the Celtic place him in.

Ironically, Murphy went on to join the Celtic committee in 1890, and the club continued to express an openly political identity. That said, personality clashes and fear of the political aspect of the club not being given continual attention, may have played a part in the desire for some to stray from Celtic.

The final factor to consider is the prominence of the temperance movement at the time. As many as 50,000 people, mostly Irish, were registered members of alcohol temperance societies in the city. In fact, some of the largest public gatherings that Glasgow has witnessed have been those of the Rechabites, abstinence societies and temperance societies demonstrating together at Glasgow Green. The cause of alcohol denial even united the traditionally Republican and Loyalist factions of the immigrant Irish, who marched side by side to deter enthusiastic drinkers during the Glasgow Fair and New Year celebrations!

The malcontents themselves are unlikely to have been concerned with alcohol issues, considering they often met one another in public houses. However, Celtic Football Club was blamed by a minority for facilitating the alcohol problem, and Quillan may have outlined this fact as a basis upon which to attract supporters of a new Glasgow Irish club.

A priest from St Mary's - of all parishes - actually stated that he "wished the Celtic club had never come into existence," when commenting on the alcohol problem that was plaguing the east end! Another parishioner, Mr Owen McGerrigan, wrote to The Glasgow Observer and said that football was "sapping the morality of the youth in St Mary's, whilst also keeping them from their religious duties." By contrast, a priest named Father Carroll lambasted Owen McGerrigan for "a cowardly attack on Celtic Football Club," in a letter of his own to The Glasgow Observer. Father Carroll went on to question McGerrigan's authority to dictate his version of morality to the club, its supporters or indeed local Catholics in general. Carroll's comments were further re-enforced by a departing clergyman of St Mary's, Father Van Der Hyde. In his farewell address, Van Der Hyde said: "There has been an increase in membership of The League of the Cross (temperance society) at St Mary's by at least 200 members per half year, and the morality of the parish has improved since the advent of Celtic."

The League of the Cross, to which Celtic fans provided wholesale support, gave birth to the Brake Club phenomenon in 1889. In line with the typically complicated nature of Celtic's history, it was only a matter of months before there were references to Celtic Brake Club carriages being accredited as "mobile drinking parlours." The oxymorons that seem to embody Celtic's history were further evidenced by the fact that some Celtic players of the time were given proprietorship of public houses. Although, in the club's defence, this was prior to the introduction of professionalism, and thus there was little conceivability that Celtic could have attracted the top players (such as James Kelly and Dan Doyle) necessary to draw seismic crowds, without using the assistance of the licensing trade.

The Celtic committee would have to wait until the AGM to discuss these factors that were potentially motivating Quillan and his followers, who were now referred to as "Quillanites" rather than the malcontents. Was it simply rule changes and management issues? Was it a clash of personalities? Could it be a battle for the soul of the club and were they planning to use alcohol abstinence as a means to build support for a rival club?

D-day arrived, and after the formalities were complete, John H McLaughlin took advantage of the opportunity to resume the debate with James Quillan in person. Sadly, the debate revealed much less than expected but appeared to suggest that Quillan and his band of Quillanites had formed a clique.

The relevant minutes from the AGM read as follows:

...The secretary was then called upon to read the minutes of the last general meeting. On these being read, Mr James Quillan said he would move the adoption of the minutes if a certain rule, (pertaining to entrance fees and subscription money) were omitted, as said rule was not the rule as passed by meeting. (Mr Quillan read his motion). A seconder being found, the chairman received the motion.

Mr Joseph Shaughnessy then rose and moved, as an amendment, that the minutes be held as a correct reflex of general meeting and be passed as such. About a dozen gentlemen sprang to their feet to second Mr Shaughnessy's amendment.

A short discussion followed. Few, very few, could understand the position adopted by Mr Quillan, for as fast as one portion of his contention was cleared away, hydra-like, another reared its head.

The amendment and motion being placed before the meeting and a vote taken, showed that for Mr Shaughnessy's amendment 104 votes were given; whilst Mr Quillan's could only total 17. This early presage of the feeling of the meeting caused jubilation and dismay to reign in each of the opposing parties.

The results of the AGM returned that Quillan's position as Vice President was opposed and he was relieved of his duties, to be replaced by Francis McErlean from Belfast. Of the 20 Quillanites, none were elected on to the committee.

Six days later, on 24 June 1889, The Scottish Referee newspaper reported:

At last, all is peace and quietness in the camp of Celtic FC. The Quillanites have been squashed and the original leaders of the club now go on their way rejoicing. The doings in the legislative chambers of the Celtic are kept so quiet that it is hard to say what the row was about. The objects of the club are praiseworthy, and it is hoped that the new offices and committee will work towards this end as one man.

Undeterred, the Quillanites decided to explore the possibility of relocating Edinburgh Hibernians to Glasgow. Rumours of a splinter group from Celtic negotiating a resettlement of their club boiled the blood of Hibernian fans. The Edinburgh club had already begun to view the Glasgow Irish with a degree of contempt, for even though Celtic donated £45 to Hibernian, it scarcely passed as compensation for the signature of players, in the eyes of Hibs supporters. This point was demonstrated when a section of the home support angrily invaded the pitch at Easter Road, whilst 3-0 down against Celtic earlier in the season.

In order to silence the rumoured move of the Edinburgh side, Michael Whelahan, (co-founder of the club) said less than phlegmatically: "Hibernian are the Edinburgh Irishmen and will carry on as the Edinburgh Irishmen. There will be no move to Glasgow or anywhere else."

Subsequently, one local newspaper ran the headline:

The men of the west are unable to come to an agreement with the men of the east.

The Quillanites persevered, holding a public meeting in Bridgeton to announce their next move. Before a reasonable crowd, James Quillan revealed that he hoped to establish another club of the Glasgow Irishman, with an almost identical raison d'être to that of Celtic.

By the time the curtain was lifted on the 1889/90 season, a new team had successfully applied to become members of the Glasgow and Scottish Football Associations. The club established by James Quillan had secured a six-acre site near the Oatlands district, south of the River Clyde, with the perk of an entry point from Rutherglen Road. The venue was level, drained and prepared for the erection of an athletic enclosure, complete with a grandstand and cinder athletics track. The arena would be known as Hibernian Park.

The roots and optimisms of James Quillan's club appear very similar to Celtic, yet there was one key difference in ideology. Glasgow Hibernians would have an openly exclusive signing policy, which meant that the club would only adopt the services of players from Irish Catholic backgrounds.

As Celtic represented the Irish Catholic community, whose footballers were generally not given the opportunity to sign for clubs such as Queen's Park or Rangers, the Celts themselves made little attempt to reach outside of the Glasgow Irish domain for players in the first season. However, the door to such possibilities was never closed at Parkhead and, despite having an all Catholic team in the club's formative year, the lack of desire to enshrine a sectarian or exclusive policy may have played a role in some of the Quillanites wanting to depart the club. Indeed, Celtic would complete the signing of their first non-Catholic, a goalkeeper named Jamie Bell, in 1890. At that time, the goalkeeping position was becoming difficult to fill and it was beneficial to look beyond the Irish community for footballing talent. One year later, Bell was replaced by Orange Order member, Thomas Duff, who was nicknamed 'The Cowlairs Orangeman!'

Willie Maley further describes the psyche of the Celtic committee, who stayed beyond the 1889 AGM, in his book, The Story of the Celtic (published in 1938):

We have always been a cosmopolitan club since our second year, and we have included in our list of players a Swede, a Jew and a Mohammedan. Much has been made in certain quarters about our religion, but for forty-eight years we have played a mixed team, and some of the greatest Celts we have had did not agree with us in our religious beliefs, although we have never at any time hidden what these are.

Men of the type of McNair, Hay, Lyon, Buchan, Cringan, the Thomsons, or Paterson, soon found out that broad-mindedness, which is the real stamp of the good Christian, existed to its fullest at Celtic Park, where a man was judged by his football alone.

There were predictions from some quarters that the serious ambition of Quillan's Glasgow Hibernian could lead to a decline in gate receipts at Celtic Park. However, any hopes of this feat being achieved by the followers of Glasgow Hibernian, were soon scuppered.

Glasgow Hibernian's audacious launch in opposition to Celtic began with a glimmer of hope, when they defeated Shettleston 3-1 in their first game. Interestingly, Shettleston were drafted in as a makeshift opponent, after Edinburgh Hibernians declined the invitation to provide opposition to this latest Glasgow Irish club.

From debut victory, nothing but desperate despair ensued.

The club was eliminated from the first round of the Scottish Cup by Thistle, who defeated the Glasgow Irishmen 3-1 at Hibernian Park, on 7th September 1889. A solid fan base was not mustered, and as few as 500 spectators were among the terraces. Meanwhile, Celtic were prospering with crowds of over 20,000 on a regular basis.

The writing was on the wall. Glasgow Hibernian were declared bankrupt, quicker than a Buggati Veyron cruising down an open stretch of the Autobahn.

It may have been the end for Glasgow Hibernian, but for James Quillan the story was very much ongoing. In a remarkable twist of events, he was welcomed back to Celtic Football Club a short time later, and he stayed committed to the Bhoys throughout the remainder of his involvement in football! He stood for re-election to the committee in 1896, and failed to win a place, but he did remain a club member and keen supporter.

James Quillan's life was in turmoil in the late 1890s. He lost his wife in July 1897 and was then involved in a slander case with his brother-in-law and Celtic club member, Peter Winn. Quillan was found guilty and had to pay out £300, which was a gargantuan sum back then.

To make matters worse, Quillan's once-successful business failed in 1901, and he had to sell off assets to pay for court costs. By August that year, the stress had taken its toll and, sadly, he suffered a fatal heart attack.

Chapter 19:

JOHN HERBERT MCLAUGHLIN: THE MAN WHO BROUGHT PROFESSIONAL LEAGUE FOOTBALL TO SCOTLAND

John Herbert McLaughlin was born in Glasgow in 1863. His family roots were in Donegal, and he frequented St Mary's parish. In that sense, he was a typical Glasgow Irishman and shared a similar story to many of Celtic's founding fathers.

By now, you will know that many of the men behind Celtic's formation were taught by the Marists, and indeed by Brother Walfrid, at St Mungo's. John McLaughlin was no different. He was educated by Walfrid at the school and then went on to the famous Jesuit seminary of Stoneyhurst College in Lancashire, where he obtained the highest honours and was gold medallist for two consecutive years. John also studied at St Aloysius, where he performed in shows alongside others who would go on to establish Celtic. On returning to Glasgow, McLaughlin studied law at the city's university, however, as a graduate, he decided not to venture into the industry. Instead, he elected to join the commercial department of John Tullis Ltd, leather manufacturers in Bridgeton, working as a cashier.

In 1882, at the age of 19, John McLaughlin married Elizabeth Ann Shannon in the Cathedral Lodge. Three months into married life, the couple had their first child, born in Elizabeth's mother's home at 381 Duke Street. This was almost a home birth, for the McLaughlin's lived at number 300 on the same road!

Outside of family life, John devoted a lot of his spare time to music. Like his brother, James McLaughlin, who was a Catholic priest based at Ampleforth Abbey in Yorkshire, John was heavily involved with the local church, and would regularly play the piano or organ during mass at St Mary's. Interestingly, he also played the piano at many social functions in the city, which led to him performing as part of the Rangers FC Glee Club in March 1888!

Prior to his strange combination of piano commitments, McLaughlin had moved residence to Comleypark Street in 1887. His new address was in the Calton, and it is likely that his contacts through the Catholic Church, coupled with his skill set as a cashier, meant that he was brought into the Celtic project. At 24 years old, he was one of the youngest founding fathers and he had no experience in football. Yet, make no mistake, McLaughlin would soon become the best legislator that the sport had ever seen. His involvement in football would lead to professionalism being introduced in Scotland, together with the establishment of a competitive national league.

John McLaughlin was at the preliminary meetings held to establish Celtic, including the meeting on 7 November 1887, when the club was officially constituted. A member of the original committee, McLaughlin was elected as club Treasurer in 1890, becoming the youngest office-bearer in the process. One year later, at the 1891 AGM, he became club Secretary. This post was held by John for two years, until 1893, when he was elected Vice-President.

As previously mentioned, McLaughlin's involvement at Celtic had big ramifications for Scottish football. The game in Scotland was amateur when he first served on the Celtic committee. The notion of professionalism was something that appalled many establishment clubs, including Queen's Park, who were the most successful team in the world at the time. This stance became problematic, as the game in England turned professional. Inevitably, Scottish clubs lost their prize assets, as players were lured south by better wage offers, and the growth of the game was halted north of the border.

John McLaughlin was one of two Celtic representatives sent to attend a meeting between Scottish clubs at the Commercial Hotel in Glasgow, on 20 March 1890. The discussions that evening centred around establishing a league with competitive matches. McLaughlin cast his vote in favour of the idea, and then played a huge part in setting the wheels in motion, becoming the Scottish League's first Secretary. Though not alone in his efforts, the Scottish League would never have come to be, or sustained its success until the present day, without the administrative and organisational input of John H McLaughlin.

With his work underway in terms of the Scottish League, McLaughlin stepped up to the mark for Celtic in 1892. When the landlord attempted to raise Celtic's rent from £50 to £450 per annum, McLaughlin remarked, "Being an Irish club, it is but natural that we should have a greedy landlord." According to the combined research of Pat Woods and Tom Campbell, in their incredible book, 'Dreams & Songs to Sing,' McLaughlin was partly the originator of the Paradise nickname for the new Celtic Park, which a local pressman then famously utilised in the headline, 'From The Graveyard to Paradise.' It is said that the Celtic AGM in 1892 witnessed John McLaughlin telling his peers that, when the new stadium was complete, "a desert would become a garden of Eden." In response, one member said: "Would the players dream of Paradise when flitting on its sword?" Shortly afterwards, the local press described the ground as "like moving from the graveyard to Paradise." It seems too peculiar to be a coincidence.

It wasn't long after the club's move to Paradise that the debate over professionalism divided both the Celtic committee and Scottish football as a whole. The SFA called a vote on the matter in 1893, and amateurism was preserved by 20 votes to four. President of the national football authority, Thomas Lawrie, moved that, "All associations should unite to stamp out professionalism." However, John McLaughlin told those present, "You might as well attempt to stop the flow of the Niagara with a kitchen chair, as to endeavour to stem the tide of professionalism."

During this period, John McLaughlin moved into the liquor trade, like so many members of the Celtic committee. His family moved to Hamilton, and it was there that he took over as a licensee of a local public house. Concurrently, McLaughlin took his first steps into politics at this time. He was by far the least politically-minded of any Celtic founding father, something which he later took public flack for during an argument with James Quillan. However, in 1893, he joined the Irish National Foresters, whose constitution called for 'government for Ireland by the Irish people in accordance with Irish ideas and Irish aspirations.'

New businesses and debut political memberships did not abate McLaughlin's campaign with the SFA to introduce professionalism. Most clubs used underhand payments to capture players in this era, so the notion of amateur football carried little credibility. Eventually, football became professional in Scotland, in late 1893. Willie Maley spoke of the ground-breaking conversion: "With the legitimisation of professionalism, influenced by convincing arguments of John H McLaughlin, football seemed in a fair way to becoming a more honest and better organised sport."

After securing professional football in the country, McLaughlin was then at the forefront of taking Celtic down the business route. He felt that Celtic had to become a limited company in order to survive, grow and realise its full potential. Despite the romance of preserving charity, Celtic would not exist as a giant of world football today, had the likes of McLaughlin not taken the club in that direction. Perhaps more poignantly, Celtic would not have been able to contribute to charitable causes in the way it has done over the years, without being a club boasting vast finances and a huge global fanbase who carry forward the club's ideals at supporter's functions and fundraising events.

John McLaughlin, together with John Glass and Joseph Shaughnessy, led the charge towards limited liability. It was a heated and dreadful debate, which left those wanting to preserve Celtic's origins in full purity feeling outcast. Insults were thrown both ways. Those against limited company status were called "soup kitchen cranks' and "dinner table soreheads." Meanwhile, McLaughlin took more flack than any of those members supporting a different direction for Celtic. So tempestuous was the argument, that, in 1896, John H McLaughlin sued club member, Frank Havlin, for slander. McLaughlin asked for £100 in damages, however, the case was laughed out of court.

Limited liability ultimately won the day. It disgusted many committeemen and parishioners, who saw the move as a betrayal of Celtic's roots, considering the club was specifically formed to provide funds for charities operating within St Mary's, St Michael's and Sacred

Heart, all largely ran by the Catholic Church. Undoubtedly, some felt that the club had been taken over by people wanting to line their own pockets. Others suggested that those favouring limited company status simply had greater foresight, noticing that the move was essential. John Glass also remarked that the club, "would be only too willing to continue supporting charities once debts were cleared."

Regardless of the debate, the show went on. John H McLaughlin became the first chairman of Celtic in 1897. He held 150 shares, which later rose to 300, and he remained in the position for the next 12 years. His time at Celtic steered the club into its earliest glory days of six league title triumphs in a row, however, just like his fallouts with some committeemen at the club, and the disappointment felt by some within the parishes that Celtic were born to assist, McLaughlin got into further arguments. He fell out with Irish Nationalists in Glasgow and many of his board members at Celtic in 1899, when he donated 100 guineas to a patriotic fund for the families of British soldiers fighting in South Africa. The donation was made by the SFA, of whom McLaughlin was President, whilst also acting Chairman of Celtic. Two former Celtic players, John and James Devlin, who were also brothers, were serving in the war, however, Irish nationalists and, indeed, Celtic Football Club, were very publicly opposed to the British role in the war and campaigned against British involvement.

Though John McLaughlin had been a member of the Irish National Foresters, he was not politically-minded, and, indeed, was not involved in politics for much of his life. Thus, he was completely out of step with the political ideals that Celtic and many board members represented. His political naivety was further demonstrated when he denounced Irish Nationalist opposition to the British government's policy in South Africa, which led to the Anglo-Boer War, as "being the prerogative of demented Irish politicians." Among the so-called demented politicians was Michael Davitt, Celtic's second Patron and a convicted Irish Republican, who resigned his parliamentary seat.

The issue of British imperialism split public opinion. In Glasgow, the Irish community felt some empathy with the soldiers as individuals, and also with the Boer farmers, who were fighting to defend their country. Yet many abhorred the political decisions of the British government. The likes of John Glass, James Kelly, Arthur Murphy and John McKillop on the Celtic board, were all publicly anti-war. Strangely, McKillop did make a 10 guineas donation to the same British soldier fund as McLaughlin, due to his sympathies with men doing a job on the battlefield, whilst Archbishop Eyre, Celtic's English-born Patron of the time, did likewise. A few other members of the board had sympathies with British forces in this instance too, and, in typically complex Celtic fashion, the 1900 Patriotic Games, which were held in support of the soldiers in South Africa, took place at Celtic Park!

Complex as the whole saga may have been, the majority of the Celtic board were certainly not supportive of British imperialism in any way whatsoever. Thus, moves were made to have John McLaughlin removed from his seat at Parkhead. These moves failed, and he kept his position as Chairman of the club until his death in August 1909.

Among Irish Nationalist-minded Celtic supporters, who comprised the majority at the time, McLaughlin was never forgiven. He appears to have been held in some contempt by his peers within the club too. Only Tom Maley moved to comment that professionalism and the Scottish League were monuments to his labour. He was well-represented by Celtic members at his funeral, although the likes of Arthur Murphy from the club were absent. This could have been due to McLaughlin's role in leading Celtic's primary aim away from charity. It could also have been due to McLaughlin's pro-British stance in the Anglo-Boer War and his disrespect towards Irish Nationalists at that time, though it could equally have been due to McLaughin's attempt to sue Celtic member, Frank Havlin, for £100 (the equivalent of two years wages for Havlin, who was a gas labourer).

Politics aside, John H McLaughlin was a man who helped found the club we love. He steered Celtic to a future few could argue has helped bring immense joy to many through memorable victories on the pitch and charitable contributions off it. These would not have been possible if Celtic had remained amateur or had not prioritised business. McLaughlin's legacy is the success of Celtic Football Club, a European Cup, the millions of fans the club has worldwide, the ability of the club to make a big difference to charitable causes (even if it is now a secondary aim) and the presence of both professional football and a League in Scotland.

His life was summarised by the Evening Telegraph, on 12 August 1909, who reported the following in his death notice:

By the death of Mr. John Herbert McLaughlin, chairman of the Celtic Football Club, a well-known figure in Scottish Athletics has been removed. Mr. McLaughlin had been ill for eighteen months, and his death did not come in the nature of a surprise. Indeed, about a year ago his illness was of a severe nature.

Mr. McLaughlin died at his residence, Strathmore, Hamilton. He was one of the founders of the Celtic Football Club in 1888 and, on its formation as a Limited Liability Company in 1897, he became chairman. He also acted as secretary and treasurer of the club at various times. He took an active interest in the affairs of the Scottish Football Association, serving for a time as its president, and also filled the office of treasurer. He represented Scotland on the Football International Board, and his opinion on football matters commanded much respect on both sides of the Border. Kindred sports also claimed a good deal of Mr. McLaughlin's attention, especially bowling, and he was president for three years of the Hamilton Caledonian Club.

The deceased, who was 46 years of age, is survived by a widow and family. A native of Glasgow, he was educated in St. Mungo's School and finished at Stoneyhurst College, where he took the highest honours and was gold medallist for two years in succession. An accomplished musician, he was organist for many in St. Mary's Church, Abercromby Street, Glasgow, and latterly he held a similar appointment with much acceptance in St. Mary's Catholic Church, Hamilton.

The funeral takes place on Saturday to Dalbeth Cemetery, and a pathetic coincidence is that, on the same day, the annual athletic meeting of the Celtic Club, in which the deceased always took a great interest, will be held.

Chapter 20:

JOHN ALOYSIUS MACCREADIE: KEEPING FAITH WHEN HIS PARISH WITHDREW

Not a man with a prominent role in the establishment of Celtic, John Aloysius MacCreadie was present prior to the creation of the club and thus qualifies as a founding member to a certain degree. His father, Dominick MacCreadie and brother, Dominick Junior, were also around the club in its embryonic days.

The MacCreadie family were originally from Donegal. Dominick Senior arrived in Scotland during the height of the famine, in 1847. Having worked as a labourer, constructing roads around the country, he settled in Glasgow and set up a business as a rag dealer. A mark of his success was that he was able to move into the licensing trade, owning the Old Empire Bar in the Saltmarket. The pub made him a popular Irishman, not least because it was the first watering hole that Irish immigrants stumbled across after arriving at the Broomielaw.

The MacCreadie's lived on Steel Street, less than half a mile from the family bar. It was there that John MacCreadie grew up, following his birth in 1856. The first child of the family, John played football with a local youth team, which was quite unusual with the sport being in its infancy at this time. Aside of his sporting pursuits, John attended St Andrew's School. From there, he went on to St Mungo's, where he was taught by Brother Walfrid, before completing his education at St Aloysius College. His younger brother, Dominick Junior, would follow in his footsteps, taking the same educational path.

In 1887, around the time of Celtic's formation, John married an Irish immigrant of some prestige, Catherine Hegerty. Catherine hailed from

Dundalk and was the sister of the mayor of Louth. Interestingly, the MacCreadie clan expanded their business portfolio beyond the Old Empire Bar at this time, opting to delve into the metal, machinery and boiler businesses. Within a couple of years, John was working on his own as a machinery dealer. He then furthered his independence, moving with his wife and child, also named John Aloysius MacCreadie, to their own house on London Road, in Glasgow's East End.

As representatives of St Andrew's Parish, the MacCreadie family were involved in the discussions between Celtic and the church, alongside the other parish leaders of St Mary's, St Michael's and Sacred Heart. The latter three parishes, of course, stuck with the Celtic project and became benefactors, however, St Andrew's withdrew. Nevertheless, according to Willie Maley's book, 'The Story of the Celtic,' John MacCreadie remained interested and joined the burgeoning committee of men seeking to establish Celtic Football Club in a personal capacity. Perhaps this was due to his Celtic connections within the Home Government Branch of the Irish National League, of which he was a member. He was also the first President of the Donegal Reunion Society, a lead member of the Catholic Literary Society and founder of the St Aloysius Association, with the assistance of prominent Celtic founding fathers, Joseph Nelis, Joseph Shaughnessy and Dr John Conway.

Until the arrival of the Maley brothers in September 1887, John MacCreadie was one of the few people that had any footballing knowledge, in terms of actually playing the game! Though not prominent among the founding fathers, he was party to the discussions taking place and was a member of the club's committee within a couple of years. He was a pragmatic individual, sitting on the fence throughout the debates over paid officials and then limited liability, however, he did make up part of the sub-committee organised to put plans in place for the conversion to a limited company in April 1897.

Shortly after Celtic's conversion to a limited company, John's personal life took an upturn. He took over a pub on Greendyke Street. This was a trade he was familiar with, thanks to his father running the Old Empire Bar, and it was also in a profitable location, being situated just along the road from the Glasgow Highlanders headquarters.

The financial reward of such entrepreneurship was short-lived for John MacCreadie, for in late 1907, he suffered with flu, which put strain on his body owing to an underlying heart condition. On 2 January 1908, he passed away at his home, leaving behind his wife and 17-year-old son. As a mark of the respect John courted, almost all leading members of the Glasgow Irish community were present at his funeral, together with a large Celtic delegation, which was held at Dalbeth Cemetery.

The MacCreadie legacy continued at Celtic Football Club through his brother, Dominick Junior, who was an original and lifelong member of the club, just as the pair's father was, despite John being the only committee member of the trio. In terms of his more immediate family legacy, his own son, also John Aloysius MacCreadie, never involved himself with Celtic, but he made his own mark volunteering to fight in Salonika in the First World War. Meanwhile, John's wife, Catherine, took over the running of their pub on Greendyke Street.

As stated at the top of the piece, John MacCreadie wasn't one of the leading founding members or an office-bearer at Celtic, however, he did take part in discussions to form the club and was a long-time committee member. For that reason, he should be remembered in Celtic circles.

Chapter 21:

BROTHER WALFRID: THE KEY FOUNDING FATHER

I often think it unfortunate that the vast majority of the Celtic faithful only seem to be aware of Brother Walfrid, in terms of the club's establishment. This is perhaps the case because he was the leader of the founding fathers, the man who had the inspiration to bring a group of people together to form the football club. Indeed, it was once said that Brother Walfrid was the main man who founded Celtic and John Glass was the person who then established the club.

Born Andrew Kerins in Ballymote, South Sligo in 1840, Brother Walfrid was the son of John Kerins and Elizabeth Flynn, two dedicated Catholics. Andrew studied teaching, joining the Marist Brothers Teaching Congregation in 1864. It was not long before he moved to Glasgow, making the trip across the Irish Sea on a coal ship.

Upon arriving in the Dear Green Place, Walfrid began teaching at St Mungo's Academy in Townhead, where he tutored many of the future founding fathers of Celtic. He was a major player in the local Irish community, and as an academic, he was very interested in playing his part in the Gaelic cultural revival that was being experienced by Ireland and her diaspora. Indeed, Walfrid established a literary society for local Irish linguists, took a keen interest in local Irish friendly societies and enjoyed listening to music that was Nationalist in nature.

Having previously been the protégé of Brother Procope, Walfrid was promoted to an assistant teaching position on 13 May 1870 and was transferred to St. Mary's School. Four years later, he was appointed headmaster of the newly opened Sacred Heart School in Bridgeton. Despite managing his own institution in Bridgeton, Walfrid was still sent to teach in St Mary's, and the working relationship that grew between himself and St Mary's Headmaster, Brother Dorotheus, was to prove pivotal in the development of The Poor Children's Dinner and Breakfast Tables.

Ten years into the role as headmaster of Sacred Heart, Brother Walfrid was increasingly faced with the challenges arising from a trio of issues – the appalling social conditions of Glasgow, a lack of school attendance and Catholic children converting their faith, due to proselytism within Protestant-ran soup kitchens. Walfrid identified the school's attendance record as his primary concern, as with greater attendance, the government would increase the funding allocated to each educational institution. A rise in government grants would mean that he, as a lead member of the St Vincent De Paul Society, could then seek to tackle wider issues with greater resources.

The Penny Dinner Scheme was one of the projects established by Walfrid in the hope that children would be encouraged to attend school in order to enjoy a substantial meal. The payment of one penny was a suggested token, to avoid embarrassment for parents who may feel a loss of pride at being seen to depend on charity, although payment was never compulsory. To acquire premises for serving these school dinners, Brother Walfrid approached the local St Vincent De Paul Conference for assistance. The Society duly obliged, renting a shop property behind Sacred Heart School in Savoy Street. The shop was turned into a makeshift kitchen and was to be the first location used to provide food for The Poor Children's Dinner and Breakfast Tables.

Brother Walfrid worked closely with his confrere, Brother Dorotheus, who headed St. Mary's Catholic School in the Calton district of the city and who had set up the Penny Dinner Scheme for pupils at St. Mary's. As the year progressed, the scheme's success rocketed, to such an extent that it became challenging to continue to satisfy the increasing demand, and other initiatives needed to be explored to sustain benefit for the children.

A mark of the problematic overgrowth of the scheme was that Sacred Heart provided 48,500 dinners and 1,150 breakfasts in its debut year. Added to this huge level of service was the fact that the school capacity had quadrupled and was to educate over 1,200 pupils for the school year of 1886. Similarly, St. Mary's started the first six months of 1886 by serving 26,421 meals to students, 17,707 of which were free of charge. Rather than make the suggested donation of one penny compulsory, the decision was made to reach out to other aspects of social assistance.

The two Marist Brothers soon branched into football, having seen the enjoyment that not only their pupils, but the working-class people of Britain had received from playing the sport. The pair set up youth football leagues for former and current pupils of each school, whilst Walfrid also founded a few teams of his own, which were associated with his other community organisations, including one outfit born from the literary society that he had developed for local Irish linguists.

The rapid growth of football attendances, particularly at Edinburgh Hibernians matches, led Walfrid and Dorotheus to spot a fundraising opportunity. Indeed, Walfrid had already invited Edinburgh Hibernians to travel to the east end of Glasgow, on 26 September 1885, where a reserve team fulfilled a charity game against a junior club named Glasgow Hibernian. After that match, the Edinburgh side were fed and entertained by the St Vincent De Paul Society at St. Mary's Church Hall.

The initial match had been disappointing. On the park, Edinburgh Hibernians won 6-0 whilst off it, only a small amount of money had been raised. Undeterred, it was on a balmy mid-May afternoon in 1886 that Brother Walfrid managed to get Dundee Harp, one of approximately 40 Irish teams in Scotland at the time, to accept Clyde's invitation of a charity match at their home pitch, Barrowfield Park.

Harp 'stole' the win, with a late goal to make the scoreline 2-1 in their favour, and this time, the match was a resounding success as a fundraiser. All proceeds from the event went towards The Poor Children's Dinner and Breakfast Tables, which was the charity within which the 'Penny Dinner Scheme' operated. Therefore, it was perhaps fitting that both teams were then invited to Sacred Heart School for a post-match meal.

The Marist Brothers organised a further match, Walfrid's Eastern Rovers visiting Glengarry Park on 18 September 1886 to face Columba, a team that he had also formed in St Peter's Parish (St Columba brought and preached Catholicism to the Scottish Highlands). Funds continued to roll in, thanks to a crowd of over 1,000 on that occasion.

Interestingly, John Glass (who would later become the founding father to whom Willie Maley claimed Celtic owe their existence) had formed a club named Eastern Hibernian, who also locked horns with Columba in this period, thus bringing Walfrid, Dorotheus and Glass together within the footballing arena.

Another team of note at this time was Western Hibernians, who played in exhibition matches and who were also instituted to The Poor Children's Dinner and Breakfast Tables. The Western Hibernians donned white shirts, black shorts and green-and-black hooped socks. In an exhibition match in February 1888, they fielded no fewer than seven of the 11 players who would play in Celtic's first match, three months later!

The initial seeds of Celtic were sewn with the success of Walfrid's aforementioned charity match between Dundee Harp and Clyde in May 1886. Walfrid was the main organiser, the one with the ideas behind founding the Poor Children's Dinner & Breakfast Tables and the 'main man', in terms of founding football clubs. Yet Dorotheus followed him every step of the way, acting as an assistant and carrying through the ideas with his great friend. Make no mistake, these charity matches, which supported their Penny Dinner Scheme, were very important ingredients in the establishment of Celtic Football Club.

Hibernian's Scottish Cup triumph of February 1887, and the comments subsequently made at the reception held in celebration at St Mary's Church Hall, which Walfrid and Dorotheus were both present at, also played a major part. The Glasgow Irish were encouraged to, "Go and do likewise," (form a major Irish football club) that day by Hibernian Secretary, John McFadden. Dr John Conway led the victory speeches, and responded to the suggestion by saying to his peers: "Glasgow Irishmen, we can emulate the Hibernian's example, not only in social but in political matters too, so that the goal of every Irishman's ambition

– legislative independence of his country – will soon be attained."

The idea behind Celtic was in place among a prestigious few in Glasgow Irish circles, yet a final event confirmed the notion of a football club being formed for charitable purposes in the minds of the Marists.

A charity exhibition match was organised at Glengarry Park on 26 May 1887. This time, it was evident that Brother Walfrid and an embryonic committee of men, who would go on to found Celtic, were behind the match. The organisation was much better than previous charity games in Bridgeton. A trophy had been offered up to the winner, which enabled the clash to be labelled 'The East End Catholic Charity Cup'. A major coup was also secured, when the competing teams were announced as Edinburgh Hibernians and Renton. The magnitude of this contest should not be understated, for Hibernian were Scottish Cup-holders, whilst Renton held the Glasgow Merchant's Charity Cup (the cup committee invited some teams located on the periphery of Glasgow to compete) and Dunbartonshire Cup trophies.

The improved planning paid off, when 12,000 fans paid entry to the fixture, a larger crowd than that which had attended the Scottish Cup Final three months earlier! The match finished 1-1, meaning a replay and another pay-day beckoned. The replay was pencilled in for the beginning of the new season, on 6 August 1887, and a reduced yet respectable crowd of 4,000 arrived, excited at what lay in store. They were not disappointed, as Neil McCallum, who would go on to score Celtic's first-ever goal, struck five times in a 6-0 win for Renton.

Following the match, the Renton and Hibernian parties were cordially invited to the Sacred Heart Boys Club for a post-match reception. There, it was revealed that the combined crowds of 16,000 over the course of the two games had raised some £120 (equivalent of £15,000 in today's money), which was primarily donated to The Poor Children's Dinner and Breakfast Tables, but which was also dispersed among charities in Edinburgh and West Dunbartonshire.

The Sacred Heart parish had witnessed a revolution of football for good. The football became a leather tool, introduced to local school playgrounds as a means of encouraging educational attendance, whilst the charitable fundraising power of the sport had confirmed the convictions of those behind the foundation of Celtic. From this point, nothing could stop the founding of Celtic Football Club.

Brother Walfrid was the organiser who took all the important steps which preceded founding the club. He started the Penny Dinner Scheme within the Poor Children's Dinner and Breakfast Tables. He arranged the charity football matches, when demand became an issue, and he brought together all the characters necessary to form a successful Irish football club. His work, with Dorotheus' help, demonstrated to others that they had the capabilities to produce an Irish football club which could not only be the stand-out one of its kind in Glasgow, but could also raise significant funds to ease the poverty within their local community.

During preliminary meetings to establish Celtic, Walfrid had proposed that the focus of the fundraising should be on three Catholic parishes in the East End of the city. Almost all of the founding fathers had connections in these communities, and after discussion, the churches would be on board following one parish withdrawing from the project. This is reflected in the club's first circular:

The main objective of the Celtic Football Club is to supply the East End conferences of the St Vincent De Paul Society with funds for the maintenance of the "Dinner Tables" of our needy children in the missions of St. Mary's, Sacred Heart and St. Michaels. Many cases of sheer poverty are left unaided through lack of means. It is therefore with this principle object that we have set afloat the "Celtic", and we invite you as one of our ever-ready friends to assist in putting our new park in proper working order the coming football season.

The identity of Celtic was reflected in its founding members, its early patrons and public campaigns, however, the club needed a suitable name. At the inaugural meeting to set afloat the club in November 1887, the name suggested was Celtic, a suggestion made by Brother Walfrid.

There are many theories as to why the name was chosen. Some speculate that it was to reflect a blend of Scottish and Irish cultural integration, however, there is no evidence to suggest this and Celtic was very much established as a club with an Irish identity in the beginning. Another theory suggests that Celtic was more Irish in its connotation than Scottish. This idea stems from the fact that other Irish clubs in Scotland, such as Partick Celtic, used the name, but likewise 'The Celts' was a name initially suggested for Queen's Park, and they were a Scottish establishment team.

The more likely scenario is that Walfrid chose the name to be a little more subtle than the likes of Hibernian, who faced a tough time from the SFA and Scottish media because of their overtly Irish title. Indeed, Walfrid put the name Celtic up against the suggestion of Glasgow Hibernian. When 'Celtic' was passed, Hibernian's Secretary, John McFadden, was critical. In The Scottish Umpire newspaper, on 7 August 1888, McFadden said: "Patriotic Irishmen, truly, the Celtic and its supporters; patriotic Irishmen indeed who, in order to raise the name of Celts – a name which may cover Welsh, Highland Scotch, French, and all the nations of that family – dealt as they thought, and by means which are apparent to everybody, a death blow to the Hibernian club."

Regardless of the reasoning behind the name, one thing beyond doubt is that Walfrid intended for Celtic to be pronounced with a K (Keltic). He maintained this pronunciation until his death, despite the fact that most people referred to the club in the current way, Celtic with a soft C (Seltic). In 1909, Tom Maley wrote in the Glasgow Observer that the current pronunciation is a result of the supporters mispronouncing the name, which just stuck. Due to lack of evidence, this comment has never been challenged, although it does seem bizarre, given that multiple Irish organisations bearing the word Celtic, were all pronounced with a K.

Walfrid was heavily involved with the club for which he played such a great role in founding. Celtic were a huge success, raising funds he could only dream of for his Penny Dinner Scheme and Poor Children's Dinner and Breakfast Tables, among other Catholic charities. In sporting terms, the Bhoys were performing superbly for such a young club too.

Talks to change the financial status of club were soon underway. The old guard of Walfrid et al were very much against this. The concept of the club they created for charitable causes being taken away from its roots was unthinkable, however, Brother Walfrid would leave Celtic before the shift in status came about, his Church superiors transferring him to London, in August 1892.

In the English capital, Walfrid continued his work in combining football with charity. He set up football matches for the barefoot children in Bethnal Green and Bow. Meanwhile, he also took charge of a school, and worked to reduce crime in his very deprived area. Beyond those domains, Brother Walfrid immersed himself in community organisations and even set up a Marist Brother Sanctuary, at Ferry Grove in Kent.

An attempt by the traditionalists to influence the committee took place in 1893, when they read out a message from Brother Walfrid at the Celtic AGM. In the letter, Walfrid assured the club members that he gave his continued support and had sincere interest in the club from afar. The thought of Brother Walfrid keeping an eye on the club of which he was the main founder, was enough to halt the process of limited liability taking effect for the time being at least.

Walfrid's support of Celtic never wavered whilst he was living in England, even after limited liability status was secured. Indeed, he met the Celtic team and delegation in London, on their return from a continental tour, after the club had gone down the limited company route. Walfrid appears to have accepted the direction of the club, knowing that whilst it did not totally encompass the values he envisioned, it was a necessity for survival. He also understood that the charitable heritage would be carried forth by the supporters.

Tom Maley recorded Brother Walfrid's words of the day:

"Well, well. Time has brought changes.
Outside of ourselves, there are a few left of the old brigade.
It's good to see you all so well and I feel younger with the meeting.
Goodbye, God bless you."

Brother Walfrid passed away in Dumfries on 7 April 1915. He was buried in Mount St Michael Cemetery, where a commemoration was recently held by the club and Celtic Graves Society. Every Celtic fan owes the club's ethos and values to him and has to be thankful for him leading the way in terms of founding the club. Other founding fathers should not be forgotten, however, Walfrid was the key man, more than deserving of his statue outside Celtic Park. It could be argued that only John Glass held the same level of importance in terms of bringing Celtic Football Club to fruition.

Section 2:

CELTIC'S FIRST SEASON

By Matt Corr

For the six months following the decision to establish Celtic Football club in November 1887, the founding fathers, committeemen, volunteers and supporters involved had moved heaven and earth to create a suitable new home for the club.

Remarkably, by early May of 1888, they had achieved that objective, and Celtic Park was open for business. A slice of Paradise in the east end of Glasgow.

There were still some significant challenges to be faced, not least of which the club required to secure a squad of players fit to wear the colours, to be part of a team which would attract paying customers to the new ground, thus allowing the charitable objectives of this wonderful new initiative to be fulfilled.

At this time, football had been part of the fabric of Scottish sporting society for two decades, with the pioneering Queen's Park, multiple Scottish Cup-winners and inventors of the passing game which had transformed the sport, now facing a challenge from the West Dunbartonshire triumvirate of Vale of Leven, Dumbarton and the all-powerful Renton.

Then there was the potent threat from the east of Scotland, where Edinburgh's Hibernians, 'the men of Ireland', had caused a sensation by beating favourites Dumbarton to win a first Scottish Cup in February 1887.

It would be a daunting prospect for any newcomer to the Scottish football scene.

But this was Celtic.

Nothing would ever be quite the same.

The following section is a month-by-month account of the progress made by the new football club emerging in Glasgow's east end in the spring of 1888, including a look back at some of the key characters and fixtures which shaped the early history of one of the world's great sporting institutions.

This is how it felt to be Celtic, in season 1888/89.

Chapter 1:

MAY 1888: A NEW HOME & A WINNING START

Excitement was intense amongst the Irish community in the east end of Glasgow as April turned to May, with Celtic's first football ground nearing completion. Indeed, its construction had been a labour of love for many of those within that community, who had participated as part of the volunteer labour force assisting the main building contractor, Pat Gaffney, and who would later will 'their team' on to victory from or around those same wooden enclosures.

Progress had been quite remarkable, Celtic's new uncovered wooden grandstand, capable of accommodating 1,200 spectators and incorporating a suite of modest facilities for players and officials on its ground floor, now ready, willing and waiting to embrace its first customers in early May 1888. Just six months earlier, the new club's founding fathers had leased a stretch of grassland between Janefield Cemetery's eastern perimeter and Dalmarnock Street (later renamed Springfield Road), adjacent to the main tramcar terminus at Parkhead Cross.

The initial proposals for Celtic Park had included a second grandstand, to run alongside that perimeter wall, opposite the main structure, however, a combination of time and budgetary constraints would defer that addition for a further two years. The new ground would include a second playing field, which would be used for training purposes, and an ash track around the circumference of the main pitch. This would enable non-football events to take place on the new facility, providing additional income streams for the Celtic Football & Athletic Club.

So it would be on that basis that the first Celtic Park was officially inaugurated on the evening of Monday, 8 May 1888, with a friendly match between 1887 Scottish Cup-winner's Hibernian and Cowlairs FC, a few hours after the Prince of Wales - the future King Edward VII – opened the Glasgow International Exhibition at Kelvingrove Park, over in the west end of the city.

Current Scottish Cup-holders, Renton, had been the preferred opponents for the Edinburgh side for the stadium's grand opening, the two teams having played a charity game at Brother Walfrid's request the previous year, with more than 12,000 fans turning out at Barrowfield Park - Clyde FC's Dalmarnock home - raising much-needed funds for the poor of the East End. Sadly, a fixture conflict would prevent a lucrative battle between two of Scotland's giants, Renton in action against Rangers in the Glasgow Charity Cup semi-final at Second Hampden the same night, the West Dunbartonshire outfit winning that one 5-1. Readers of a certain vintage will know Second Hampden better as Cathkin Park, home to Third Lanark from 1903 until their sad demise in 1967, and currently the focus of some really dedicated people, working hard to uncover the remains of the old terracing and preserve its football heritage.

The enterprising Celtic committee had then turned their eyes south, inviting Preston North End, the strongest side in England at that time, to play Hibernian. They had suffered a shock defeat at the hands of West Bromwich Albion in the FA Cup Final at Kennington Oval six weeks earlier, having been so confident of victory that they reputedly asked to be photographed with the cup before the game! They would make no such mistake in the season to follow, becoming the first side to win the League and Cup double in England by going through both competitions unbeaten, the original 'Invincibles'. Those plans would soon be scuppered when the fee requested by the Lancashire club was deemed by the Celtic committee to be too hefty.

There were still several high-profile Scottish options, given the exclusion of Renton, Rangers, Dumbarton and Cambuslang, the last four Charity Cup participants. Like Hibernian, Queen's Park, 3rd Lanarkshire Rifle Volunteers (3rd LRV, later renamed as Third Lanark in 1903) and Vale of Leven had all lost their first-round tie in the above competition, and, presumably, would have been available. However, for whatever reason, it was a lesser-known team from Springburn who would be chosen to grace the original hallowed turf first.

Cowlairs had won the Glasgow North-Eastern Cup for the third successive season, just three days earlier, beating local rivals Northern

1-0 in the final at Barrowfield Park. They had been formed 12 years earlier, in 1876, as the Springburn area became a focal point for the railway sector of the Industrial Revolution, the club playing their home games at Gourlay Park. Whilst the exact location of this ground is unknown, the chances are that it may have been on the site of the latter-day Cowlairs Park, a recreational facility at one end of Gourlay Street in Springburn. It was from that park that a 9-year-old Matt Corr ran the short distance home on Wednesday, 6 May 1970, to catch the start of what would surely be Celtic's second European Cup Final win in four years. That night didn't end so well, after a promising start.

The Springburn club had been regular participants in the Scottish Cup since September 1880 and had taken part in the previous season's English FA Cup, beating Darwen Old Wanderers and Rossendale before losing to Rangers, in the last season such involvement was allowed by the Scottish Football Association. Cowlairs would then go on to play a key role in Celtic's early search for competitive honours. More on that to follow.

For the first-ever match at Celtic Park, Cowlairs would field recently-defeated Northern FC's goalkeeper, Burnside, in place of Duff, their regular stopper. Tom Duff would later feature in the Celtic story, albeit perhaps mainly for the wrong reasons. Having developed an excellent reputation at Gourlay Park, the Ayrshire-born 'Cowlairs Orangeman' had signed for Celtic in August 1891, a key part of the side who won the Glasgow Cup the following December, the Bhoys beating Clyde 7-1 at First Cathkin Park, the 3rd LRV's old drilling ground off Dixon Avenue. That final would be the first to feature goal nets, thus Tom Duff would have the perhaps-unwanted record of being the first Parkhead goalkeeper to literally 'pick the ball out of the net'. A few weeks later, he would enter notoriety for real, as League champions Dumbarton visited Celtic Park for a friendly match on New Year's Day 1892. The Sons were on course to retain their Scottish title, shared with Rangers the previous season, however, they had been beaten 2-0 in the League fixture in Glasgow's east end in September, whilst the Celts had been undefeated since an opening-day loss at Tynecastle. The 15,000 fans present saw the introduction of the new goal net phenomena to Celtic Park. They also watched poor Tom Duff pick the ball out of the new nets no fewer than 11 times over the 90 minutes. The only consolation was that three of those strikes were disallowed. The 8-0 defeat by Dumbarton remains Celtic's heaviest-ever home loss. Tom Duff was the obvious scapegoat and he would not feature again for the club, the keeper returning to Cowlairs within weeks.

The Cowlairs team of 8 May 1888 also featured the McPherson brothers, James and John. James would make two guest appearances for Celtic in October 1890, a 2-2 friendly draw against Sunderland, playing alongside Willie Maley, James Kelly and many of the Hibernian side who would line up against him on that opening evening, and a 3-1 Scottish Cup replay win over Carfin Shamrock two days later, albeit his latter involvement remains unconfirmed. His younger brother John would go on to become one of only two players capped for Scotland whilst playing with Cowlairs, scoring in Scotland's 4-1 win in Belfast in March 1890 then again in the 1-1 draw with England at Second Hampden the following week. He then joined Rangers for the inaugural Scottish League season, scoring the first hat-trick in the new competition and notching just under a century of goals over a 12-year spell, before becoming a director at Ibrox, a position he held until his death in 1926.

For the Celtic Park clash, Cowlairs would line up in their distinctive brown-and-blue half-and-half jerseys for perhaps the final time, before adopting a new look with white shirts and navy shorts for the following season's campaign. Hibernian would be in their usual dark green shirts and white shorts. Incredibly, nine of the eleven men who took the field in their colours that evening would later wear the green and white of Celtic. These included full-backs Dan Doyle and Mick McKeown, wing-halves Paddy Gallagher and James McLaren, wingers Willie Naughton and Johnny Coleman, inside-forwards Jimmy McGhee and Mick Dunbar and centre-forward 'Darling' Willie Groves. It would actually have been ten had the goalkeeper listed, John Tobin, taken part, however, he was replaced on the night by a stand-in called Docherty.

Just before 6pm on the evening of Monday, 8 May 1888, Founding Fathers Dr John Conway and Joseph Shaughnessy led the two teams on to the new Celtic Park surface, before more than 5,000 spectators. Honorary President Conway then kicked off the match and Celtic Park history, to the cheers of the faithful. The game itself finished goalless, the football Gods thus kindly allowing a Celt to be the first on the scoresheet at the new ground, later that month.

Three weeks later, on Monday, 28 May 1888, Celtic Football Club played its first-ever match, facing Glasgow outfit Rangers in a friendly. As Celtic were still in the process of securing a team for the new season (players' contracts were renewed annually in those days), the home side comprised of players still contracted to other clubs, including both Renton and Hibernian.

The Celtic line-up on this historic occasion consisted of guest players from the Irish community in Scotland, and was as follows:

Michael Dolan *(Drumpellier)*;
Eddie Pearson *(Carfin Shamrock)* & **James McLaughlin** *(Whitefield)*;
Willie Maley *(Third Lanark)*, **James Kelly** *(Renton)* & **Phil Murray** *(Cambuslang Hibernian)*;
Neil McCallum *(Renton)*, **Tom Maley** *(Third Lanark)*, **Johnny Madden** *(Dumbarton)*, **Mick Dunbar** *(Hibernian)* & **Charlie Gorevin** *(Whitefield)*.

There are a number of legendary Celtic characters in there, including perhaps a couple who are not so well-known outside of club historians.

James McLaughlin was born on 16 September 1864, at 447 Springburn Rd, just a few hundred yards from where I grew up at 399a. He started his career as a junior at Cowlairs and was the senior team captain there before joining Hibernian in 1887, then Celtic, one year later, although he is listed above as belonging to Whitefield in May 1888. He played at full-back in the inaugural match with Rangers, then, remarkably, he later took over as goalkeeper and was between the sticks for Celtic's first-ever trophy win in May 1889 (more on that to follow). James left the club the following year to join Battlefield and, on his retirement from playing, he became one of the top referees of the era, representing Celtic in that role for many years. James passed away in March 1946 and lies in rest in St Kentigern's Cemetery, Lambhill.

Willie Maley took his place at right-half. He is listed as belonging to Third Lanark, although that club was known as the 3rd Lanarkshire Rifle Volunteers (or 3rd LRV) until 1903. His elder brother Tom was actually the signing target for Brother Walfrid and Founding Fathers John Glass and Pat 'Tailor' Welsh, when they called at the Maley household in Cathcart on that September evening in 1887. Tom was out 'courting' at the time but would then be joined at Celtic by his brother Willie, who just happened to be at home and was told to 'come along'. The rest, as they say, is history.

Then there was the Renton pair of James Kelly and Cornelius 'Neilly' McCallum.

To put some context around their importance, I'll take you back to Saturday, 28 January 1888, as Cambuslang win the first-ever Glasgow Cup competition, the only one not to feature Celtic, who had only been founded in November of the previous year and had yet to play a game. Cambuslang had beaten Rangers 3-1 in the final at Second Hampden that day. It would prove to be their only Glasgow Cup success. The following Saturday, 4 February 1888, the newly-crowned Glaswegian champions would face the best team in the land, Renton, in the Scottish Cup Final at the same venue. Cambuslang would find Renton a different proposition, being on the wrong end of a 6-1 scoreline, a Scottish Cup Final record unchallenged until May 1972, when a John 'Dixie' Deans hat-trick inspired Celtic to beat much-fancied Hibernian side by the same margin. For over 130 years, Renton's feat that day has never been bettered.

In the victorious Renton team that day were two men who would later carve their names into the history of another club, James Kelly and Neil McCallum. Kelly was the Billy McNeill of that era, a dominating central defender and leader. He left Renton to become Celtic's first captain and would eventually be chosen as Scotland's skipper. Kelly's signing is widely considered to be one of the most critical in Celtic's history, as he would be the catalyst for a host of other top players to flock to the new club. There was a saying at the time, 'No Kelly, No Celtic.' Whilst the club would undoubtedly have progressed without him, there is a question as to whether that progress would have been so great from the outset, without the acknowledged best player in Scotland in its ranks. In a decade of service to the 'Bould Bhoys', James Kelly was part of the first Celtic side to win both the Scottish Cup (1892) and Scottish

League (1893), the first of his three Championship titles. On his retiral in 1897, he became a director at Celtic, a post he held until his death in 1932. James spent five years as chairman from 1909 and was the father of Bob Kelly, who carried out the same role between 1947 and his own passing in 1971, having succeeded his late father as a Celtic director back in 1932.

Winger Neil McCallum had scored twice for Renton in that 6-1 Scottish Cup Final win against Cambuslang at Second Hampden four months earlier. Together with James Kelly, he was also part of the Renton side which had become unofficial 'World Champions' just nine days earlier, beating English FA Cup-winners, West Bromwich Albion, 4-1 on the same ground. Neil would carve his own name into Celtic folklore in the inaugural game against Rangers.

The line-up featured Dumbarton's John Madden at centre-forward. Followers of early Celtic history will know that Johnny moved to Slavia Prague in the early part of the 20th century, making such an impression that he is revered to this day as 'the Father of Czech football'. Celtic played a match in Prague in July 2017, to commemorate a stand named in his honour.

Inside-forward, Mick Dunbar had played for Hibernian in that first game against Cowlairs, before signing for Celtic. Mick would perform at both Celtic Parks over the next five years and would be part of the side which won our first 'major' honour, the Glasgow Cup of 1891, before clinching the Scottish League title in his final season of 1892/93. He will feature prominently in the review of the season to follow. By the time he retired in 1893, Mick Dunbar's first-team spot had been taken by the great Sandy 'Duke' McMahon. He returned to the club as a Director in 1897, a role he retained until his death in 1921. Mick was joined on the Board at that time by his May 1888 colleagues James Kelly and Tom Maley, whilst a third, Willie Maley, became Celtic's first-ever team manager at the same time, at the tender age of 29 years.

The Rangers XI who would face Celtic featured a number of reserve players, known as 'Swifts'. In front of 2,000 spectators, on-loan Renton winger Neil McCallum had the honour of scoring the first-ever goal at the new ground and in the history of Celtic, with a header in the opening 10 minutes. Future captain and chairman James Kelly scored the second goal before half-time, whilst Tom Maley, playing beside his brother Willie, notched Celtic's inaugural hat-trick in the second half, as the white-shirted Celts won 5-2. Interestingly, whilst McCallum's first goal is widely known amongst the Hoops support, Kelly's is much less so and, even more bizarrely, the fact that Tom Maley scored the club's first hat-trick that day rarely gets mentioned.

Chapter 2:

JUNE 1888: MIXED MONTH FOR THE CELTS AS THEY SUFFER A FIRST DEFEAT

On Saturday, 9 June 1888, 12 days after the inaugural victory over Rangers, Celtic played the second game in its history, the visitors to First Celtic Park for the friendly match being Dundee Harp.

Harp had been founded in 1879, five years after Edinburgh Hibernian, to satisfy the needs of the large Irish community in Dundee, at that time reflecting around one-fifth of the city's population. They played in green shirts with a harp on the chest, the emblem of Ireland, white hose and black socks.

Dundee Harp is the club who could have been world record-holders but for an honest committee man.

On Saturday, 12 September 1885, they beat Aberdeen Rovers 35-0 at their Harp's Athletic grounds in East Dock Street, in the first round of the Scottish Cup...or did they? The referee had actually noted 37 goals as being scored, however, he was then corrected by the said club official, who had been keeping a tally of the individual scorers. Remarkably, the referee then reported the lower of the two scores to the Scottish Football Association at their Carlton Place headquarters in Glasgow, and the result stood.

Eighteen miles along the Tayside coast, Harp's bitter rivals Arbroath were entertaining another Aberdeen side, Bon Accord, at the same stage of the competition. Incredibly, Arbroath won by 36-0, although claims were later made that this scoreline was actually even higher. In any event, their 36-0 victory over Bon Accord remains a world record to this day.

Legend has it that Tom O'Kane, signed by Dundee Harp from Arbroath at the start of that campaign, sent a telegram to the Gayfield club that evening, 'winding his old friends up' about the record score which his new team had racked up that day, blissfully unaware that his old side had gone one better the same afternoon until he arrived back at what was still his home city in the early hours. O'Kane would be a signing target for Celtic, following their initial meeting in Glasgow three years later, however, he chose to remain with Dundee Harp at that time, before returning to Arbroath in 1889.

The Harp would enjoy Scottish cup victories over local rivals Dundee Our Boys (forerunners to the present Dundee FC) and Vale of Teith, before succumbing by 6-0 to the previous year's beaten finalists, Vale of Leven. James Kelly's Renton, the cup-holders, would then eliminate Vale of Leven in the fifth round in a repeat of the 1885 final, although they, in turn, would suffer a 3-1 defeat at the hands of Queen's Park at First Cathkin Park in the February 1886 final, a record eighth triumph for the Spiders.

Celtic's second visitors had actually played in Glasgow's east end before, notably In May 1886, Dundee Harp travelling to face Clyde at Barrowfield Park, their original Dalmarnock home, to raise funds for Brother Walfrid's Poor Children's Dinner Tables in his Sacred Heart parish in nearby Bridgeton.

Just over two years later, Harp faced the new group of Irishmen from Glasgow in front of around 6,000 spectators in their shiny new stadium, a mile or so north-east. Celtic made several changes to the team which had faced Rangers in May, with Eddie Pearson, James Kelly, Neil McCallum, Tom Maley and Johnny Madden all unavailable for various reasons. The hosts would win the match 1-0, thanks to a goal scored by debutant left-winger, Johnny Coleman, with just ten minutes remaining.

Coleman had been born in Dublin in June 1863 and had only recently signed for the fledgling club, having played for Hibernian against Cowlairs in the first-ever game played at Celtic Park, the previous month. He would go on to make 18 League and Scottish Cup appearances for the Bhoys over the next five years, scoring three goals, later becoming Celtic's reserve team trainer in November 1895. Despite being over-age, Johnny would join the first world war effort, before eventually settling in Canada, where he passed away in March 1927, aged 63.

As Johnny Coleman was scoring Celtic's first late winning goal, at the other end of the field, goalkeeper Michael Dolan was celebrating the first clean sheet in the club's history.

The 28-year-old Dolan had moved to Celtic from his local side Drumpellier, having played in the 5-2 win over Rangers just under two weeks earlier. Although he remained at Celtic Park on-and-off until 1894, his career was spent largely in the reserves, playing only three League games at the end of the inaugural season, in spring 1891, as the title was shared between Dumbarton and Rangers. He then moved to the wonderfully-named Coatdyke Gaelic in 1894. During his spell at Parkhead, Mick would not have had far to travel to and from games, as he lived on the Great Eastern Road (now split between Gallowgate and Tollcross Road), just a few minutes' walk from the ground. Dolan died in July 1910, aged 50. Both Johnny and Mick have been honoured by the wonderful folk at the Celtic Graves Society.

Mick's younger brother, Francis, also played for the club, between 1890 and 1894, so the Dolans may have a good claim to be Celtic's second set of siblings, after Tom and Willie Maley. Francis was a centre-half, who had the misfortune to understudy captain James Kelly, widely acknowledged as the finest player of the time. Largely as a consequence of that, he would play only twice in the Celtic first team.

A few years after their meeting with Celtic, Dundee Harp would run into severe financial problems, often struggling to pay their players. By 1894, suspended by the SFA, they had played their final game, ironically against a team from the same city, who had been formed as an amalgamation of East End and Our Boys. This new combined side would now be known as Dundee FC and it survives to this day.

In 1909, a new club would be established to fill the vacuum in the lives of Dundee's Irish community. They took the name Dundee Hibernian, and played, as the Harp had, in emerald green. By 1923, the new side themselves struggling in a financial sense, they changed their name twice in an attempt to appeal to a wider audience, first to Dundee City then to Dundee United, whilst changing their colours to black and white. United would then retain those colours for over 40 years until the adoption of the present tangerine and black combination under Jerry Kerr in the late 1960's.

Back in June 1888, there would be two further games for Celtic, following the defeat of Dundee Harp, the original Irish club from Tayside.

The following Saturday, 16 June 1888, Mossend Swifts made the journey through from West Lothian to Glasgow to take on the Bhoys, in front of 4,000 spectators. They would arrive in good spirits, having recently beaten holders Hibernian 5-3 to win their first East of Scotland Shield, no mean feat, given that the Edinburgh side had also won the Scottish Cup that same 1886/87 season.

Celtic welcomed back some of its big guns, James Kelly, Neil McCallum and Johnny Madden, as well as giving a debut to yet another Hibernian star who had played in the match against Cowlairs back on 8 May, Jimmy McLaren. It was McLaren who equalised for Celtic after 20 minutes, with Charlie Gorevin doing likewise before the interval, to cancel out a double from Mossend's Reid. Boyd would then put the West Lothian side ahead for a third time in the second half, and it took an 85th-minute strike from Neil McCallum to preserve Celtic's unbeaten record, as the teams declared at 3-3 for Celtic's first draw.

As a footnote to this clash, it should be said that the Swifts must have been a decent team. Within two months, they would claim the scalp of the Irish club from Edinburgh for a second time. On Saturday, 1 September 1888, as Celtic were taking on Shettleston in our first-ever Scottish Cup-tie, Mossend would cause a huge shock, knocking the 1887 winners, Hibernian, out of the competition. The little West Calder club would then go all the way to the last 16, before they were beaten by Dumbarton.

The final game played that month, four days later on Wednesday, 20th June 1888, would constitute Celtic's first derby fixture, as the visitors this time were Clyde, their east end opponents based just a short distance away on the boundary of Dalmarnock and Bridgeton, Brother Walfrid territory. The Glasgow Evening News of the time states the crowd as being 'several thousand' and they would see Lambie give Clyde an early lead with a header, before James Kelly turned the game around with a quickfire double. Jimmy Britton then decided to enter his name into the Parkhead history books, by equalising before half-time then adding a further two goals in the second half to score the first hat-trick by a visiting player against Celtic. With Clyde reduced to 10 men following an injury to their first goalscorer, Lambie, the Bhoys fought hard to reduce the 4-2 deficit, however, a solitary strike from Johnny Madden near the end could not prevent the home side from suffering a first-ever defeat.

The month would end on a more positive note, with several top players committing their services to the club for the 1888/89 season. This included the critical signing of James Kelly and Neil McCallum from Scottish Cup-holders Renton, plus a number of stars moving west from Hibernian, including 1887 Cup-winners Willie Groves and Jimmy McLaren, Johnny Coleman, Mick Dunbar and Paddy Gallagher.

More would follow before the new season kicked off in August.

Chapter 3:

JULY 1888: BIRTH OF A FUTURE CELTIC LEGEND

There were no games played in July 1888, as the new club in the east end of Glasgow made plans for its first competitive football season, due to begin the following month. However, there was an event that month which would produce a star player for Celtic beyond the turn of the century.

On Monday, 2 July 1888, Andrew McAtee was born in the village of Cumbernauld, just north-east of Glasgow. Raised in the mining community of nearby Croy, as was the mighty Jimmy Quinn, young Andy developed as an exciting right-winger with Mossend Hibernian. On 12 September 1910, he signed for Celtic, making his debut two weeks later on a Monday night at Firhill, in a game which ended 1-1.

Willie Maley's champions, that first great side of Jimmy McMenemy, Jimmy Quinn and Peter Somers, were going for seven League titles in a row in 1910/11, however, a disappointing campaign would see them finish in fifth place, 11 points behind Rangers. There was a first medal for the 22-year-old McAtee though, Celts winning the Scottish Cup with a 2-0 replay victory over Hamilton Academical, after a goalless first game, strikes from Quinn and another local man, near-namesake Tom McAteer of Smithstone, Cumbernauld. Both matches were played at Ibrox, Hampden having ceased to be used for the showpiece game following the riot Scottish Cup Final between Celtic and Rangers, two years earlier. The following season, 1909/10, McAteer had captained Clyde all the way to the Scottish Cup Final, his side defeating both Glasgow giants before losing to Dundee in a second replay at Ibrox.

Andy McAtee would repeat his own Scottish Cup success in April 1912, as Celtic defeated local rivals Clyde by 2-0 at Ibrox, in front of a 45,000 crowd. By this time, McAtee had a new partner at inside-right, a certain Patsy Gallacher. The career of the little man from Milford, Donegal, known as the 'Mighty Atom', would almost shadow that of McAtee, starting and ending one year later. Patsy scored the first goal in that 1912 final, with the second coming from another Hoops legend, 'Napoleon' McMenemy. Andy, Patsy and Celtic would also beat the Bully Wee in the final of the Glasgow Charity Cup at the present Hampden Park the following month, winning 7-2 on corners after a goalless draw!

On 3 March 1913, Andy McAtee made his only appearance for the full Scottish international side, in a 0-0 draw with Wales at the Racecourse Ground in Wrexham. Playing on the right for the Welsh team that day was Billy Meredith, perhaps football's first superstar. Born in July 1874, the winger made over 300 League appearances for both Manchester City and Manchester United in an incredible 30-year career, playing his final match for City in March 1924, just 100 days shy of his 50th birthday.

Five days after Andy's international debut, Celtic's third bid to win a hat-trick of Scottish Cups was ended at Celtic Park at the quarter-final stage of the campaign by Hearts, just as they had done at Ibrox in the 1901 Final to deny the first attempt. Ironically, it would be against the Edinburgh side some 118 years later when that particular Scottish Cup bogey would be laid to rest, as the Hoops won the world's first Treble Treble, on 25 May 2019. The infamous Riot final of 1909 had put paid to Celtic's second attempt, both sets of fans storming the ground in protest at the lack of extra-time, following a second drawn game, angered by suggestions that the two clubs had been complicit in the agreement to play a third match instead. That third game was never played and instead, the old cup was withheld.

Celtic's only silverware of the the 1912/13 season was claimed two months later, the Hoops retaining the Glasgow Charity Cup in front of 30,000 spectators at Parkhead. The Bhoys came back from two goals down within six minutes to beat Rangers 3-2, thanks to strikes from Patsy Gallacher and Bernard Connolly, who scored twice. Four days earlier, the semi-final victory against Third Lanark at Cathkin Park had marked the debut of legendary Celtic goalkeeper, Charlie Shaw.

The following season saw Celtic complete their third League and Cup double, finishing six points clear of Rangers and defeating Hibernian 4-1 in the Scottish Cup Final replay, after a goalless draw, with doubles from John Browning and Jimmy 'Sniper' McColl. Incredibly, Celts would then have to wait exactly 40 years for their fourth double, when Jock Stein captained Jimmy McGrory's side in 1954. McColl was also on the scoresheet in May 1914 as Celts added a third trophy, with a 6-0 victory over Third Lanark at Hampden in the final of the Glasgow Charity Cup, our third successive victory in this competition. Thirds had beaten the Hoops in the semi-final replay of the Glasgow Cup at Cathkin the previous October, thus preventing the very real possibility of a first-ever 'clean sweep' for Celtic.

Although the Scottish Cup competition would then be suspended until 1919, due to the outbreak of war, the League did continue, Celts winning four-in-a-row between 1914 and 1917, whilst extending their run of successive Glasgow Charity Cups to seven by 1918, with victories over Partick Thistle (twice), Queen's Park and Rangers. There were also two Glasgow Cup Final wins in 1916 and 1917, with victories over Rangers and Clyde, as Andy McAtee's medal haul became increasingly impressive.

He had missed out on one of the above medals, the Glasgow Charity Cup of 1917/18. Having worked in the reserved occupation of mining for the first three years of the conflict, whilst playing for Celtic each Saturday, Andy was then conscripted into military service, based in Italy with the Royal Field Artillery from April 1918 until January 1919. He returned in time to celebrate another League championship success, in May of that year, Celtic taking the title by one point from Rangers.

Season 1919/20 saw a silverware double for Andy and Celtic, with both the Glasgow and Glasgow Charity Cups won with victories over Partick Thistle and Queen's Park, respectively.

Both trophies were then retained the following season, the Charity Cup with a 2-0 victory over Rangers and the Glasgow Cup with a single-goal win over Clyde at Celtic Park in October 1920, with Andy McAtee's strike just before half-time proving to be the matchwinner, in front of 40,000 fans. And the winger struck another vital goal in April 1922, his late header rescuing a point against Scottish Cup-holders Morton at Cappielow, a game marred by violence, as Celts again won the title by a single point.

There would be one final medal for the veteran Celt.

The Hoops 1922/23 Scottish Cup campaign began on Saturday, 13 January 1923 in Lochgelly, the local United beaten 3-2 on their own ground. The following week saw the Celtic debut of a certain James Edward McGrory, in a 1-0 League defeat by Third Lanark at Cathkin, the Garngad Bhoy replacing the legendary Patsy Gallacher to partner Andy McAtee on the right flank. Further home cup wins against Hurlford, East Fife and Raith Rovers took Celtic through to a semi-final tie against Motherwell at Ibrox, in front of 75,000 spectators. Goals from Joe Cassidy and Andy McAtee then set up a final meeting with Hibernian, at Hampden Park on 31 March 1923. Cassidy was again on target to give the Bhoys a 10th Scottish Cup success, equalling the record set by Queen's Park in the previous century.

After 14 trophy-laden years at Parkhead, Andy McAtee left Celtic in 1924, joining his old goalkeeping colleague Charlie Shaw at New Bedford Whalers, Massachusetts in the American Soccer League. With 6 League titles and 4 Scottish Cup-winner's medals, he is one of the most decorated of the early Celts. He also won a further 10 winner's medals between the Glasgow and Glasgow Charity Cups. With 407 League appearances, only ten other Celtic players are ahead of him in the all-time list. He hit 65 League goals and managed another 2 from 32 ties in the Scottish Cup. All in all, he had a fantastic Celtic career.

Andy McAteer passed away in Condorrat, on the outskirts of Cumbernauld on Sunday, 15 July 1956, aged 68 years. He is buried in the same Kilsyth cemetery as another Hoops legend, Jimmy Quinn.

Chapter 4:

AUGUST 1888: 'THE IRISHMEN' TASTE COMPETITIVE ACTION AT KELVINGROVE

August 1888 was by far the busiest month in the short story to date of the fledgling football club in Glasgow's east end, with no fewer than nine games to be played, including six scheduled by their 20-year-old Match Secretary, Willie Maley, who combined those duties with his playing role at Celtic Park.

Wednesday, 1st August 1888 - 1.8.88 - was the appropriate date of Celtic's first competitive fixture, a first-round Glasgow International Exhibition Cup match against Abercorn, played on the University of Glasgow playing fields at Kelvingrove, near the site of the current Art Gallery & Museum. As would be the case 50 years later, at Bellahouston for the 1938 Empire Exhibition, the football tournament would run alongside the main event being held at the adjacent Kelvingrove Park. Sixteen clubs were invited to participate, although, for whatever reason, none of the great sides of the day - such as early Scottish Cup-winners Queen's Park, Vale of Leven, Dumbarton, Renton or Hibernian - were involved.

Celtic's opening round opponents, Abercorn, were based in the Ralston area of eastern Paisley. They had been formed within months of local rivals, St Mirren, 11 years earlier. Both sides would make their opening appearances in the Scottish Cup of 1880/81, clashing in the third round of the heavily-regionalised tournament on 23 October 1880 at Abercorn's Blackstoun Park. The hosts had already beaten Renfrewshire rivals Barrhead and Morton by those famous Celtic scorelines of 7-1 and 4-2, however, on the day, St Mirren would prove too strong, eventually prevailing by four goals to one. Abercorn would gain revenge with a 2-0 victory in the first round at the same venue, five years later.

Abercorn's finest hour had come in the season leading up to the clash with Celtic, the club going all the way to the semi-final of the national competition, drawing 1-1 with Cambuslang at home before succumbing to a 10-1 hammering in the replay, in January 1888. Cambuslang themselves would find the going tough in their first Scottish Cup final, the following month at Second Hampden (later Cathkin Park, home of Third Lanark from 1903). As discussed in an earlier chapter, they faced the new 'world champions' Renton, featuring James Kelly and Neil McCallum, losing 6-1, a record scoreline which would not be matched until a certain Dixie Deans destroyed Eddie Turnbull's Hibernian at Hampden in May 1972, some 84 years later, the favourite Celtic game of my childhood.

Both Kelly and McCallum had since left Renton and would feature against Abercorn in Celtic's first-ever competitive line-up, which was as follows:

Willie Dunning; James Coleman & Mick McKeown; Paddy Gallagher, James Kelly & Jimmy McLaren; Neil McCallum, Willie Groves, Johnny Madden, Johnny Coleman & Charlie Gorevin.

Details of the game itself are sketchy, although Celtic did score first before Abercorn equalised just before the break. Reports of the day suggest that many within the 4,000 crowd were not so kindly disposed to 'the Irishmen.' I guess the more things change, the more they stay the same. In any case, Abercorn declined the offer of a replay on Monday, 13th August, the tie thus awarded to the Bhoys as a walkover. They would face Dumbarton Athletic in the next round, at Kelvingrove, three weeks later.

In the interim, Willie Maley had arranged friendlies on the next three Saturdays.

The first game was the very definition of a 'grudge match', Celtic facing Hibernian at Celtic Park three days later, on Saturday, 4 August 1888. Six of the Edinburgh club's players had made the switch to the west - the lure of employment being key in the still-amateur world of Scottish professional football - fuelling antagonism between the two which would last for decades. The irony that Hibernian had built their own squad by previously plundering other clubs in exactly the same way - and would continue to do so moving forward – was somewhat lost in the ensuing arguments. Indeed, Hibernian had tried to lure both James Kelly and Neil McCallum from Renton that spring, and had been favourites to do so, before both men joined the new project at Celtic.

A combination of that background and a 4.30 Saturday afternoon slot drew a healthy crowd of 5,000 to the new ground on Dalmarnock Street, now Springfield Road. All five former Hibernian stars who had played in the midweek clash with Abercorn - McKeown, Gallagher, McLaren, Groves and Johnny Coleman - were in the starting line-up for Celtic, whilst the sixth to defect, Mick Dunbar, missed out.

One of the 'Leith Six', Paddy Gallagher, would draw comparisons with a modern-day footballer who served both clubs with distinction, Scott Brown. His all-action, aggressive play made him both a firm favourite of the Celtic support and a target for abuse from opposition fans. Indeed, in October of that year, he would three times be the focus for invading Hibernian spectators in a so-called 'friendly' in Edinburgh. Gallagher was the vice-captain to James Kelly, succeeding the legendary Celt in the main role in 1891, so becoming the first Celtic skipper to lift the Scottish Cup, following the 5-1 victory over still-mighty Queen's Park in April 1892. Definitely, the 'Broony of his day' was our Paddy Gallagher.

Gallagher was in his normal wing-half role for that initial clash with Hibernian, as Greenock Bhoy John O'Connor made his Celtic debut up front, together with Pat Coogan, from Port Glasgow. Interestingly, the green-clad visitors from the east seemed to enjoy much of the crowd's support, taking the lead in the 20th minute through George Smith, with Willie Groves equalising for Celtic shortly afterwards. Hibernian then suffered a real blow, losing their star centre-forward Jimmy McGhee to an ankle injury shortly after the break. Undaunted, the Edinburgh side soon regained the lead through Willie Naughton, Johnny Coleman levelling things for a second time five minutes later before, with time running out, Groves notched his own second, Celtic's winner. Thus, the first-ever clash between Edinburgh and Glasgow's Irishmen ended 3-2 to the hosts.

As an aside, Jimmy McGhee would become yet another Hibernian player to sign for Celtic, albeit not until the original Edinburgh club had ceased to function in late 1890. McGhee had captained the side to its first Scottish Cup victory over Dumbarton at Second Hampden in February 1887, having lined up with teammate James Lundie to make history at the same stadium in April of the previous year, by becoming the first Hibernian players to gain a cap for Scotland, Wales beaten 4-1 in front of 5,500. He would later emigrate to the USA in 1910, and 20 years later, his son Bart would also create a piece of history by scoring the first goal for their national side at a World Cup Finals, netting in a 3-0 win over Belgium in Montevideo.

Paddy Gallagher would be replaced by Willie Maley the following Saturday, 11 August 1888, one of two changes, as Celtic travelled to Mavisbank to face the local Airdrieonians in another friendly. Alec 'Abe' Collins made his first appearance for the club, becoming the first Donegal-born Celt, replacing James McLaughlin at left-back. Neil McCallum scored the only goal of the first period on 30 minutes, to give the visitors the breakthrough, the Celtic players then helping themselves to five second-half goals to win 6-0 in front of what The Scotsman described as 'an immense gathering' in their first outing in Lanarkshire. Typical of newspaper reports of the time, whilst the first half is described in some detail, there is a throwaway line to cover the five strikes after the interval, with no reference to who was credited with those goals.

There would be 10,000 spectators crammed into Clyde's Barrowfield Park seven days later, as the two east end rivals clashed, two months after the hosts had dealt Celtic their only defeat to date, by 4-3 in the June friendly at Celtic Park. There would be no such negative outcome for the new Bhoys today, Celts running out 5-1 winners thanks to doubles from Neil McCallum and Tom Maley and another goal from Willie Groves, with Clyde reduced to 10 men in the second half after losing McLure to injury.

Celts had again made a couple of changes for the short trip to Bridgeton. Tom Maley had returned to the forward line in place of Pat Coogan, whilst this game marked the only Celtic appearance of full-back Tom O'Kane. As mentioned in an earlier chapter, he had starred for Dundee Harp in their 1-0 defeat at Celtic Park in June, the Bhoys then rumoured to be keen to sign up the Arbroath-born man. Instead, O'Kane chose to remain on Tayside, flirting between Harp and his hometown team. As related previously, Tom was the key figure in one of the more intriguing stories to come out of Scottish football that decade. Just under three years earlier, on Saturday, 12 September 1885, he had been part of the Dundee Harp side which had recorded a 35-0 victory over Aberdeen Rovers in the first round of the Scottish Cup, setting up his chairman to send a mocking telegram to his old club, Arbroath, boasting of the huge score. Incredibly, the Red Lichties had beaten another Aberdonian side, Bon Accord, by 36-0 at Gayfield the same afternoon, a score which is still regarded as the all-time record to this day.

Just to twist the knife further, it would later transpire that the referees in both games had experienced some difficulty in keeping track of the scores, the official in Dundee knocking two goals off his tally after a Harp official had queried his original total of 37! The legend remains on Tayside that Dundee Harp had actually outscored their local rivals Arbroath by three or four goals on the day!

Three nights after the victory over Clyde, on Tuesday, 21 August 1888, Celts played their last-eight tie in the Glasgow International Exhibition Cup against Dumbarton Athletic at Kelvingrove. Athletic had beaten Morton 2-1 in the first round and would be merged (or perhaps, more accurately, absorbed) with local rivals Dumbarton the following year. The new combined club would then win the inaugural Scottish League in March 1891, sharing the title with Rangers after a drawn play-off at First Cathkin, despite having a better goal difference, goal average and head-to-head record than the Ibrox side.

As an aside, Celtic would be the only team to remain unbeaten against either of those sides that season, taking three of the four available points from each, however, the Parkhead club would suffer through the imposition of a 4-point penalty for allegedly fielding ineligible players, eventually finishing eight points behind the joint-leaders in third place.

Dumbarton and Rangers would fare very differently over the next 120 years. The Sons would go on to retain their Scottish title in 1892, however, to date, they have not managed a third success, whilst the Govan club would claim 53 League Championships in their own right, before their demise in 2012.

Details of Celtic's Glasgow International Exhibition Cup quarter final against Dumbarton Athletic back in August 1888 are difficult to come by. What is known is that Bathgate-born goalkeeper John Tobin, yet another veteran of Hibernian's Scottish Cup-winning side of February 1887, made his debut for Celtic, who led by three goals before Athletic pulled one back before the break. There would be no further scoring in the second half, the Bhoys recording a first-ever competitive victory to advance to the semi-final by 3-1. John Tobin would 'enjoy' a rather strange Celtic career. More of that later.

Curiously, the Bhoys would play matches on each of the following two evenings.

On Wednesday, 22 August, a strong Celtic side lined up at the original Cathkin Park to face the 3rd LRV in a friendly, the Bhoys suffering a 4-3 defeat in front of 3,000 spectators, despite another Willie Groves effort and an own goal, with the third goalscorer undetermined. Only the result is known for the game played 24 hours later, on Thursday, 23 August, Celtic emerging as 4-2 winners in their second meeting that month with Glasgow International Exhibition Cup rivals Abercorn, this game played at Blackstoun Park, Paisley.

The final friendly match that month took place at Hyde Park in Springburn, on Monday, 27 August. This would mark Celtic's first visit to the area where I would grow up (that statement is a matter of opinion, obviously, rather than fact!), around 80 years later.

Cowlairs had not been the only side from Springburn to feature in the early part of Celtic's history. By the time they were formed, in 1876, Northern FC had already been established for two years on the other side of the main Springburn Road.

Details of the Northern club's origins are vague, however, it would appear that they played for their initial season at Lodge Park (exact whereabouts unknown) before moving to Hyde Park, which would be their home for the remainder of the club's existence. Their Hyde Park ground was adjacent to the massive engineering works of the same name, on the corner of Flemington and Ayr Streets, to the east of Springburn Road. If the two bases of Cowlairs FC, Gourlay and Springvale Parks, would have been close to my home growing up, then Hyde Park, if anything, would have been even nearer. Indeed, the front window of my last 'Springburn residence', in Adamswell Street, would have looked directly into the ground. A century after Northern FC was set up, a Celtic supporters' social club would relocate from Angus Street to new premises in Flemington Street, around the corner from the old park. The Northern Area Celtic Club would be the meeting point for us Springburn Bhoys through the 1980's and beyond, where great victories were enjoyed and disastrous defeats dissected, over a few pints.

Northern's initial club colours were blue-and-red 2" hooped shirts, with dark blue shorts. These were changed for halved shirts of light and dark blue the following season and retained thereafter. In 1883, they absorbed (or merged with) Petershill FC, not to be confused with the current Junior club of the same name. Not everyone was enamoured by this move, a new 'breakaway' club being set up as Springburn FC for the 1884/85 season. That year also saw the introduction of another football team on the local scene, Springburn Hibernian. Again, details are difficult to come by, however, the success of the established Edinburgh club in supporting its local Irish community is perhaps more likely than not to be the inspiration behind that move.

All the clubs in the area at that time competed in the Glasgow North Eastern Cup, with Cowlairs the dominant team as we entered 1888. On Saturday, 5 May 1888, they won the trophy for the third successive season, following a single-goal victory over old foes Northern in the Barrowfield Park final. Three days later, the newly-crowned North-Eastern champions Cowlairs would meet Hibernian, in the first-ever fixture to be played at the original Celtic Park. The world was about to change for all of us.

Northern FC's first game with Celtic would take place at Hyde Park on Monday, 27 August 1888, in front of 3,000 spectators. It would be the 12th game in the short three-month history of the new club, Celts winning the friendly 3-0, Neil McCallum to the fore, scoring the second goal before the interval.

Two nights later, Celtic were back at the University of Glasgow's grounds at Kelvingrove for the semi-final of the Glasgow International

Exhibition Cup. Their opponents were local favourites Partick Thistle, at that time based just a stone's throw away, in Overnewton Park, Yorkhill. The Jags had beaten Airdrieonians 5-2 then Kilbirnie 2-1, to set up a first meeting with Celtic. It would prove to be a tight game, the two key moments occurring in the final 20 minutes. First, Thistle winger Ferguson sustained a bad leg injury, which sadly ended his participation in the night's proceedings. Then, as a draw seemed inevitable, a Celtic attack produced a dramatic late goal for the cup-tie winner, the first such event for which the club would later become synonymous. The identity of the scorer is at this point unknown.

By the end of the evening of Wednesday, 29 August 1888, just three months after playing its inaugural game, Celtic Football Club had reached its first cup final. Their opponents would be...Cowlairs.

Chapter 5:

SEPTEMBER 1888: REVENGE IS A DISH BEST SERVED WITH EIGHT GOALS

September 1888 was a memorable month in the short history of Celtic Football Club. It included a couple of significant milestones, as Celts entered the Scottish Cup for the first time and took part in first-ever cup final.

The first day of the month saw no fewer than 166 clubs across the country play in the first round of the major national football competition of that time, the Scottish FA Challenge Cup, better known as the Scottish Cup. It would be a further two years before the inaugural Scottish League championship would kick in, in the summer of 1890. Celtic had gained entry to the SFA just ten days before the first round, on 21 August 1888, together with another seven clubs, whose names make interesting reading some 130 years or so later.

From Glasgow came the wonderfully-named Temperance Athletic, whilst the Irish community in Coatbridge would now be represented by Whifflet Shamrock. Further east, Champfleurie hailed from Linlithgow, Adventurers were from Edinburgh and Leith Harp would provide local competition for the original Edinburgh Hibernians, the Scottish Cup-winners in February 1887. Over on the west coast, any 19th-century Oban ultras could support Balaclava Rangers, whilst down in Ayrshire, Darconner Britannia would deliver Scottish Cup football to the banjo-playing goatherds of Auchinleck.

Of the eight new entrants, only Celtic and Adventurers would survive the first round, with some severe maulings dished out. Just three years earlier, as mentioned previously, Arbroath and Dundee Harp had managed 71 goals between them in defeating their respective opponents from Aberdeen, Bon Accord and Rovers. Whilst those staggering performances were not quite repeated, there was some serious scoring taking place that Autumn day, with many of the new clubs sadly on the receiving end of that.

The draw was heavily regionalised, producing a number of local derbies.

Britannia were definitely not ruling in Ayrshire, beaten 5-1 at Annbank, whilst Whifflet Shamrock lost 6-1 to their Carfin namesakes. Leith Harp also shipped six, this time without reply at Bathgate to Erin Rovers. Three of the others lost by double-figures. Champfleurie were beaten 12-0 by Armadale, whilst Balaclava Rangers would have been thankful for their headgear on the way home from Lochgilphead, having lost 15-1. Faring worst of all were the good folk of Temperance Athletic. I suspect a few may have fallen off the wagon in need of a stiff drink after a 18-2 defeat at Gourlay Park from Cowlairs.

Celtic and Adventurers did strike a blow for the new guys, the Edinburgh side beating Linlithgow Athletic 6-2 away from home in their first foray in the senior competition. At Celtic Park, the fledging club played its initial Scottish Cup tie against a side from just along the road, Shettleston.

The Celtic team lined up for this momentous occasion as follows:

Willie Dunning; James Coleman & Mick McKeown; Paddy Gallagher, James Kelly & Jimmy McLaren; Neil McCallum, Johnny Coleman, Willie Groves, Mick Dunbar & John O'Connor.

Five of the Celtic team had been plundered from Hibernian, allegedly due to the promptings of their former teammate Tom Maley, whilst a further two, James Kelly and Neil McCallum, had joined from Renton, having previously promised their services to the Edinburgh club. As these sides had won the previous two competitions, there was plenty of Scottish Cup experience in that Celtic eleven, indeed Willie Groves had scored the winner for Hibernian against Dumbarton at Second Hampden in the 1887 final, whilst Neil McCallum had netted his customary double in Renton's 6-1 rout of Cambuslang at the same venue 12 months later.

The resentment felt by Hibernian towards Celtic for more than a century can almost certainly be traced back to these events of 1888, the fortunes of the Edinburgh side plummeting whilst the Celts went from strength to strength, thanks to the input from many of their former stars. There was a humorous nod to this almost 120 years later, in the Gordon Strachan era, when the Celtic manager, himself a boyhood Hibernian supporter, took his charges to play at Easter Road on 23 September 2007. This would mark Scott Brown's first return to Leith since his summer transfer, the midfielder one of five Celts involved that day who had previously plied their trade in the green and white of the capital side, Gary Caldwell, Paul Hartley, Derek Riordan and Chris Killen being the others. The visiting fans displayed a banner proclaiming Hibs as 'Celtic's feeder club since 1888!' Sadly, the joke would be on us that day as the Hibernian player I always felt we should have signed, striker Steven Fletcher, was on target in a 3-2 home victory.

Celtic's initial Scottish Cup match with Shettleston on Saturday, 1 September 1888, was a one-sided affair, the Bhoys 1-0 up after five minutes then adding a second just before the interval. A spate of three goals within several minutes midway through the second half took the score to 4-1 before Celts added a fifth as we entered the closing stages, the hosts eventually running out comfortable 5-1 winners. Curiously, some records assign all five goals to left-winger John O'Connor (sometimes known as Connor), although newspaper reports of the time would appear to have ignored that feat and Celtic themselves have not acknowledged this, to the best of my knowledge. Perhaps tellingly, there is no reference to it in either the definitive 'Celtic Story' history books by Willie Maley or Dr James Handley.

There were a number of other Scottish Cup ties of interest in that first round, played on the same day.

Dundee Our Boys beat Dundee East End 5-4. These two clubs would amalgamate five years later, in 1893, to form the present Dundee FC. Within another two years, on 26 October 1895, they would lose 11-0 to Celtic in a Scottish League game at the new Celtic Park, still a club record win to this day.

Dumbarton's 13-1 win over Kirkintilloch Central at Boghead included a goal from Johnny Madden. He had featured for Celtic the previous month in the Glasgow Exhibition Cup match against Abercorn and would later star at Parkhead before making his name as the Father of Czech Football in the new century with Slavia Prague.

Perhaps the biggest shock was the 2-1 defeat of 1887 Scottish Cup-winners Hibernian by Mossend Swifts at West Calder, whilst holders Renton, minus the departed James Kelly and Neil McCallum, were still far too strong for neighbours Bowling, emerging victorious by 8-0. Eight-time Scottish Cup-winners Queen's Park won a five-goal thriller in Springburn, by edging out Northern at Hyde Park.

Two nights later, Monday, 3 September 1888, a strong Celtic side travelled to Copeland Park in Govan, recovering from the loss of an early goal to win the friendly with Whitefield by the same 5-1 scoreline as they vanquished Shettleston in the previous weekend's Cup-tie. Jimmy McLaren had helped himself to a first-half double to put Celts 3-1 ahead by the break, however, the other scorers are unknown.

The following Thursday, 6 September 1888, would mark another key date in the history of the new Parkhead club, as the Bhoys faced Cowlairs in Celtic's first-ever cup final, to contest the Glasgow International Exhibition Cup at the University of Glasgow's grounds at Kelvingrove.

This was the Celtic line-up charged with securing the club's first trophy that evening.

Willie Dunning; Alec 'Abe' Collins & Mick McKeown; Paddy Gallagher, James Kelly & Jimmy McLaren; Neil McCallum, Johnny Coleman, Willie Groves, Mick Dunbar & John O'Connor.

The Springburn club would field two players who would later turn out for Celtic, goalkeeper Tom Duff – the 'Cowlairs Orangeman' – and James McPherson, as well as the latter's sibling John, who would go on to play for Rangers and Scotland, before becoming a director at Ibrox. The McPherson brothers were amongst six Cowlairs players who had taken part in the inaugural match at Celtic Park against Hibernian, just four months earlier. They would be further strengthened by the inclusion of Renton's Jimmy McCall, playing as a guest. The Scotland striker would be up against his old teammates, James Kelly and Neil

McCallum, part of their 'World Champions' line-up from earlier that year. As an aside, both Celts would later play with their old friend in a Renton Select team, pulled together for Jimmy's testimonial. The match was held at Celtic Park in May 1890, the Bhoys providing the opposition, with the aforementioned Tom Duff playing that night between the Celtic sticks! A small world is football.

In the absence of most of the leading Scottish clubs of the day, the 'Irishmen' had been the favourites for the competition in the eyes of many observers. However, in front of 6,000 spectators, many of whom taunted and abused the Celtic players throughout, goals either side of the break from Stewart and Bishop without reply saw the trophy heading for Springburn. At a reception afterwards, legendary Celtic chairman and co-founder John Glass vowed that those who had abused his representatives would be "taught a lesson they would not forget." Perhaps, this was the occasion when his oft-quoted speech, now appearing on the new storyboard in the Jock Stein Lounge at Celtic Park, was first aired.

"Let them scoff and jeer. Celtic will yet win to their proper position by their merits and those who scoff today will one day have to applaud."

He would not have long to wait.

Two days later, Saturday, 8 September 1888, Celtic hosted Dumbarton Athletic in a friendly fixture, less than three weeks after knocking them out of the Glasgow International Exhibition Cup at Kelvingrove. The Bhoys line-up on this occasion would include yet another of Hibernian's 1887 Scottish Cup-winners, goalkeeper John Tobin, whilst James Coleman represented the visitors, having played for Celts in the Scottish Cup-tie against Shettleston the previous Saturday! Willie Groves opened the scoring after half an hour, with Mick Dunbar adding a second just before the break. Athletic would appear to have enjoyed the better of the second half, however, Celtic's defence stood firm, allowing John O'Connor to wrap up a 3-0 victory towards the end.

There would be a step up in class the following Saturday, 15 September 1888, as Celts travelled through to face Athletic's local rivals Dumbarton in another friendly, a first-ever visit to Boghead Park for the new Glasgow club. Dumbarton and Dumbarton Athletic would later amalgamate to form the club who would go on to win the first two Scottish League championships in 1890/91 and 1891/92.

A couple of noteworthy Celts featured in the home ranks. Johnny Madden had played in Celtic's first match, the 5-2 victory over Rangers, and had been a signing target for the club before being allegedly 'kidnapped' by Dumbarton during the Glasgow International Exhibition tournament the previous month, such a description used by Willie Maley to describe the scenario where the player disappeared shortly before playing for Celtic in their inaugural competition. He would later return to Dumbarton, his hometown club, before eventually signing on at Parkhead in August 1889, before enjoying not one but two glorious football careers, firstly as a player with Celtic then as a coach with Slavia Prague.

Between the sticks for the hosts at Boghead that afternoon was Jamie Bell. He would also join Celtic, 12 months after Madden, in August 1890, and would then be at the centre of a bizarre series of events. For Celtic's first-ever League game, against Renton at Celtic Park on Saturday, 16 August 1890, the Bhoys, incredibly, had no recognised goalkeeper, wing-half Jimmy McLaren the unlucky outfield player chosen to literally 'adopt the position.' Perhaps not surprisingly, Renton would win 4-1 on the day, the aforementioned Jimmy McCall helping himself to a double after Cameron had opened the scoring for the visitors in the first minute. Winger Hugh Gallagher then pulled a goal back just before half-time to make it 3-1 at that point, thus putting himself into the record books as Celtic's first League goalscorer.

Or did he?

Apparently not. On 30 September 1890, Renton were accused of 'professionalism' at a disciplinary hearing and thrown out of the Scottish League, with the four fixtures played to that date by the Dunbartonshire club, including their victory at Parkhead, subsequently wiped from the record books.

Seven days after that Renton 'defeat', a Celtic squad with new signing Jamie Bell in goals travelled to Tynecastle, for what would ultimately become their maiden Scottish League game. Bell's former Dumbarton teammate, Johnny Madden, would have the honour of scoring the first League goal in Celtic's history, when he crashed a shot in off the Hearts crossbar after 10 minutes. He would also claim the second, with Willie Groves making it 3-0 at half-time. Groves would add his own second after the interval with a long-range drive before Peter Dowds sealed an emphatic 5-0 win towards the end.

There would be one final twist in the tale, however.

At a meeting on 4 September 1890, the Scottish League deemed that a full fortnight had not elapsed between Jamie Bell's final appearance for Dumbarton and his Celtic debut at Tynecastle. The Parkhead club were thus docked four points for fielding an ineligible player. Playing catch-up on the League leaders, Dumbarton and Rangers, Celts would ultimately finish eight points behind both after the 18 valid matches had been completed, despite taking six points from a possible eight to remain unbeaten in the clashes involving the top three clubs. Who knows how significant that penalty turned out to be?

Celtic had also beaten champions Dumbarton in that friendly at Boghead back in September 1888. It was the Bhoys free-scoring right-winger Neil McCallum who headed the opener in the first half, with Chapman equalising for the hosts (referred to as the 'ground side' in the language of the day in the Press) after the break. With 10 minutes remaining, McCallum scored his second goal, the ball going in off a post, Dumbarton by this time reduced to 10 men following an injury to their forward, Robertson.

Seven days later, on Saturday, 22 September, the second round of the Scottish Cup took place, with 39 ties played across the country. Cowlairs' reward for the 18-2 slaughter of Temperance Athletic was a trip to Celtic Park, just 16 days after the ill-natured encounter at Kelvingrove Park in the final of the Glasgow International Exhibition Cup.

With feelings running high, a large crowd of over 7,000 packed into Celtic's new ground in Dalmarnock St. Cowlairs had once again secured the services of one of Renton's 'World Champions', this time wing-half Bob Kelso teased north from Newcastle West End to take part. All three

Scottish international players associated with the Springburn club in its 20-year existence, full-back William McLeod and inside-forwards Tom McInnes and John McPherson, also took to the field, as did goalkeeper Tom Duff, suggesting that this was perhaps the strongest Cowlairs side of all time.

There was revenge in the air, and it was a dish served red hot for the Springburn club, the on-fire Celts, wearing a distinctive all-green outfit to avoid a clash with their white-shirted opponents, scoring four goals in each half for a resounding and no doubt, extremely satisfying, 8-0 victory. This could have been anything but for the heroics of Duff in the visitors' goal. Both Maley brothers played, with the elder sibling, Tom, on the scoresheet, making it 5-0 early in the second half. Mick Dunbar scored Celtic's first competitive hat-trick (in the absence of confirmation of John O'Connor's tally against Shettleston), Neil McCallum hit yet another double and solo strikes from Willie Groves and James Kelly completed the rout. John Glass would have been a contented man that particular Saturday evening, as his Celts, described as 'the wearers of the green' in one newspaper report, ran riot.

The final Saturday of the month featured a lower-key friendly, this time against Airdrieonians in front of around 1,000 spectators at Celtic Park. A brace from – yes, you've guessed it, Neil McCallum, set Celts up for a 4-1 victory, Willie Groves and John O'Connor also getting in on the act as September ended with another win.

Thoughts and dreams for those of a Celtic persuasion could now turn to the next round of the Scottish Cup, where their opponents would be Airdrieonians' neighbours, Albion Rovers from Coatbridge.

Chapter 6:

OCTOBER 1888: CELTIC JOY AS RANGERS ARE HIT FOR SIX AT IBROX

Another month brought another first, as Celtic made their maiden appearance in the Glasgow Football Association Cup, better known simply as the Glasgow Cup.

For someone like myself, brought up in the 60s, when the six senior clubs in the city became five after Third Lanark's liquidation in 1967, it is difficult to imagine a version of the Glasgow Cup where no fewer than 25 teams competed. This was the case as the competition kicked off for the second edition, on Saturday, 15 September 1888, as Celts were travelling to Dumbarton for the friendly mentioned in the previous chapter, having become the only side to receive a bye in the first round. The major shock of that round would be the humiliating 6-0 defeat by holders and inaugural winners Cambuslang, at the hands of 3rd LRV at First Cathkin.

Celtic would thus enter at the second round stage, scheduled for Saturday, 6 October 1888, their first involvement in the competition seeing Shettleston make the short trip to Celtic Park, just as they had for the new club's initial Scottish Cup-tie the previous month, when the hosts had won 5-1. The Bhoys would more than double the pain inflicted that afternoon by scoring 11 goals to their neighbour's 2, in front of 7,000 spectators. The contest, such as it was, was over long before the interval, by which time the Celts were 8-0 ahead. The second half would then be more even, with the young Shettleston side pulling a couple of goals back, although one would assume Celtic had taken the foot off the gas. On the same day, there would also be heavy wins for Clyde, Northern, Queen's Park and Rangers, whilst Cowlairs, Partick Thistle and 3rd LRV enjoyed the luxury of a bye into the third round.

Two days later, Monday, 8 October 1888, the Celts were in high-scoring action again, having taken the road and the miles to Dundee to take on the local Harp, at their Athletic's ground on East Dock Street. The visitors were without Tom and Willie Maley and Mick Dunbar, whilst Tom O'Kane was missing for the green-shirted hosts. The 4,000 crowd would witness a fine display of attacking football by the Bhoys on that autumn holiday afternoon on Tayside, Harp doing well to hold them to 2-0 at half-time. Celtic then stepped up a gear after the break, Willie Groves involved in most of the goals as the visitors secured the first 7-1 victory in Celtic's history. It would certainly not be the last one of those.

The following Saturday, 13 October 1888, saw Albion Rovers visit Celtic Park for the third round of the Scottish Cup, by some distance the most prestigious competition in Scottish football at that time. The Coatbridge side had enjoyed a 'walkover' win in their first-round tie with Bellshill before destroying Rutherglen 9-1 at home in the next match. The main casualties from the second round of matches had been three-time winners Vale of Leven, beaten 4-2 by Dumbarton Athletic, and the side Vale had twice defeated in the Scottish Cup final, Rangers, who lost a home replay with Clyde by 3-0. Those two sides would join 1887 winners Hibernian, beaten in the first round by West Lothian outfit, Mossend Swifts, on the sidelines as the competition progressed. As I have mentioned previously, the draws for the early stages of the national tournament were arranged very much on a regional basis

For their third successive home Scottish Cup-tie, Celtic lined up as follows:

Willie Dunning; James McLaughlin & Mick McKeown; Paddy Gallagher, James Kelly & James McLaren; Neil McCallum, Johnny Coleman, Willie Groves, Mick Dunbar & Tom Maley.

Albion Rovers started on the front foot, taking the lead in the 10th minute, before strikes by Paddy Gallagher and Mick Dunbar saw the hosts reach the break 2-1 ahead. The visitors again pushed Celtic hard in the second half and so it was somewhat against the run of play when Tom Maley made it 3-1 from close-range near the end. With the pressure now off, Willie Groves added a fourth before the final whistle, to secure Celtic's place in round four.

Things would not be so pleasant the following Saturday, 20 October 1888, as Celts paid their first visit to Edinburgh and Easter Road with a side including several who had previously plied their trade with or pledged their support to opponents Hibernian. The fixture was billed as a friendly, however, given the bad blood between the two clubs at this time, it would turn out to be anything but that. Celts emerged to a storm of jeering and insults which would not let up all afternoon. Former Hibernian skipper, Jimmy McLaren was missing from the Celtic line-up, as was Tom Maley, the latter's brother Willie and John O'Connor taking their places.

Former Hibernian favourite Johnny Coleman opened the scoring for his new club within 10 minutes, whilst another Easter Road favourite, Mick Dunbar, piled on the agony with a double before the break, the first the subject of an offside claim which heightened the tension around the stadium. This would manifest on the hour mark, as several hundred home supporters ploughed on to the pitch behind Mick Dunning's goal. Celtic players found themselves surrounded on the field as the situation threatened to get out of hand, a full 10 minutes elapsing before order was restored. Apparently with the blessing of the two clubs, the referee then blew for full-time with a further 10 minutes of the original 90 still remaining. This provoked another burst of tempers flaying, with the hosts looking to play on and Celts trying to get the hell out of Dodge as quickly as possible. It had been a difficult afternoon all round.

Seven days later, there was yet another first, as Celtic travelled to Ibrox Park for their Glasgow Cup quarter-final tie with Rangers. The original stadium was located adjacent to the site of the current ground, just off Copland Road. The Govan club would continue to play there until the final days of the 19th century, in December 1899. Rangers had enjoyed a 10-0 romp over United Abstainers in the previous round of the competition, as Celts enjoyed a bye. However, that afternoon would be a different matter entirely.

The following Celtic team lined up for the first competitive meeting with a club who would become their fiercest rivals for the next century and beyond.

Willie Dunning; Paddy Gallagher & Mick McKeown; Willie Maley, James Kelly & Jimmy McLaren;

Neil McCallum, Johnny Coleman, Willie Groves, Mick Dunbar & Tom Maley.

The 4,000 crowd that day would include the first travelling Celtic support inside Ibrox, with Press reports of the time stating that the roar greeting goals scored by the visiting team drowned out those made by the hosts. Rangers centre-forward Wilson had struck first on 20 minutes, with Willie Groves equalising directly from the restart before Mick Dunbar quickly added a second. Whilst Celtic enjoyed the bulk of the play after the interval, the score remained at 2-1 until 20 minutes from time, when the roof caved in on the Ibrox men. Tom Maley set up Johnny Coleman for a third before heading the fourth himself. And with the tie finished at 4-1, the visitors turned the screw, Dunbar grabbing his second before captain James Kelly rounded it all off just before the final whistle, setting up his former Renton colleague Neil McCallum to maintain his goal-a-game record against Rangers by making it 6-1.

The only other Glasgow Cup tie played that afternoon saw Clyde beat Cowlairs 4-2 at Barrowfield Park, to join Celtic in the draw for the semi-final. The remaining quarter-final matches would be played in November. This would include a rematch between the 3rd LRV and Partick Thistle, the visitors having successfully protested about Third's equaliser in the original drawn match earlier in the month, although with the second game again to be played at Cathkin rather than at Thistle's home ground, Inchview, I am struggling to understand the point of that appeal. The fourth tie would see Queen's Park start strong favourites against another club from Springburn, Cowlairs' great rivals, Northern.

Chapter 7:

NOVEMBER 1888: A ST BERNARD'S WALTZ FOR THE BHOYS IN EDINBURGH

The first Saturday in November saw the Celts return to Edinburgh, this time to face St Bernard's in the fourth round of the Scottish Cup at Powderhall. The east-coast club had originally been formed in 1874, around the same time as fellow capital sides Heart of Midlothian and Hibernian, as the 3rd Edinburgh Rifle Volunteers. Like their Lanarkshire equivalents, later known as Third Lanark, they had originated from a Territorial Army unit, however, rather than becoming 'Third Edinburgh', they would adopt their name from the parish in which they played, St Bernard's Well on the nearby Water of Leith becoming the focal point of their club badge.

St Bernard's Scottish Cup run of 1888/89 had commenced with a 7-0 victory over neighbours Leith Athletic, before a trip to Norton Park, in the shadow of Easter Road, saw them return as 3-1 victors. The previous round had seen them on the road again, this time to Fife, Saints edging a three-goal tie with Kirkcaldy Wanderers. The big shock of that third round had been the defeat of eight-time winners Queen's Park at the hands of local rivals 3rd LRV, the Crosshill side winning 4-2 in the rematch after their 2-1 victory at First Cathkin seven days earlier had been declared void.

The other high-profile tie had seen holders Renton, now shorn of many of their star players, still prove too strong for Glasgow Cup-winners Cambuslang, beating them 4-1 in a repeat of their Scottish Cup Final clash eight months earlier. The two sides had also met in the Glasgow Charity Cup final on May 12, their semi-final appearances earlier that week ruling both out of appearing in the inaugural match to be played at Celtic Park. The Dunbartonshire side, at that time still featuring their legendary players such as Bob Kelso, James Kelly, Neil McCallum and Jimmy McCall, had again been far too powerful for their opponents, a McCall hat-trick the platform for a comfortable 4-0 win at Second Hampden.

Like Cowlairs in an earlier round, St Bernard's colours at that time were white shirts and navy socks, meaning a clash with their Glaswegian visitors. Celts would, therefore, again be wearing green strips.

The Celtic team charged with progressing to the fifth round in their maiden Scottish Cup adventure on Saturday, 3 November 1888 was as follows:

Willie Dunning; Paddy Gallagher & Mick McKeown; Willie Maley, James Kelly & James McLaren;

Neil McCallum, Johnny Coleman, Willie Groves, Mick Dunbar & Tom Maley.

In front of over 6,000 spectators at Powderhall, Celts would enjoy the bulk of first-half possession, Neil McCallum opening the scoring after half an hour, despite strong St Bernard's protests for offside. The Saints' response was a shot from Dorkin, which came crashing back off Willie Dunning's crossbar, with many in the home crowd cheering, believing the ball to have crossed the line. Just before the break, Tom Maley grabbed a crucial second goal for the visitors. James Kelly would prove to be a formidable obstacle in the second period, time and again foiling St Bernard's attempts to pull a goal back, Willie Groves taking advantage of the hosts relentless attack to grab a third goal for Celtic with a strong shot. Corson then provided the highlight of the day for the home crowd, beating Dunning all ends up to make it 3-1, however, this merely served to awaken the Bhoys from their slumbers, Groves finishing the match with a tremendous goal, as Celts won 4-1 for the second successive Scottish Cup-tie.

Seven days later, as the club founded for the very best of reasons passed the first anniversary of that inaugural meeting in St Mary's Church Hall in East Rose Street, Renton would provide the opposition for a charity match played at Celtic Park in aid of the St Vincent de Paul Society. This would be the first game between the two clubs viewed by many as the joint favourites for the Scottish Cup, a crowd in excess of

10,000, Celtic's highest to date, drawn to the east end for the occasion. The Celts were unchanged, whilst Renton had their talismanic forward Jimmy McCall available to play. A keenly-contested match was settled by a second-half header from Jimmy McLaren, following a corner kick.

This match also has a special significance in Celtic's history, as it was the first appearance of the green-and-white vertically-striped jersey which would become the club's strip of choice for the next 15 seasons or so, the precursor to the iconic Hoops which would then be adopted in August 1903. It is a design most regularly associated nowadays with Real Betis Balompie, a club based in Sevilla in Spain.

On the same day, Saturday, 10 November 1888, the remaining two quarter-final ties in the Glasgow Cup would be played off. Partick Thistle would edge 3rd LRV 2-1 at First Cathkin, in the rematch following the earlier protest, as Queen's Park were handing out a 6-0 mauling to Northern in their replayed tie at Second Hampden, the sides having drawn 5-5 at Hyde Park the previous weekend. Clyde would be the last four opponents for Partick Thistle, whilst the Spiders' reward was a semi-final trip to Celtic Park the following Saturday, to take on newcomers Celtic for the first time.

Despite the horrendous weather, another excellent crowd of 7,000 turned out to witness the historic clash, the traditional powerhouse versus the new Bhoys on the block, Celtic again fielding the same line-up. Queen's Park attacked the London Road end from the kick-off and sensationally went ahead within the first minute, Berry beating Willie Dunning low at his post. Still 1-0 down at the break, Celts started the second half on the front foot, in search of that elusive equaliser, however, as often happens, when the next goal arrived, it was at the other end, this time Robertson's header doubling Queen's advantage. There was a worrying moment, as one of the officials appeared to be manhandled by someone in the crowd, before order was established on and off the pitch as the Spiders controlled the remainder of the match to progress to a December Glasgow Cup final with either Partick Thistle or Clyde. Those two sides had fought out a 1-1 draw just a mile or so from Celtic Park at Barrowfield Park, the home of Clyde, with a replay scheduled for the first day of December at Thistle's Inchview base in Whiteinch, near the northern entrance to the Clyde Tunnel, to put that location in a current context. The Jags would not move further east to their present Firhill HQ in Maryhill until 1909.

As it turned out, the final fixture of the month for the Bhoys was a Scottish Cup fifth round tie with Clyde, seven days later, played at Celtic Park on Saturday, 24 November 1888. The Bully Wee had begun their campaign on the road, with a 4-2 win at Linthouse before knocking Rangers out a few miles along the road in a second-round replay at Ibrox, following a 2-2 draw at Barrowfield Park. The next round saw a comfortable 4-0 home victory over Cambuslang Hibernian set up a lengthy trip north-west to Oban, where they hit the local side for six goals without reply.

The Bhoys were forced into making two changes for the visit of their east end neighbours, John Tobin replacing Willie Dunning in goals, whilst John O'Connor came in for the injured Johnny Coleman up front. A tremendous attendance in excess of 8,000 watched a match played on a waterlogged surface, the dreadful conditions no doubt adding to the excitement for the crowd but perhaps restricting the free-flowing football style normally enjoyed by Celts. Despite laying siege on the visitors' goal, Clyde forward Jimmy Britton scored the only goal of the game in the first half, as the side previously thought to be invincible appeared to be facing a second home elimination from a major tournament within a week.

However, Scottish football in the 1880's was slightly different, if you haven't already picked that up. I have seen suggestions that the protests which followed next from the Parkhead club were based around a lack of light and/or delays attributed to some of the Clyde players changing footwear. Neither would appear to be the case.

I'll let Mr Celtic himself, Willie Maley, who actually played that afternoon, pick up the narrative from his fantastic tome 'The Story of the Celtic,' covering the first 50 years of his beloved club's existence.

"On a day of rain, with a ground absolutely waterlogged, we lost by 1-0 after a wonderful display by Clyde's goalie, W. Chalmers, but on the advice of many prominent officials who were present (it is to be remembered [that] we were still novices as far as legislative work was concerned), we protested on the unplayability of the ground, in which we were supported by the referee, and the tie was ordered to be replayed."

So, we would live to fight another day and the great Scottish Cup dream was still very much on.

Chapter 8:

DECEMBER 1888: CELTS GO MARCHING ON IN THE SCOTTISH CUP

The opening day of December 1888 saw the Celts head 'doon the water' for a friendly match with Port Glasgow Athletic at Clune Park. Details of the match are sketchy, although the Celtic Wiki records that outside-left Tom Maley scored twice for the Bhoys in a 5-2 victory, in a contest where only 30 minutes were played in each half.

The following Saturday, 8 December 1888, Clyde returned to Celtic Park for the rematch of the Scottish Cup fifth-round tie which they had won 1-0 two weeks earlier, prior to a protest being raised by the Parkhead club around the state of the playing surface. The fallout had been acrimonious since the day of the tie, Clyde officials indignantly insisting that the grounds for such protest were flawed, whilst Celtic countered that the club's displeasure had been appropriately represented, both in terms of its content and timing. Celtic's protest was upheld with Clyde's subsequent appeal only narrowly failing.

Thus, on the back of some strong feelings and resentment between the two clubs, 8,000 spectators packed into the ground to watch the following Celtic side have another go at their east-end rivals.

Willie Dunning; Alec Collins & Mick McKeown; Paddy Gallagher, James Kelly & Jimmy McLaren;

Neil McCallum, Johnny Coleman, Willie Groves, Mick Dunbar & Tom Maley.

Celts started as if they meant business, Tom Maley's close-range finish and Jimmy McLaren's header giving the hosts a 2-0 lead within 10 minutes. Back came Clyde, with their own 'double-whammy' to level things before another similar period had elapsed. First, Bully Wee centre-half Cherrie struck a low drive which went in off Willie Dunning's upright with the Celtic goalkeeper not looking too clever, then the same player took advantage of a second bite at the Celtic defence, to equalise in the next attack with an excellent finish. Maley then seized on a perfect through ball from James Kelly to restore the Bhoys lead just before the half-hour mark, as the play raged from end to end.

The interval arrived with Celts narrowly in front by 3-2, after a hard-fought contest. I suspect that very few of those spectators could have predicted the eventual outcome at that point.

Two key moments swung the second half and ultimately the tie in Celtic's favour. First Neil McCallum got that crucial 'next goal' by heading powerfully past Clyde keeper Chalmers in the early exchanges of the second period. Then, as the visitors threw everything into remaining in the Scottish Cup, their left-back Hart suffered a bad shoulder injury, which effectively finished his afternoon. Within minutes, 4-2 had become 6-2, as Maley secured his hat-trick and Willie Groves got in on the scoring action, with a sublime finish. With 20 minutes remaining, 'Darling Groves' struck again with another unstoppable effort. There would then be further punishment inflicted on Clyde in the closing stages, as Celtic took their final tally to an improbable 9-2, albeit the scorers of those last two goals remain unconfirmed.

It had been a remarkable turnaround in two weeks, the initial 1-0 defeat from Clyde now consigned to the dustbin of Scottish Cup history, as Celts prepared for a quarter-final tie with East Stirlingshire. The Falkirk-based club had enjoyed their best-ever run in the national competition to reach the last eight, having begun their campaign with a 10-1 victory over local rivals Stenhousemuir followed up with an 11-2 mauling of Vale of Bannock. These remain the only 9-goal winning margins in the club's history to this day. The third round saw a 4-0 triumph over King's Park (later known as Stirling Albion) with the same scoreline achieved in a fourth-round replay win over Dunblane, the teams having shared eight goals in the first match. East Stirlingshire were then handed a bye into the quarter finals.

The four ties were scheduled to take place the weekend after Celtic's

Plaque marking the site and history of First Celtic Park.

Brother Dorotheus

Pat 'Tailor' Welsh

Dr John Conway

Michael Davitt lays the first sod of turf at Celtic Park

Joseph Shaughnessy

Joseph Nelis

David Meikleham

Born to wear the Hoops on 2 July 1888. Andy McAtee in action for his beloved Celtic.

Fan's favourite Andy McAtee honoured by the St Andrew's Celtic Brake Club.

James McKay

Gold medal won by the players of Cowlairs FC, following the Glasgow International Exhibition Cup final v Celtic, at Kelvingrove, on 6 September 1888. First Cup final.

John H McLaughlin

Brother Walfrid in later life.

Celtic team v Vale of Leven, 22 December 1888 with six founding fathers, (back row); James Quillan (2nd left), Daniel Malloy (centre), John Glass (2nd right) & John C MacDonald (right), with John O'Hara and William McKillop immediately in front.

James Kelly

Sandy McMahon

The four annual trophies Celtic competed for in their first season, 1888/89. From left; Scottish Cup. Glasgow Cup, Glasgow North Eastern Cup & Glasgow Charity Cup.

Barney Battles

Willie Maley

Dan McArthur

One view of the Celtic vs Third Lanark Scottish Cup Final at (Second) Hampden Park. The match was played in wintry conditions under protest and was dubbed 'The Snow Final'. The strong and established Third Lanark side defeated Celtic, completing their first season in existence, by 3-0 and later won the replay by 2-1. The full name of Celtic's opponents was 3rd Lanark Rifle Volunteers and they were affiliated to a military regiment. (Second) Hampden Park was later owned by the Thirds and re-named Cathkin Park.

Dan Doyle

Jimmy Blessington

Johnny Campbell

Celtic's first game in England, v Corinthians at Kennington Oval, 16 February 1889.

Tom Maley

Johnnie Madden

Jimmy Quinn

Alec McNair

Celtic win the Glasgow North Eastern Cup, beating Cowlairs 6-1 at Barrowfield Park, Dalmarnock, on 11 May 1889, our first-ever trophy success.

Sunny Jim Young

Peter Somers

Willie Loney

Celtic beat the original 'Invincibles', English Double-winners Preston North End.

Davie Adams

Jimmy McMenemy

James 'Dun' Hay

Celtic FC (before switching to the hooped jerseys). Probably the Celtic side which beat Blackburn Rovers 1-0 at Celtic Park in October 1889. Back row: McLaughlin (Goalkeeper), Middle row, left to right: Madden, Coleman, McKeown, Reynolds, Dowds, Cunningham. Front row: Gallagher, M. Dunbar, J. Kelly, Groves. Several committee men are included:Willie McKillop (extreme left, back row), Tom Maley (wearing hat, third from left in the back row), John Glass, Club President, (middle row, next to Reynolds), John O'Hara, Secretary, (next to Dowds), D. Malloy (next to Cunningham).

Founding fathers William McKillop, John Glass, John O'Hara, Hugh Darroch, Joseph McGroary, Daniel Malloy & Celtic team v Blackburn Rovers, October 1889

Celtic team of 1890–1

Left to right: Back row: Mick Dunbar, Joe Anderson (trainer), Gerry Reynolds, J. Boyle, J. Bell, Mick McKeown, committeeman John O'Hara, James Kelly. *Centre row:* linesman P. Gallagher, Frank Dolan, J. McGhee, Willie Maley, Tom E. Maley. *Front row:* Johnny Madden, John Coleman, Peter Dowds, Sandy McMahon, Johnny Campbell

Celtic FC 1890/91. Ready for the inaugural Scottish Football League campaign.

The Proud, proud Celts. An early version of the Celtic Huddle? The Glasgow, Glasgow Charity and Scottish Cups are shown in the shamrock leaves, all won by Celtic in 1891/92.

Founding fathers Michael Cairns & James Curtis in Celtic's Second XI Cup-winners' team photo, Feb 1891. The Glasgow North Eastern Cup is also displayed on the left

The first Celtic team to win the Scottish Cup, beating Queen's Park 5-1 at Ibrox on Saturday, 9 April 1892

Monument to Celtic's Founding Fathers at Dalbeth Cemetery

....

The authors would like to take a moment to acknowledge the tremendous work carried out by the Celtic Graves Society.

Established in 2010 by Celtic supporters with an objective of cherishing the memory of those whose contribution, large or small, has been the cornerstone of the club's history, the group have succeeded in locating and honouring the final resting places of countless Celts across the world, including our founding fathers, our first-ever team and other early heroes.

Devotion above and beyond the call of duty and yet another example of why our beloved Celtic is so much more than a football club.

Support these wonderful Celts at **www.celticgraves.com**

rematch with Clyde, Saturday, 15 December 1888. Celts would travel to Falkirk to meet East Stirlingshire with Third Lanark, or 3rd Lanarkshire Rifle Volunteers to give them their full name, entertaining outsiders Campsie at First Cathkin. The other two ties would take place in Dumbarton, the 1887 runners-up facing St Mirren whilst Dumbarton Athletic took on neighbours and holders, Renton. As was the case with East Stirlingshire, both Campsie and Dumbarton Athletic had been given byes in the previous round, so only five of the eight teams remaining in the Scottish Cup had qualified. Seems quite incredible now.

Celtic were unchanged for the visit to Merchiston Park, Bainsford, just north of Falkirk, in front of 3,000 spectators, whilst the reigning Stirlingshire Cup-holders featured two half-backs who would gain international honours with the club, Welsh captain Humphrey Jones and Scotland's Alexander Ritchie. It would be another star man for the hosts who would break the deadlock, prolific marksman Lawrence McLachlan netting just before the break. Celtic had enjoyed the majority of possession and would continue to do so as the second half progressed, however, with three minutes remaining, they still trailed East Stirlingshire by that McLachlan strike. Then into the breach once more stepped Neil McCallum, like his skipper James Kelly, a Scottish Cup-winner with Renton earlier that year. Firstly, he would take a long ball from Jimmy McLaren in his stride before beating home keeper Sharp to draw Celtic level. Then, with all eyes on a replay, he broke Shire hearts by immediately grabbing the winner. It had been yet another close shave in a thrilling cup run, with another of Celtic's lucky lives used up.

Saturday, 22 December 1888 saw the Celts on the road again, this time heading to Alexandria for a friendly match with Vale of Leven. The Dunbartonshire club had been a powerhouse in the first decade of the Scottish Cup, emulating Queen's Park's three successive wins by repeating that feat between 1877 and 1879, twice at the expense of Rangers. They would then achieve an unwelcome if not still-commendable record, by reaching but losing three consecutive finals from 1883, Dumbarton, Queen's Park and Renton the victors on those occasions. As with the Renton friendly the previous month, this was another event which would leave its mark on the club for reasons other than the play itself. The photo taken outside the Millburn Park pavilion remains the earliest surviving image of a Celtic team. Press reports at the time would suggest the occasion was the opening of Vale of Leven's new ground.

Willie Maley had been a late replacement for Alec 'Abe' Collins at right-back, the future Celtic manager thus appearing in this line-up, which has now been immortalised in the fledgling club's history.

Willie Dunning; Willie Maley & Mick McKeown; Paddy Gallagher, James Kelly & Jimmy McLaren;

Neil McCallum, Johnny Coleman, Willie Groves, Mick Dunbar & Tom Maley.

Photographs duly taken, the home side started well before an enthusiastic 2,000 crowd, winger Bruce giving them the lead within the opening twenty minutes. Willie Groves then snatched an equaliser before the break, with the third and decisive goal being plundered by Neil McCallum on the hour.

The following Saturday, 29 December 1888, saw Celtic enter its fourth tournament, with a first appearance in the Glasgow North Eastern Cup. The competition did what it said on the tin, allowing entry to clubs from the north or east of the city to participate. It had first been played in season 1881/82, Petershill FC – no connection to the later junior club of the same name – beating Tollcross 5-0 in the final. The trophy had never left Springburn, Cowlairs dominating with five wins from the six editions played since, twice defeating Clyde and near-neighbours Northern in those finals. Hyde Park-based Northern were the only other club to have won the tournament, their sole success coming in 1885.

Celtic's initial North Eastern Cup opponents were Clydesdale, based in Rutherglen, the visit of the Bhoys drawing another record attendance to their Southcroft Park home. Neil McCallum opened the scoring in the fifth minute as the Celts marked their arrival in the latest competition open to them just as they had in their inaugural Scottish Cup tie with Shettleston, by running out 5-1 winners on the day.

And the calendar year of 1888 was rounded off with another first, the maiden visit of a non-Scottish side to Celtic Park, a fixture arranged to generate funds for the East End Poor Children's Dinner Tables.

Birmingham St George's were the team who created such history, on Monday, 31 December 1888. The Midlands club had only recently changed its name from Mitchell St George's, having earlier been formed as an amalgamation of the two entities making up that title.

Celtic took the opportunity to field a new goalkeeper, John Kelly, recently signed from Renfrewshire outfit Mearns, together with a right-back named Gallagher, of whom little is known. It is likely that he was appearing as a guest player on loan from another club, as was the custom of the day.

The full line-up was as follows:

John Kelly; A. Gallagher & Mick McKeown; Paddy Gallagher, James Kelly & Jimmy McLaren;

Neil McCallum, Mick Dunbar, Willie Groves, Tom Maley & Johnny Coleman.

Press reports of the day are inconsistent to say the least, in terms of the attendance and goalscorers on the day. What is factual, is that Celtic recovered from the loss of an early goal to lead 3-1 at the interval, with Willie Groves and Neil McCallum to the fore. After the break, the English side struggled badly, particularly following the loss of two players to injury. The second half became a procession towards the St George's goal, the Bhoys eventually declaring once again at that perfect-sounding 7-1.

It was perhaps a rather harsh way to wish a Happy New Year to our English guests!

Chapter 9:

JANUARY 1889: A TRICKY TRIP TO 'FATAL BOGHEAD'

The new year was brought in with another glamour friendly match in aid of 'catholic charities', this time against Corinthians, the famous English amateur side, at Celtic Park on Thursday, 3 January 1889. Interest in the game was phenomenal, with over 20,000 tickets sold, most of those, it would appear, cramming into Celtic's home ground to witness the occasion, unprecedented numbers for those times.

Celts fielded Hibernian's full-back Pat Dowling as a guest player, whilst the Corinthians utilised Queen's Park's wing-half Allan Stewart and winger William Lambie on the same basis. Lambie had actually played against his own side as the two famous amateur outfits met for their annual friendly match at Second Hampden on New Year's Day, two days earlier, his goal giving Corinthians a 2-1 first-half lead before Queen's snatched a late winner to edge a five-goal clash.

The full Celtic line-up that lunchtime was as follows:

John Kelly; Pat Dowling (Hibernian) & Mick McKeown; Paddy Gallagher, James Kelly & James McLaren;

Neil McCallum, Mick Dunbar, Willie Groves, Tom Maley & Johnny Coleman.

Just as they had done on Hogmanay against Birmingham St George's, the Bhoys would destroy their latest English visitors with a powerful display of attacking football despite the atrocious condition of the pitch, the Celtic forwards ploughing through the mud to overcome their guests by six goals to two.

John Kelly would show up well in the early exchanges as the visitors pressed for an opener, however, it would be Neil McCallum who would strike first, after wonderful work from Willie Groves in the 5th minute. Five minutes later it was 2-0, this time Johnny Coleman on target as the hosts began to flex their muscles. Two goals within a minute then took the score to 3-1, first Dewhurst getting Corinthians off the mark following a corner only for Mick Dunbar to force a third home goal over the line with his chest. Before the interval, Tom Maley would finish the match as a contest by adding a fourth for Celtic.

The visitors would grab the opening goal of the second half, guest player Stewart setting up one of the Walters brothers for 4-2, however, this only served to re-energise Celtic, McCallum and Coleman both securing personal doubles as the hosts ran out winners by 6-2, another 'very Celtic' scoreline.

An under-strength Celtic side made the short visit to Beechwood Park, Dalmarnock, two days later, Saturday, 5 January 1889, for a friendly match with near-neighbours Thistle FC. Minus star names such as Paddy Gallagher, Jimmy McLaren, Neil McCallum and Tom Maley, and again featuring Hibernian's Pat Dowling at right-back, the Bhoys XI managed to build up a 2-0 half-time lead through goals by James Kelly and a young reserve by the name of McGuire. It would prove to be the proverbial game of two halves, however, as the blue-and-white hooped hosts Thistle fought back strongly in the second half, eventually securing a 3-2 victory on the day.

The following Saturday, 12 January 1889, would be the biggest match in Celtic's short history, as they travelled to face Dumbarton in the semi-final of the Scottish Cup, a quite incredible achievement for a club in its first season. The game would be played on their rival's home ground, famously described by Willie Maley as "Fatal Boghead," such was the dominance they enjoyed on their own patch. The Bhoys could claim a perfect record there, however, having won 2-1 in the first-ever meeting of the two clubs back in September 1888, thanks to a double from Neil McCallum.

As had been the case in September, Dumbarton would field two players who would later (and before in one case) play their own part in Celtic's history, goalkeeper James Bell and centre-forward Johnny Madden.

The chapter covering that calendar month provides the supporting detail for those players.

Dumbarton had serious Scottish Cup pedigree. Formed in December 1872, they first appeared in the final of the country's most prestigious football competition in April 1881, losing 3-1 to Queen's Park at Kinning Park, as Dr John Smith wrote his way into the history books with the first hat-trick to be scored in a Scottish Cup final, as the amateurs notched up their fifth success in the opening eight years.

The same two sides would contest the 1881/82 final, 12 months later, the Spiders again coming out on top, this time defeating Dumbarton 4-1 in a replay at First Cathkin, following a 2-2 draw in March.

The Sons of the Rock would finally gain some revenge on Saturday, 3 February 1883, when they beat the defending champions 3-1 at Boghead in the following season's quarter-final. They would then go on to claim their first national success by defeating Vale of Leven 2-1 in the final at Second Hampden.

Dumbarton would reappear at the same venue on Saturday, 12 February 1887 for the 1886/87 final. Their opponents that day would be Hibernian, a change in the balance of power perhaps illustrated by the fact that the two beaten semi-finalists the previous month had been the clubs who dominated the first decade of the competition, Queen's Park and Vale of Leven. Hibernian had been knocking on the door of their first Scottish Cup final, having lost out at the semi-final stage in each of the previous three seasons. They would finally strike gold at the fourth attempt with a 3-1 victory over Vale of Leven, having earlier beaten rivals Heart of Midlothian by a 5-1 scoreline - which we would see again in the final of 2012 – to become the first side from eastern Scotland to contest a Scottish Cup final.

There had then been an anxious wait as the club awaited the outcome of an appeal by Vale of Leven over a suggestion of illegal payments being made to their star player of that semi-final. The name of the player involved was none other than 'Darling' Willie Groves, later to shine for Celtic. Three days before the final, Hibernian were cleared of any wrongdoing by the Scottish Football Association panel, albeit that peculiar 'not proven' verdict and a casting vote was required to do so. A further appeal by Vale of Leven was subsequently withdrawn at the last minute, bringing that process to an end.

Dumbarton would start strong favourites on the day, whilst the bulk of the 15,000 crowd were rooting for the 'Irishmen.' The Sons would score first, through Aitken, early in the second half, before Phil Clarke equalised for Hibernian. The football gods would then conspire to ensure that the man at the centre of the controversy had the final say, quite literally, Groves waltzing through the Dumbarton defence to win the cup for Edinburgh's Little Ireland community, and many more ex-patriots across Scotland. No-one would have known this then, however, that 1887 Scottish Cup final success would have huge implications for victors Hibernian and another, as yet unnamed, club which would spring up to support the Irish community in Scotland later that year, some 45 miles to the west of Leith.

As previously discussed, that would have been the subject of much acrimony long before Celtic took the field at Boghead in front of 6,000 spectators for their own date with Scottish Cup destiny on Saturday, 12 January 1889. Two of Hibernian's cup-winning heroes against Dumbarton that afternoon, Jimmy McLaren and Willie Groves, would now line up in the striped jerseys of Celtic, as would a duo who would repeat that success with Renton, 12 months later, James Kelly and Neil McCallum, and a further four players plucked from the Edinburgh club during 1888, Paddy Gallagher, Mick McKeown, Mick Dunbar and Johnny Coleman. Indeed, it was more difficult to pick a Celtic player who did not snugly fit into one of those three categories, as they lined up for the huge match as follows:

John Kelly; Paddy Gallagher & Mick McKeown; Willie Maley, James Kelly & James McLaren;

Neil McCallum, Mick Dunbar, Willie Groves, Tom Maley & Johnny Coleman.

As it transpired, the semi-final would turn out to be much more comfortable for Celtic than had been widely anticipated, goals scored five minutes into the game and just before the interval by Willie Groves and Mick Dunbar had pretty much assured the Bhoys' progression to the Hampden final by half time. The goal of the game arrived just after the hour, Groves running virtually the length of the pitch with Dewar trailing helplessly in his wake before beating James Bell for the second time. Dunbar then secured his own brace to make it 4-0 before, rather poignantly, Johnny Madden, who had played for Celtic in its first-ever game in May 1888, then apparently reneged on a promise to join the club permanently during that summer but who would later wear the green-and-white colours again with great distinction, pulled a late consolation goal back for his hometown team.

In the other semi-final, played at First Cathkin on that same afternoon, 3rd LRV beat holders Renton 2-0 to reach their third Scottish Cup final, having lost the 1876 and 1878 deciders to Queen's Park at Hamilton Crescent then Vale of Leven at First Hampden. Thus, the one certainty was that there would be a new name on the trophy at the end of the 1888/89 final the following month, a sixth club eligible to join the illustrious roll of honour, as follows:

Queen's Park (8 wins)
Vale of Leven (3 wins)
Dumbarton
Renton (2 wins)
Hibernian

In the meantime, there would be two friendly fixtures to conclude Celtic's January commitments.

On Saturday, 19 January 1889, the club made its first visit to Cappielow Park, Greenock to take on local outfit Morton, named after its first patron and Lord Provost of the town, James Morton. Celtic were without a number of their established stars, the most worrying of which was Neil McCallum, who was suffering from what The Scotsman described as a "sudden and severe illness". The aforementioned Dowling and McGuire turned out to fill the gaps, as did Hibernian's cup-winning skipper from 1887, Jimmy McGhee, and a guest player named Graham from Port Glasgow Athletic, who would later bring the scores level at 4-4. On the plus side, there was a welcome return for right-back Alec 'Abe' Collins.

This was the craziest of games, as Celts led 2-0 then trailed 2-4 before Tom Maley's last-gasp winner. Mick Dunbar, Johnny Coleman and Mick McKeown supplemented the strikes from Graham and Maley.

The final game of the month saw the Bhoys return to Celtic Park for the first time since the visit of the Corinthians, Airdrieonians the visitors on Saturday, 26 January 1889. With Neil McCallum still out and Willie Maley unavailable, Hibernian's regular stand-in Pat Dowling was joined in the Celtic line-up by Harry Groves, brother of star centre-forward Willie. A shortened duration of 70 minutes' play had been agreed for the game, with both goals coming either side of the interval. Stark opened for the visitors on the half-hour before Mick Dunbar ensured that Celts would not go into the following week's Scottish Cup final on the back of a loss, the inside-forward equalising after good work by Willie Groves.

So only seven more sleeps remained until the biggest game in the short history of Celtic Football Club.

Chapter 10:

FEBRUARY 1889: OH, HAMPDEN IN THE SNOW!

Excitement would have been at fever pitch within the Irish community congregated in the east end of the city of Glasgow on the morning of Saturday, 2 February 1889.

The team, their Bhoys, would later that day appear in the biggest showpiece event of Scottish football, the Scottish Cup Final, to be played at Second Hampden Park on the south side of the River Clyde.

It was a staggering achievement.

Around six months earlier, the new Celtic club had no signed players.

Now here we were.

The opposition on the day would be provided by the 3rd LRV and the cup final venue would be somewhat ironic. Within four years, they would be known as Third Lanark and the ground would be renamed New Cathkin Park, after the club had moved from their old Cathkin home - a Territorial Army drilling ground off Dixon Avenue - to replace Queen's Park as the occupiers, the Spiders then moving a few hundred yards south along Cathcart Road to their current Mount Florida base.

The Volunteers would be appearing in their third Scottish Cup final after an absence of 11 years, having lost both times at the last hurdle. They had commenced their latest assault on the much-cherished trophy with a walkover victory against fellow-Glaswegian outfit Whitefield before travelling to inflict an 8-0 destruction on Kelvinside Athletic in the second round. The third round saw them pitted against neighbours and eight-time winners Queen's Park, the volunteers emerging triumphant with a 4-2 win in the replayed match, their initial 2-1 victory having been declared void.

There was another emphatic win over Ayrshire's Hurlford in the next round, this time by 7-1 at Cathkin, before 3rd LRV endured a marathon tie with Paisley's Abercorn, who had been opponents of Celtic in our first-ever competitive match, in the Glasgow International Exhibition Cup back in August 1888. It would take four matches to separate the teams, after the initial 5-4 home victory achieved by the Volunteers on Saturday, 24 November 1888 was rendered invalid. The teams would play out two 2-2 draws, one at each of their home grounds, before the Glasgow side finally forced themselves through with a 3-1 win at First Cathkin on Saturday, 22 December 1888, by which time the other three quarter-final ties had already taken place.

Seven days later, 3rd LRV would beat Campsie 6-1, to set up a January last-four clash with Renton. Having earlier disposed of Queen's Park, the Volunteers would then claim the scalp of another former winner, beating the cup-holders 2-0 on the same day that Celtic were beating Dumbarton at "Fatal Boghead."

There was no doubt they had come through a difficult path to the final. They would provide formidable opposition for this new club, Celtic, consisting of a group of men with Ireland in their blood.

Neil McCallum was deemed sufficiently fit after his recent health scare to start the match, meaning that the Celtic team chosen to win its first-ever trophy was along the usual lines, as follows;

John Kelly; Paddy Gallagher & Mick McKeown; Willie Maley, James Kelly & James McLaren;

Neil McCallum, Mick Dunbar, Willie Groves, Johnny Coleman & Tom Maley.

Sadly, the day itself would turn out to be a huge anti-climax.

Snow had fallen constantly that morning to the extent that by the time of the allotted kick-off, 3.15pm, the entire Hampden pitch was a sea of white, several inches deep. Both clubs registered protests at that point, as was their right, with an agreement then reached within themselves that the match be played but essentially as a friendly, a deal apparently not endorsed by the SFA committee or conveyed to the 20,000 shivering souls in the stadium, a record attendance in Scotland at least at that time. The farcical scenario continued with the sight of the cup final teams having a snowball fight on the pitch.

One has to assume, however, that some spectators believed they were watching the 1888/89 Scottish Cup final play out that wintry February afternoon, outside-right Johnny Marshall striking first for the locals when he headed the ball past John Kelly midway through the first half, somewhat against the run of play at that stage. The difficult conditions would continue to deteriorate further as the snowfall grew heavier by the minute, making the passing game enjoyed by the Bhoys well-nigh impossible. There would be no further scoring before the interval, despite incessant pressure from Celtic.

That pattern continued after the break, 3rd LRV keeper Robert Downie performing heroically time and again to stop the ball passing between his posts. The concern amongst those wearing the green in the crowd was that this all-out attack would leave Celts susceptible to the sucker punch, and this duly arrived as John Oswald made it 2-0 on 70 minutes, the ball by this point covered in snow as it squirmed through Kelly's frozen fingers. Press reports suggest that, shortly afterwards, snow fell to such an extent that many spectators took their leave, perhaps realising that the result would not stand. Those who did would not witness the final act of the match, Jimmy Hannah's drive ending it at 3-0.

The fallout from the game dubbed forever as 'The Snow Final' illustrates how different the protocols involved were in those days, whilst that old chestnut of 'self-interest' would manifest itself back then.

What happened next is perhaps best summarised by a man who played that afternoon for Celtic, right-half Willie Maley, recalling the events of February 1889 half-a-century later, in 'The Story of the Celtic.'

"It goes without saying that, following the 'snow' game, there was considerable discussion as to whether the result would stand. At the SFA meeting it transpired, although there was no secret about it, that the officials had, previous to the game, given instructions that both teams should play under protest. Indeed, both had actually intimated their objections to the conditions. The referee [Charles Campbell] and the two umpires were questioned, and, having stated that in their opinion the ground was unplayable, the Association decided that the game should be replayed on the following Saturday."

"The conditions on this occasion were fairly good, the only fault to be found being that the surface was very hard owing to frost. 3rd Lanark, having claimed that the previous game should stand, despite their agreement to protest against the ground conditions, now performed a rather comical volte-face by intimating a protest against the ground in the replay, owing to its hard condition – and they also protested against the Association's decision [to replay the match]!"

Seven days later, on Saturday, 9 February 1889, another 16,000 supporters made their way back to Second Hampden for the replayed Scottish Cup final of 1888/89. After the protest by the Volunteers had been received, on the two points of issue as described above, the two unchanged elevens went back into battle on the hard surface.

There would be a double blow for Celtic early on, which ultimately would prove crucial in their search for a first trophy win. First Neil McCallum blasted in the opening goal, his joy short-lived as an offside decision was given against him. Then Celts inside-left Johnny Coleman failed to recover from an injury and was helped from the field, the Bhoys thus reduced to 10 men for the remainder of the cup final.

Despite this, there was a Groundhog Day feel to proceedings as Celtic forwards contrived to make and miss several clear chances, Tom Maley, Willie Groves and McCallum amongst the main culprits, whilst the latter struck the upright with the keeper stranded. Then, as so often happens, a goal is scored at the other end, Johnny Marshall the man to open the scoring, midway through the first half, just as he had done the previous Saturday. The game had actually continued after Celtic keeper John Kelly had clawed the ball back into play, however after consultation with his umpires, referee Charles Campbell agreed with the 3rd LRV players that the goal should stand. Despite a series of near things at both ends, it would remain 1-0 to the Volunteers at the interval.

The game of cut-and-thrust continued after the break, until eventually the pressure applied by Celtic paid off, McCallum making another entry into the record books as the first player to score for the Bhoys in a cup final, heading home in the 67th minute to tremendous cheers from the bulk of the crowd. There then followed a virtual bombardment on Downie's goal, as the Celtic supporters cheered wildly for that historic winner. Surely it was only a matter of time. Then, as a replay beckoned, there was a heartbreak ending to the fairytale club's big day, as John Oswald, in a rare but deadly 3rd LRV breakaway, snatched the goal which would take the Scottish Cup to Cathkin Park for the first time.

The last word on Celtic's ultimately unsuccessful attempt to claim Scottish football's greatest prize at the first attempt goes to Willie Maley, again from his historic record, 'The Story of the Celtic'.

"And so Celtic's first bid to win the trophy ended in failure, but what a glorious failure! They had astonished the football world by reaching the final in their first year, and even in defeat had given an exhibition seldom if ever equalled, one which in the years to come was to be regarded as their own particular brand of football and of the most scientific order."

As the song created in the great man's honour would recall many decades later, right from the outset there was a desire and a passion "to play football the Glasgow Celtic way."

No doubt reeling from the disappointment of that initial Hampden appearance, seven days later the Celtic players made the long journey south to London to play the return game with Corinthians at the Oval, in those days the venue for England's FA Cup final as well as the home of the Surrey Cricket Club. Neither Maley brother was available for the Bhoys first venture outside Scotland, Pat Dowling and Phil Clarke of Hibernian joining the other nine from Celtic's cup-final team on Saturday, 16 February 1889.

Celtic had coasted to a 6-2 victory in their initial meeting in Glasgow the previous month, however, the match in Kennington would prove a very different proposition. A combination of horrendous wet weather and a competing England rugby international reduced the attendance to around one third of that anticipated, only 3,000 or so wet souls braving the elements that afternoon. Celts would struggle on the day against the strong amateur select, goals at the start and end of the first half by Currey and Veitch giving Corinthians the advantage at the interval. Guest player Phil Clarke would get Celtic on the scoresheet, however, Veitch grabbed his second in the final minute to seal a 3-1 win for the hosts.

The month ended with another unique occasion and another Celtic defeat, albeit this would be far from the strongest team available to the Bhoys.

On Saturday, 23 February 1889, Celtic Park welcomed the Clydesdale Harriers for their cross-country championships, the runners setting out from the track around the pitch before completing the race in front of the grandstand. Hence the club were living up to their name as the Celtic Football & Athletic Club. Almost as a sideshow, there would be football on the menu, with Celtic taking on a Harriers Select XI which featured the Clyde goalkeeper Chalmers, who had played so well against the Bhoys previously. He would do so again that afternoon, particularly in a first half dominated by the hosts, who took to the field minus the injured Jimmy McLaren and Mick McKeown and Neil McCallum, who were representing Glasgow against the East of Scotland in an inter-county fixture, Pat Dowling and Phil Clarke becoming Celts for the second successive Saturday whilst Carfin Shamrock's Jerry Reynolds made his maiden guest appearance in the jersey he would later wear with courage and distinction.

The final change to the Celtic line-up saw the debut of a player later described by Willie Maley as "the greatest all-round player we had seen at Celtic Park, at home in any and every position", Peter Dowds. A native of Johnstone in Renfrewshire, which is a story itself for another day, Dowds had joined the Bhoys from Broxburn Athletic that same month. He would line-up with Paddy Gallagher and James Kelly to complete the half-back line against the Harriers in the continued absence of that same Maley.

The heroics of guest goalkeeper Chalmers kept the scoreline blank at the interval, despite a Bhoys attacking onslaught, however visitors Clydesdale would score three goals without reply in the second half, as

Celtic ended a calendar month without a victory for the first time in their short history.

With the football over for the afternoon, those with Celtic in their hearts could sit back to await the return of the 50 or so hardy runners to the arena for their final lap, perhaps contemplating how far the club had come so quickly, beaten finalists in two of the three competitions entered thus far with the mighty Queen's Park ending our interest in a third. It would then be time to reflect on that progress and to regroup for the remaining challenges to be faced that season.

Chapter 11:

MARCH 1889: THE NEW BHOYS REACH A THIRD CUP FINAL

Celtic opened March with a home friendly against Abercorn on the second day of the month. The Paisley side had featured in the club's first competitive game back in August 1888, the first-round tie in the Glasgow International Exhibition Cup at Kelvingrove, which had finished with 1-1 with the Bhoys progressing after a failure to agree on a suitable replay date. A few weeks later, Celts had won 4-2 at Abercorn's Blackstoun Park home in Paisley, in a friendly played as the Kelvingrove tournament was reaching a climax. They had then taken eventual Scottish Cup-winners 3rd LRV to a fourth match before losing at Cathkin, all of which suggests they were a useful outfit at that time.

Jerry Reynolds and Peter Dowds retained their places in the Celtic line-up for this latest clash, whilst Mick McKeown and Willie Maley returned. James Kelly and Neil McCallum missed out with the latter's right-wing slot taken by William Naughton, the teenager making his first appearance for Celtic since signing from Hibernian. He would be yet another veteran of the match between the Edinburgh club and Cowlairs, which had opened Celtic Park 10 months earlier, to later wear the colours of Celtic.

The Bhoys thus lined up on Saturday, 2 March 1889 as follows:

John Kelly; Jerry Reynolds & Mick McKeown; Willie Maley, Paddy Gallagher & Peter Dowds;

Willie Naughton, Mick Dunbar, Willie Groves, Johnny Coleman & Tom Maley.

Abercorn would avoid defeat at the hands of Celtic for a second time by sharing eight goals in a highly-entertaining clash in Glasgow's East End, despite falling two goals behind early on, following strikes by debutant

Naughton and Johnny Coleman. The Paisley men had levelled matters before the break and would then take a 3-2 lead early in the second half before Mick Dunbar equalised. As was common at that time, the remaining play is described in scant detail, perhaps due to reporting deadlines. In any event, somewhere along the line both sides managed another goal, as the match ended in a 4-4 draw.

There was another 'goalfest' seven days later, Saturday, 9 March 1889, as Hibernian travelled west for a friendly at Celtic Park, the third meeting that season of Scotland's most prominent Irish clubs. On the same afternoon, across the city at Ibrox, Scotland and Ireland were in opposition in the opening match of the Home International Championship. The Scots, with Mick McKeown making his debut at left-back, would prove far too strong on the day, Willie Groves marking his own second international appearance with a hat-trick as the hosts won 7-0. The opening two goals came from Kilbirnie winger Frank Watt, with Hurlford's David Black making it 3-0 before the half-hour. Groves would then secure his own personal treble either side of the break before Cowlairs' teenage inside-forward Tom McInnes completed his first match in the navy of Scotland by grabbing the seventh with two minutes to play.

With McKeown and Groves on international duty, the Celtic line-up was shuffled yet again for the visit of Hibernian, in a match played to raise much-needed funds for the visitors, with all proceeds going into the coffers of the Edinburgh club. How quickly things change in football. Two years earlier, Hibernian were the pride of the Irish community in Scotland, winners of the Scottish Cup itself in 1887, whilst Celtic Football Club was at that time no more than an idea or a twinkle in Brother Walfrid's eye.

Alec 'Abe' Collins and James Quiqley of Campsie made up the full-back pairings for this latest battle of the greens. The Milton of Campsie outfit had caused a few raised eyebrows in their Scottish Cup run of that season, Heart of Midlothian amongst their conquests as they reached the quarter-final, before being put to the sword by 3rd LRV. James Kelly replaced Willie Maley whilst Mick Dunbar's younger brother Tom joined the half-back line for a rare appearance in the stripes. That allowed the versatile Peter Dowds to move forward to help Mick fill the gap left by the sublime forward, Willie Groves.

The Celtic team was thus set up as follows:

John Kelly; Alec Collins & James Quigley (Campsie); Paddy Gallagher, James Kelly & Tom Dunbar;

Neil McCallum, Peter Dowds, Mick Dunbar, Johnny Coleman & Tom Maley.

The Hibernian team featured an 18-year-old inside forward who would go on to become one of the all-time Celtic greats, Sandy McMahon. And it would be the man later known as 'The Duke' who would score the Edinburgh club's equaliser 20 minutes in, after Tom Maley had given the hosts an early lead. A Neil McCallum double followed by a Mick Dunbar strike saw Celts extend their lead to 4-2 by the interval, George Smith having kept the visitors in the game briefly at 3-2. The Bhoys would extend that advantage early in the second half and would eventually prevail by the odd goal in nine despite a late fightback by Hibernian. So, no less than 17 goals in two matches for the Parkhead faithful to enjoy.

It was back to competitive action for Celtic the following Saturday, 16 March 1889. A large St Patrick's weekend crowd rolled up to Celtic Park to watch the Bhoys take on Northern in the semi-final of the Glasgow North Eastern Cup. Northern had finished as runner's up to Springburn rivals Cowlairs in the 1888 final at Clyde's Barrowfield Park, losing 1-0 just three days before Cowlairs would take part in the inaugural match at Celtic's new stadium against Hibernian. In the opening round of this season's competition, Northern had returned to Barrowfield in late January, this time emerging as winners over hosts Clyde by the odd goal in five. Another victory over Celtic would set up a repeat of the previous final with Cowlairs, who had overcome Dalmarnock-based Thistle FC at the third attempt in February, before hammering Shettleston 7-1 at Gourlay Park in their semi-final tie on Saturday, 2 March 1889.

Celtic and Northern had met once before, a friendly played at Hyde Park on Monday, 27 August 1888 in front of 3,000 spectators. Neil McCallum had been the star man that night, as the visitors racked up three goals without reply, and he would again be pivotal in the last-four clash eight months later.

The Celts lined up as follows, as they attempted to reach a third cup final in their maiden season:

John Kelly; Alec Collins & Mick McKeown; Paddy Gallagher, James Kelly & Jimmy McLaren;

Neil McCallum, Mick Dunbar, Willie Groves, Johnny Coleman & Tom Maley.

It was Northern's McLeod who would be first on the scoresheet, the left-winger beating John Kelly in the home goal after 10 minutes to upset the majority of the crowd. Within two minutes, though, Celtic were level, Mick Dunbar equalising after good work from Willie Groves. Despite numerous near things, the score remained at 1-1 as the half-time whistle blew.

Ten minutes into the second period, Neil McCallum resumed his personal vendetta with the Northern defence by giving the Bhoys a 2-1 lead. This would prove to be the defining moment in the tie, as the Celts began to turn on the style. There would be a double for Johnny Coleman before the end, Celtic eventually easing through to another final by a 4-1 winning margin. Cowlairs would lie in wait in May.

In the meantime, there would be further friendlies to complete. The first of those saw Celtic travel down to Newcastle to play West End at St James Park, sharing the train journey south with a Rangers party bound for Sunderland. Newcastle West End would merge with East End in 1892 to form a new club, Newcastle United. For the match against Celtic, they would wear their navy-and-red hooped kit which would be adopted as a change strip by Kevin Keegan's Geordies more than a century later. West End also featured the former Renton legend Bob Kelso at wing-half. He would be up against his old sparring partners from those heady days, James Kelly and Neil McCallum. Newcastle united indeed.

McCallum would again prove to be the man for the big occasion, becoming the first Celtic player to score in England then repeating the dose as the Bhoys won by the odd goal in seven. Johnny Coleman and Tom Maley were the other Celts on target, thus ensuring a happy journey home in the early hours.

The last game of the month saw a rerun of the Scottish Cup final, as 3rd LRV brought their victorious squad to Celtic Park for a friendly, on Saturday, 30 March 1889. A huge crowd was attracted by the rematch of two sides who had produced such thrilling spectacles in the Hampden clashes just the previous month, despite the varying but consistently difficult conditions they endured.

Thirds were bolstered by a guest appearance from Kilbirnie winger Frank Watt, who had netted twice in his Scotland debut against Ireland just three weeks earlier. Facing him in the green and white stripes of Celtic was Willie Groves, who had gone one better by notching a hat-trick in the same 7-0 victory. He would be joined by regular stand-in defender Pat Dowling and Willie Naughton, in for Tom Maley.

The rest of the Celtic team was chosen along familiar lines, as follows;

John Kelly; Pat Dowling (Hibernian) & Mick McKeown; Paddy Gallagher, James Kelly & Jimmy McLaren;

Neil McCallum, Mick Dunbar, Willie Groves, Johnny Coleman & Willie Naughton.

In contrast to the 'Snow Cup Final' day, it was a beautiful afternoon as the teams emerged to a packed house. And Celtic came flying out of the blocks, Johnny Coleman heading them in front within five minutes, whilst Willie Groves added a second shortly afterwards. With the cup-holders reeling, Celts piled on the agony, Neil McCallum making it 3-0 on the half hour before Mick Dunbar made it 4-0 on the stroke of half-time. What a difference would just one of those strikes have made back in early February at Hampden, when chances galore were passed up before Thirds snatched a late winner?

With the game finished as a contest by the interval, there would be only one goal scored in the second half. That would fall to Jimmy Hannah, the 3rd LRV left-winger who had made it 3-0 in the dying seconds of the original Scottish Cup final tie at Second Hampden. Just as on that snowy afternoon, his strike would eventually mean little, Celts comfortably seeing out the match at 4-1 to gain a tiny piece of revenge on the Crosshill men, a first win in four attempts for the new Bhoys from the east end.

Chapter 12:

APRIL 1889: A FIRST VISIT TO IRELAND FOR CELTIC

On Saturday, 6 April 1889, Celtic made a first visit to Motherwell to take on the local side in a friendly fixture. Details of the line-ups and goalscorers are vague, however, a newspaper report from the time included in the Celtic Wiki indicates that the Bhoys scored three times in quick succession midway through the first half before Motherwell pulled a goal back, Celts then grabbing another to lead 4-1 at the interval. The 5,000 or so spectators crammed along the ropes of Dalziel Park then received further entertainment after the break, those who were favouring 'the Irishmen' enjoying a further four Celtic strikes, including one right on the full-time whistle, while the home support had two of their own to cheer as the match ended Motherwell 3 Celtic 8.

Seven days later, the 'Celtic firsts' continued as the Bhoys travelled north to Springburn for another friendly, this time against Cowlairs, who would be the club's opponents in the Glasgow North Eastern Cup final at Barrowfield Park the following month.

The sides had met twice previously, a 2-0 victory for Cowlairs in the final of the Glasgow International Exhibition Cup at Kelvingrove in September 1888 followed by a resounding 8-0 victory for the hosts in the Scottish Cup second-round tie played at Celtic Park just a couple of weeks later, however, this would be the first time that the Springburn club would welcome the Bhoys to their Gourlay Park base, just off the main Springburn Road. Both sides would be without key men due to the England v Scotland Home International clash being played at London's Kennington Oval the same day, James Kelly and Jimmy McLaren of Celtic and John McPherson of Cowlairs all starting for the Scots. That would prove to be a memorable occasion for McLaren, his last-minute shot winning the match for the visitors after Scotland had fought back from an early two-goal deficit with second half goals from Neil Munro of Abercorn and James Oswald of Scottish Cup-winners 3rd LRV. As an aside, Oswald would join Notts County at the end of that season and will reappear shortly in this chapter.

Hibernian duo Pat Dowling and Willie McCallum came in to bolster the visitors' ranks, as Celtic lined up in front of a large, noisy crowd as follows:

John Kelly; Willie McCallum (Hibernian) & Mick McKeown; Pat Dowling (Hibernian), Willie Maley & Paddy Gallagher; Neil McCallum, Mick Dunbar, Willie Groves, Johnny Coleman & Willie Naughton.

In the absence of John McPherson, Cowlairs would bring Bishop back in at inside-left. He had scored the decisive second goal at Kelvingrove the previous September, which had ensured that Celtic's first appearance in a cup final had not been a winning one. McPherson's brother James also lined up, as did home goalkeeper Tom Duff, the 'Cowlairs Orangeman'. Both men would later turn out for Celtic.

At left-back was William McLeod. He had gained his only international cap whilst a player with Queen's Park, against Ireland in Belfast three years earlier. His teammates that day had included current Celts James Kelly and Mick Dunbar, at that time playing their trade with Renton and Cartvale respectively. Dunbar had scored Scotland's fifth goal at Ballynafeigh Park that afternoon. McLeod would appear for several English sides over the years, most notably Aston Villa, before becoming a referee in later life.

Playing on the left wing for Cowlairs was Tom McInnes. His is a remarkable story. Like myself, he was born in Springburn on 22 March, although in his case slightly earlier, back in 1869. He joined his local club and at just 19-years-old was part of that Cowlairs side who beat Celtic 2-0 to win the Glasgow International Exhibition Cup. McInnes was still a teenager when he received his first international cap, against Ireland at Ibrox on 9 March 1889. He would also have two Celts for company that day, fellow debutant Mick McKeown and striker Willie Groves, the latter hitting a hat-trick in the Scots' 7-0 win. A dream day for 'Oor Tam' would be capped by a debut goal, Scotland's seventh, in the 88th minute.

In December 1889, McInnes would head south to sign for Notts County, joining fellow Scottish forward James Oswald, who had moved to Trent Bridge from 3rd LRV as the Midlands club tried to improve on their second-bottom finish in the inaugural Football League. On the eve of Tom's 22nd birthday, Saturday, 21 March 1891, both lined up at the Kennington Oval for the FA Cup Final against holders Blackburn Rovers. Oswald would get on the scoresheet, however, overall it would be a disappointing day for the young Scots, as the Lancashire side retained the trophy with a 3-1 win.

The following April, Tom McInnes became the first player to score in the Inter-League fixture between Scotland and England, netting just before the interval at Pike's Lane, Bolton, home of the local Wanderers, the inaugural game between the two fledgling League entities ending in a 2-2 draw. He was partnered that day by Willie Groves, just as he had been in his Scotland debut three years earlier, albeit by this time, Groves had moved back from his centre-forward slot to a wing-half berth. Co-incidence enough you may feel until you learn that both Scotsmen were playing for the English Football League against their native domestic League team that afternoon! Groves by that time had left Celtic to join West Bromwich Albion. Just a month before the Inter-League fixture at Bolton, he had followed in McInnes' footsteps by reaching the 1892 FA Cup final at that same Kennington Oval. Groves and Albion would succeed where McInnes, Oswald and Notts County had all failed, the Baggies beating fierce Midland rivals Aston Villa by 3-0, in the first such final to feature goalnets.

A few weeks after playing for the Football League against the Scottish League, Tom McInnes headed back north to join Rangers, albeit in some sort of guest or temporary capacity. He would turn out in the end-of-season Glasgow Charity Cup final against Celtic on Wednesday, 1 June 1892. This would be the last-ever match to be played on the first Celtic Park and, with our usual fairytale sense of timing, the hosts would complete a clean sweep of the three available domestic cups by winning 2-0 in front of 7,000 spectators, thanks to a Johnny Campbell double. The Bhoys had already won the Glasgow and Scottish Cups, with a 1-0 defeat to eventual champions Dumbarton at 'Fatal Boghead' in a virtual title-decider in April seeing them finish two points behind the Sons of the Rock, thus preventing an unprecedented 'clean sweep'. That Celtic side is still considered one of the greatest to have worn our colours. Joining McInnes in the Rangers line-up at Celtic Park would be Sunderland's Donald Gow - the third Scot in that initial Football League team at Bolton - and his former Cowlairs teammate, John 'Kitey' McPherson. There could have been a third ex-Cowlairs man on the field, goalkeeper Tom Duff, however, the stopper had been dropped from the Celtic team after shipping eight goals to Dumbarton in a friendly at Celtic Park on New Year's Day 1892, on the day, perhaps ironically, that goalnets were introduced at that venue. They would certainly have come in handy as the ball flew past the hapless and allegedly hungover Duff no fewer than 11 times in total, a further three strikes mercifully disallowed. That 8-0 loss to Dumbarton remains Celtic's worst-ever home defeat, and joint biggest loss anywhere. Tom Duff did not play for the club again, returning to Cowlairs later the same month.

McInnes would then play four times for Rangers in the 1892/93 League campaign, scoring twice in a 3-2 victory over Leith Athletic at Ibrox, before heading back to Notts County in September 1892. On his return to Trent Bridge, he was promptly served with a one-month Football Association suspension for playing in Scotland! County would be relegated at the end of that season, together with Lancashire duo Accrington and Newton Heath, the latter club being renamed Manchester United in 1902.

Tom would then spend the 1893/94 season with 3rd LRV, playing all 18 League games as they finished in seventh position, 12 points behind back-to-back champions Celtic. The two clubs would meet five times in all that season, with the Bhoys winning four and drawing one, whilst knocking Thirds out of both the Scottish and Glasgow Charity Cups at the semi-final stage at Cathkin. Meanwhile, some 200 miles south of Glasgow, many of his former Notts County teammates were celebrating as they became the first second-tier side to win the FA Cup, following a 4-1 victory over Bolton Wanderers at Goodison Park, Liverpool, on Saturday, 31 March 1894. It's all in the timing.

The new home of Everton would actually be the next port of call for Tom McInnes, who moved south again that summer. Tom would join a substantial colony of Scots at the Merseyside club, including a trio of Dumbarton's League Championship-winning sides, Dickie Boyle, Jack Bell and Abe Hartley, former Renton 'world champion' Bob Kelso and David Storrier, who would cost a record transfer fee when he left Goodison for Celtic in 1898. Jack Bell would also move to Parkhead that same year. Tom's new club Everton had been based at Anfield, on the other side of Stanley Park, before an internal dispute in 1892 led to them moving to new premises at Goodison, whilst a new entity called Liverpool FC was set up to play at the Blues' former ground. Liverpool had just won the 1893/94 English Second Division, to gain promotion and join Everton in the top tier for the first time the following season, thus the first-ever Merseyside derby would take place at Goodison Park on Saturday, 13 October 1894. The first goal in this fixture came just 10 minutes in, from an Everton corner. The scorer was Tom McInnes.

McInnes would also score the first goal of the season on his Everton debut at home to Sheffield Wednesday and would be a regular contributor as the Blues finished runner's-up in England's top-flight, five points behind champions Sunderland, in his maiden campaign on Merseyside. He would add another 8 goals from 20 appearances the following season as the Blues finished third behind Aston Villa and Derby County, before heading to Southern League outfit Luton Town in the summer of 1896.

Back in April 1889, McInnes and his Cowlairs colleagues were giving Celtic a tough afternoon of it at Gourlay Park. The only goal of the match arrived in the 20th minute, and in keeping with the tone of the match, it was a scrappy affair, Tom Duff bundled over the line, ball in arms, following a goalmouth scramble in the days when protection for keepers was unheard of, certainly by today's standards.

Next up for Celtic was a whirlwind tour of Lancashire over the Easter weekend, the Bhoys lining up at Pike's Lane, Bolton – later the scene of one of Tom McInnes' landmark goals – on Friday, 19 April 1889, to take on the host club, Bolton Wanderers, in front of 7,000. Scotland internationals James Kelly and Jimmy McLaren returned for the visitors as did Tom Maley, in the absence of his brother Willie and Neil McCallum, who had failed to recover from an injury sustained against Cowlairs the previous Saturday. At left-back for the Wanderers was Dan Doyle, who would later carve his own name in the Celtic story. He had left Grimsby Town earlier that year, after a collision with an opponent, Staveley's William Cropper, had left the forward with a ruptured bowel, from which he died in the dressing-room at the ground. Dan's Celtic career is covered in some detail in David Potter's section within this book.

Whilst Celtic would enjoy the bulk of the possession and clear chances, it would be the Lancashire men who would claim the spoils on the day, goals either side of the interval giving them a 2-0 victory. The tourists would fare better 24 hours later, 30 miles to the north-east, in Burnley. Willie Groves had opened the scoring before two minutes had elapsed, with Celts adding a further two goals before the break. A chap with that wonderful Lancashire name of Duckworth managed to pull one goal back for Burnley in the second half, however, the Bhoys would hold on comfortably to run out winners by 3-1.

With the inaugural tour of England complete, it was time to break yet more new ground, Celtic heading for Ireland, where they would play their first match in the country which had been so fundamental to its creation and existence on Monday, 22 April 1889, the landmark opponents being Belfast's Distillery.

The first Celtic side to play on Irish soil was as follows:

John Kelly; Willie McCallum (Hibernian) & Mick McKeown; Pat Dowling (Hibernian), James Kelly & Jimmy McLaren;

Neil McCallum, Mick Dunbar, Willie Groves, Johnny Coleman & Tom Maley.

Over 6,000 spectators turned out at the Broadway ground in Belfast, to watch the Celts play their third in just four days, the 'day off' consisting of a sea-journey between England and Ireland. Nevertheless, the Bhoys would prove too strong for their Irish opponents, winning the game thanks to a solitary goal from Jimmy McLaren. Broadway at that time was the home ground of Belfast Gaels. In 1891, it would play host to the initial games played by Belfast Celtic, named in honour of their Glasgow forebearers.

The day after Celtic's victory over Distillery, Tuesday, 23 April 1889, the

Glasgow version was in action again at the same venue, the opposition this time coming in the shape of United Belfast, for the final match of the tour. Paddy Gallagher and Willie Maley replaced the latter's sibling Tom and guest player Willie McCallum as another 5,000 curious Irish spectators rolled up to Broadway. They would enjoy the sight of United Belfast returning to the pavilion 2-1 ahead at the interval, however, the second half would be a different matter entirely, Celts banging in four goals to emerge triumphant by 5-2, Mick Dunbar, Johnny Coleman, Mick McKeown and Neil McCallum all in on the Irish scoring action.

As the Celtic party made their way back across the Irish Sea, there would be much to contemplate as the anniversary of their first match approached. So much had already been achieved.

And we still had May to enjoy before the players and supporters could enjoy the summer break.

Chapter 13:

MAY 1889:
A FIRST CUP IS WON AND ENGLAND'S 'OLD INVINCIBLES' ARE BEATEN

As the new club Celtic approached the anniversary of its first game, following a thrilling introductory campaign, there would be two trophies still up for grabs before the curtain fell on season 1888/89.

The first of those was the Glasgow Merchant's Charity Cup, the 'Merchant's' part of the name normally dropped whenever people referred to it. This was an invitation-only competition, which had been a feature of the city's football calendar since the 1876/77 season and, just like the Scottish Cup, had been dominated by Queen's Park, the Spiders winning seven of the initial nine tournaments.

That ascendancy had come under threat over the past three seasons, when the new kid on the block, unofficial 'world champions' Renton, had triumphed each time. The most recent occasion, a 4-0 win over Cambuslang at Second Hampden on Saturday, 12 May 1888, had been the reason that Renton, the best team in the country at that time, had been unable to open the first Celtic Park the previous Tuesday, that fixture clashing with Renton's semi-final tie with Rangers. The Charity Cup final of 1888 would be one of the last games where the stars of the day, James Kelly, Bob Kelso, Neil McCallum and Jimmy McCall, would turn out for the West Dunbartonshire club, as the shadow of professional, whilst officially shunned, reared its ugly head. Indeed, by the end of that month, both Kelly and McCallum would be scoring for the new Celtic club in its inaugural match, a 5-2 victory over Rangers.

Celtic's stunning debut campaign - and no doubt the huge crowds who were flocking to watch them - had seen an invitation to the prestigious event land on the Match-Secretary's desk at Celtic Park. Competition would be fierce, with the other three clubs reflecting the cream of Scottish football at that time.

Queen's Park were in there, of course, in their capacity as Glasgow Cup-holders, the Spiders having inflicted an 8-0 defeat on Partick Thistle in the final at First Ibrox on Saturday, 8 December 1888. They had done the hard part three weeks earlier, by beating Celtic 2-0 in Parkhead, the Bhoys having taken 17 goals off Shettleston and Rangers in their maiden Glasgow Cup matches.

3rd LRV were invited as Scottish champions. In those pre-League days, this was the accolade afforded to the team which currently held the Scottish Cup. Celtic knew all about that, and them, having suffered that agonising 2-1 defeat in their first appearance in the showpiece fixture back in February. 3rd LRV would meet Queen's Park in the other semi-final.

Celtic's opponents for their first appearance in this competition would be Charity Cup-holders Renton, the match between the clubs viewed by many as Scotland's finest attracting an incredible 18,000 spectators to Second Hampden on the afternoon of Saturday, 4 May 1889. Renton were seeking a fourth consecutive success in the tournament, having beaten neighbours Vale of Leven in both the 1886 and 1887 finals, before the rout of Cambuslang 12 months previously.

The Celtic team sent out to end that sequence by reaching a first Glasgow Charity Cup final was as follows:

John Kelly; James McLaughlin & Mick McKeown; Paddy Gallagher, James Kelly & Jimmy McLaren;

Tom Maley, Mick Dunbar, Willie Groves, Johnny Coleman & Peter Dowds.

There was a disastrous start for Celtic, as Harvey put Renton ahead within a minute of the kick-off, then despite a flurry of attacking play by the Bhoys, the same man made it 2-0 from a free-kick. When centre-forward Campbell made it 3-0 before the interval, the writing was on the wall for Celtic, some brief hope emerging as a defensive mix-up allowed Willie Groves to chest the ball between the post on the half-time whistle. That hope was extinguished on the hour, as Harvey completed his hat-trick, with either side then adding a goal apiece before the end, as the match ended Renton 5 Celtic 2. Charity had most certainly not begun at Second Hampden for Celtic.

There would be no time for self-pity as the last cup final would come along just seven days later. The Glasgow North Eastern Cup would be decided at Barrowfield Park, the home of Clyde, on Saturday, 11 May 1889. To reach that stage, Celtic had enjoyed victories over Clydesdale – 5-1 at Southcroft Park, Rutherglen back in December – and Northern, the Springburn club beaten 4-1 at Celtic Park in March.

The opposition at Barrowfield would be provided by Northern's great local rivals, Cowlairs. Those two sides had met in the previous season's final, played at the same ground on Saturday, 5 May 1888, Cowlairs winning by the only goal of the game to lift the trophy for a third successive year. Cowlairs had then faced Hibernian three days later, to christen the first Celtic Park, in that historic 0-0 draw.

The Springburn club had faced two sides from the east end of the city in the defence of their title, overcoming Dalmarnock's Thistle at the third attempt before beating Shettleston7-1 in the semi-final. And, of course, there was history between Celtic and Cowlairs.

Only 10 months had passed since that clash in the final of the Glasgow International Exhibition Cup at Kelvingrove, on Thursday, 6 September 1888, where 'the Irishmen' had been roundly abused by a hostile crowd as Cowlairs won 2-0, provoking the now-famous quote from Celtic President John Glass:

"Let them scoff and jeer. Celtic will yet win to our proper position by our own merits and those who scoff today will one day have to applaud."

The players had then gone some way to backing up that prophecy, by taking eight goals of Cowlairs in the Scottish Cup-tie at Celtic Park just 16 days later. The Bhoys had then won a friendly played at the Gourlay Park home of their opponents by the odd goal four weeks before this latest contest.

Perhaps the strangest thing about the Celtic team announced for the 1889 Glasgow North Eastern Cup final was the goalkeeper situation, where Springburn man James Mclaughlin, would be between the posts, having been in his regular full-back position the previous week against Renton.

The full team read as follows:

James McLaughlin; Pat Dowling & Mick McKeown; Willie Maley, James Kelly & Jimmy McLaren;

Hugh Gallagher, Peter Dowds, Willie Groves, Johnny Coleman & Mick Dunbar.

Cowlairs would feature all three Scotland internationalists associated with the club, as mentioned in previous chapters, William McLeod, Tom McInnes and John 'Kitey' McPherson, plus McPherson's brother James, who would later appear as a guest player for Celtic.

This would be Celtic's day, as the fledgling club secured that first-season silverware at the fourth attempt, the scoring opened following a goalmouth scramble 15 minutes in before Johnny Coleman and Willie Maley gave the Bhoys a 3-0 lead which would prove unassailable. James McPherson did pull a goal back for Cowlairs before the interval, however, the second half would serve only to emphasise Celtic's superiority, Peter Dowds netting a fourth with 20 minutes remaining before a late flurry saw the tally raised to six. The press reports of the time have rather inconveniently omitted three of the Celtic goalscorers, however, the Celtic Wiki credits these strikes to Hugh Gallagher, Willie Groves and a second for Johnny Coleman. Be that as it may, the indisputable fact is that Celts had won a first trophy, in their first season and the majority of the 8,000 crowd would have left Barrowfield for the short journey home in good spirits. They would do so again, many times, over the coming years.

With the competitive action over until the following season's Scottish Cup, there would be three more friendly fixtures to deal with before the players' collective feet could be put up for the summer.

The first of those took place at Beechwood park, Dalmarnock on the following Saturday, 18 May 1889. Host club Thistle would spend most of the afternoon defending, and would do so successfully, frustrating the Celtic forwards until 12 minutes from time, Willie Groves as he so often did, breaking the deadlock. The Bhoys would add another before the finish to run out 2-0 winners on the day.

Five days later, Celts played the first of two glamour challenge matches against English opposition, when they faced Bolton Wanderers at Celtic Park before another healthy crowd, approaching 10,000. The Lancashire side had won 2-0 in the first-ever meeting of the clubs, at their Pike's Lane home the previous month, however, they would find Celtic much too strong on their own patch, goals from Jimmy McLaren, Peter Dowds, Mick Dunbar and a Johnny Coleman double enabling the Bhoys to win comfortably by 5-1, the solitary response from the visitors coming from inside-forward Alex Barbour.

Perhaps appropriately, the final game of Celtic's inaugural season would fall on a date which would become the most significant in the club's history almost eight decades later, 25 May, which fell on a Saturday in 1889. Dan Doyle had played for Bolton Wanderers for a second time against the Celts 48 hours earlier, and he was in the 9,000 crowd to watch the hosts take on Preston North End, England's 'Old Invincibles', so-called as they had just won the inaugural Football League and the most recent FA Cup without losing a game in either, to this day the only English club to achieve that feat. They would find that their Invincible tag did not carry much weight in the east end of Glasgow.

Having played against Celtic - and his old Renton teammates, James Kelly and Neil McCallum – as a guest for Cowlairs in their 8-0 mauling in the Scottish Cup in September, Bob Kelso would again be at right-half in an opposing side at Celtic Park. He had joined the Invincibles earlier that month from Everton, having spent a brief spell at Newcastle West End following his move south from Scotland. He had also faced the Bhoys whilst at St James Park, in a 4-3 defeat for his side back in March.

Kelso would now face a third successive loss against the Parkhead club with three different teams, as the Bhoys came roaring out of the traps to score twice in the opening 10 minutes, Willie Groves with yet another strike before Mick Dunbar headed home a second. Visitors Preston, fielding a side which included nine Scotsmen, signalling the spiralling use of cross-border quasi-professionals in the English game, did manage a reply through the most impressive member of that Anglo-Scot group, Jimmy Ross. The 'Little Demon', as he was affectionately known at Deepdale, had moved south from Edinburgh's St Bernard's as a teenager in 1883 to join his elder brother Nick at North End, soon establishing himself as the quintessential goalscorer with some incredible feats, including seven goals in Preston's record 26-0 FA Cup victory over Hyde seven months earlier, a scoreline which remains the benchmark in that competition to this day. He would manage only one at Celtic Park, and even that owed more to the makeshift home goalkeeper, James McLaughlin, as his side returned to Lancashire no longer Invincible.

With the football over, it was time for those with Celtic's interest at heart to take stock of progress at the end of the club's first-ever season.

By any standards, it had been impressive.

Scottish Cup finalists at the first time of asking, and in the eyes of many observers, extremely unlucky to lose to the 3rd LRV in that replayed final in February.

Semi-finalists in both Glasgow and Glasgow Merchant's Charity Cup competitions, losing out in both instances to the established powerhouses of the day, Queen's Park and Renton respectively.

And reaching the final of the other two competitions entered, the Glasgow International Exhibition Cup, just three months after formation, and the Glasgow North Eastern Cup, on both occasions facing Cowlairs for the trophy, with one victory apiece for each club.

And then, just to cap it all off, they had managed to do what no English side could achieve, beaten the 'Invincibles' of Preston North End, sending them homewards to think again, as someone once sang.

And on the 25th May no less.

If I didn't know better, I would suspect there might be a fairytale element attached to this club.

Season 1888/89 – Celtic's Roll of Honour

Scottish Cup

1st round	Saturday, 1 September 1888	Celtic 5 Shettleston 1	First Celtic Park
2nd round	Saturday, 22 September 1888	Celtic 8 Cowlairs 0	First Celtic Park
3rd round	Saturday, 13 October 1888	Celtic 4 Albion Rovers 1	First Celtic Park
4th round	Saturday, 3 November 1888	St Bernard's 1 Celtic 4	Powderhall
5th round	Saturday, 8 December 1888	Celtic 9 Clyde 2	First Celtic Park
6th round	Saturday, 15 December 1888	East Stirlingshire 1 Celtic 2	Merchiston Park
Semi-final	Saturday, 12 January 1889	Dumbarton 1 Celtic 4	Boghead Park
Final	Saturday, 9 February 1889	3rd LRV 2 Celtic 1	Second Hampden

Glasgow Cup

2nd round	Saturday, 6 October 1888	Celtic 11 Shettleston 2	First Celtic Park
3rd round	Saturday, 27 October 1888	Rangers 1 Celtic 6	First Ibrox Park
Semi-final	Saturday, 17 November 1888	Celtic 0 Queen's Park 2	First Celtic Park

Glasgow Merchant's Charity Cup

Semi-final	Saturday, 4 May 1889	Renton 5 Celtic 2	Second Hampden

Glasgow North Eastern Cup

1st round	Saturday, 29 December 1888	Clydesdale 1 Celtic 5	Southcroft Park
Semi-final	Saturday, 16 March 1889	Celtic 4 Northern 1	First Celtic Park
Final	Saturday, 11 May 1889	Celtic 6 Clyde 1	Barrowfield Park

Section 3:

CELTIC'S EARLY STARS

By David Potter

The key thing about a football club is, of course, its players.

Administrators and hard-working Committee men are all necessary, as well, but people come to see football players performing on the field.

Two things are salient about Celtic's early players.

One is that there was a determination to choose flair players. McMahon, Campbell and McMenemy, for example, men who could score goals and who could bring the success to the club that the support so desperately craved.

The other was that - particularly when Willie Maley began to have more influence after 1897 - the religious background of the player did not matter in the slightest. Where would Celtic have been, for example, without 'Sunny Jim' Young, James Hay and Alec McNair? Maley would frequently quote Brother Walfrid's visionary dictum, "It is not a man's creed nor his nationality that counts - it is the man himself." And the breadth of the selection policy allowed so many people of all denominations to join with and to enjoy the success of 'the Celtic.'

What did matter, however, was a man's commitment to the green-and-white jersey and the special meaning that the word 'Celtic' brought to the world. Celtic means a combination of Scotland and Ireland. Bigots and fools cannot cope with that, but the early players that I have chosen all played their special and unique part in the birth and development of this great institution, which so many people all over the word still love so much.

Chapter 1:

DAN DOYLE: CELTIC'S WILD ROVER

Tall, handsome, curly-haired, Dan Doyle was an immediate hit with the Celtic fans. It is often said that crowds, particularly Celtic crowds, love a small player like Patsy Gallacher or Jimmy Johnstone, with whom they can identify as being the underdog, just like they perceived (and possibly still do in some cases) themselves to be against the wicked, powerful bully, referee or landlord. But they also love to identify with someone who has clearly 'made it', who has got a lot going for him. Dan could look like that.

Dan was born in Paisley on 16 September 1864 and played for many teams, some of them with quaint names like Slamannan Barnsmuir and Broxburn Shamrock (as well as a more familiar one called East Stirlingshire) before he joined Hibs for a spell. In fact, he played for Hibernian in the first game to be played at Old Celtic Park on 8 May 1888 against Cowlairs. He tried his luck in England (where professionalism was legalised) with Newcastle East End, Grimsby Town and Bolton Wanderers, before this happy mercenary arrived at Goodison Park to play for Everton in August 1889.

While he was with Grimsby, he was involved in a tragic incident which plagued him the rest of his life. It was a total accident, but it did give some indication of the strength that he had. It was 12 January 1889, when Grimsby were playing against Staveley, who featured a player called William Cropper, better known as a cricketer with Derbyshire. He and Doyle went for a ball together and Cropper was unfortunate enough to receive the full impact of Doyle's knee in his stomach and never recovered.

It was with Everton that Doyle made his name, attracting a great deal of attention in both the English and the Scottish press when Everton won the English League championship in 1891. But happy though he was at Goodison, he hankered after a return to Scotland, particularly when feelers were put out to him by this new Glasgow Irish club. But the problem was that Celtic were, theoretically at least, an amateur team and could not be seen to pay him. Doyle would make out that he was homesick and wanted to return to Scotland, but there seems little doubt that the perspicacious John Glass and other Celtic founding fathers were prepared to break laws in order to attract Dan Doyle.

When Doyle went to Glasgow, Everton were furious, threatening legal action for breach of contract, offering him £5 and a job running a public house in Liverpool. But Celtic had already trumped that one, for they had installed him in his own public house. This was always a successful way of attracting a footballer in Victorian Britain, for there was a great deal of money (as always) to be made in drink, particularly when patrons were very happy to spend money just to see Dan, or 'Ned' as he quickly became known, behind the bar in his hostelry in Airdrie.

On the field, Doyle was an instant success. Season 1891/92 saw Celtic win three Cups – the Scottish Cup, the Glasgow Cup and the Glasgow Charity Cup – and had it not been for a reverse on the opening day of the season to Hearts and a crucial 0-1 defeat to the eventual champions Dumbarton towards the end of April, then the League would have been won as well. Doyle settled into this team instantly, turning out to be all that a left-back could be expected to be. He was a strong tackler, could clear the ball accurately and he was also a fine taker of free-kicks.

Spring 1892 was a heady time for Celtic and for Doyle. On 6 February 1892, Celtic beat Rangers 5-2 to reach the Scottish Cup final for the second time in four years of history. Their opponents were Queen's Park on 12 March, but the game had to be abandoned and played out as a friendly because of the huge Celtic crowd turning up at Ibrox and catching the authorities by surprise. But Celtic's joy would only be delayed.

But before the Scottish Cup final could be played again, on 9 April, Doyle was selected to play for Scotland against England at Ibrox on 2

April. It was Doyle's first full cap, but it was a sad occasion. Far happier was the following week, as Celtic lifted the Scottish Cup for the first time in their history. The enthusiasm of the Celtic fans surprised the watching journalists, but it was nothing to the ecstasy which prevailed in the underprivileged East End for days afterwards as Doyle and company brought home the Scottish Cup. And it hadn't finished there, for Celtic then went on to win the Glasgow Charity Cup as well. Thus, Doyle's first season ended with three medals to be shown off to patrons of his public house, and there could not have been the slightest doubt that he had made the right decision in coming north.

Dan was a well-known personality in Victorian Glasgow. Being the hero of the ethnic minority was one aspect of him, but he was also well respected by others who were not of the same persuasion. The 1890s was the first decade of the almost total domination of football over any other aspect of life, and players were recognised and pointed out in the street. His full-back partner Jerry Reynolds was similarly famous, and the phrase 'Reynolds and Doyle' became as much a catchphrase as 'Gilbert and Sullivan', the writers of Victorian opera.

Naturally Doyle, being such a clean-cut, handsome man, was good copy for newspapers and was much admired by women. Media coverage was nothing like what it would become 100 years later, but it was substantial nevertheless, and gossip was not slow to attach stories, apocryphal or otherwise, to the name of Dan Doyle. The frequent trips made by Celtic to England merely added to his reputation. Like many a Scotsman in England, his behaviour off the field was not always a credit to Scotland, but this did little to take away his 'tourist attraction'.

The reputation of the Celtic team continued to grow apace with his own. In 1893, Celtic won the Scottish League championship for the first time. Their successes included impressive victories over Dumbarton, Hearts, Third Lanark (3rd LRV) and Rangers, and the press talked grandiloquently about "Dandy Dan" or "Dynamite Doyle". He won his second Scottish cap that year in an 8-0 win over Wales at Wrexham and was disappointed not to be given a game against England at Richmond.

There was one other major disappointment in 1893 for Doyle and Celtic, and that was the failure to retain the Scottish Cup. Queen's Park gained a little revenge for the previous year's defeat in the final, but Celtic were sore about what happened. The wind was dreadful, and Queen's Park indulged in questionable tactics which caused many injuries to Celtic players, not least to Willie Maley, who lost a few teeth in the game. To crown it all, Dan Doyle conceded what looked to all the spectators like a corner, but the Queen's Park players were convinced that the ball had passed on the other side of the post (there were no goal nets in 1893). One of them said to the referee: "It's a goal, Mr. Harrison," and the goal was given! Then Willie Maley, however, in his series of articles that he wrote for the Weekly News in 1936, singled out the "immense courage" of Doyle in what was "a forlorn hope" as "(Doyle) inspired the rest of us to put up a glorious fight right to the end."

But Dan had one major success that season, and that was in the Charity Cup final against Rangers when Celtic beat them 5-0. Doyle played right-back that day, but it mattered little for he could play equally well on either side, and it was he who orchestrated the massive victory with his runs down the wing and long, accurate crosses which "perpetually brought applause and approbation" from the crowd. The game itself was remarkable for the 5-0 score line at half-time, followed by a second half in which Celtic toyed with their opponents without adding to the score. Indeed, it was the opinion of many that the referee shortened the second half, for Celtic had no real desire to score any more goals, and the supporters were beginning to sing, a clear sign that boredom was setting in.

Oh, my darling, oh my darling, oh my darling Danny Doyle
How I love my football champion, oh my darling Danny Doyle!

The honours were similarly distributed in the 1893/94 season, with Celtic once again proving their consistency by winning the League and the Glasgow Charity Cup but falling a little short in the Glasgow Cup and the most prestigious trophy of all, the Scottish Cup. The League was won very comfortably in spite of a 0-5 defeat from Rangers in September on Doyle's first day back from injury. After that reverse, Celtic, inspired by Doyle, did not lose again until after the League had been comfortably won.

On April 7 1894, Doyle was invited to captain Scotland against England. It was strange that he was asked to skipper the international side, for he had only captained Celtic on the rare occasion when James Kelly was not playing, but perhaps the fact that the game was being played at the new, smartly-completed Celtic Park had a great deal to do with it. Scotland played very well. Their forwards missed a few chances, but even so they were well pleased with themselves to be leading 2-1 as the game entered its final stages. But a goal was scored in the final minute and the 45,000 were stunned into silence. Doyle and the rest of his team were shattered. It cannot have been easy for Dan to call for the traditional three cheers for England that night.

Strange goings-on occurred, however, the following year when Scotland went to England to play at Goodison Park. Doyle travelled down to Liverpool on the Friday with the rest of the party, but suddenly disappeared. He had, of course, played for Everton four years previously and so it was assumed that he was visiting an old acquaintance. The 'old acquaintance' may or may not have been a member of the opposite sex, but certainly Doyle failed to reappear at the team's hotel on the Friday night.

Then suddenly Doyle reappeared, apparently none the worse for his disappearance, which he was remarkably shy about discussing. The instant reaction of the selectors was to keep him out of the team because of his irresponsible behaviour, but then they realised that he was such a big name, and such a great player, that the cause of Scotland would be much diminished without Dan. He was given the nod.

Clearly it was the wrong decision. Doyle had a shocker of a game, playing very badly (and such a good player having an 'off-day' did matter) as Scotland went down 0-3. He and Neil Gibson were involved in a dreadful mix-up. which led to an own goal, and the Scotland forwards, missing Doyle's long passing, never really got themselves into the game.

In addition, Celtic lost the Scottish League to Hearts that year, and departed anonymously from the Scottish Cup in the early rounds. They did win the two Glasgow tournaments, but that was scant consolation for the large and unhappy support. Yet Dan, for all his faults, remained a personality figure, attracting crowds wherever he went.

Like many Victorian footballers, Doyle also played other sports – bowls, quoits, cricket, athletics and billiards. He was a superb athlete with broad shoulders, flat chest and long legs, very fast, supple and lithe, and he had the common sense to realise that although he could occasionally indulge in some of the earthly pleasures, the necessity to keep fit was paramount. Professionalism meant that he simply had to keep fit, for all the opponents that he faced were at least as fit as he was. They may have lacked some of the ability that Doyle possessed, but they were all as athletic.

The 1895/96 season was a better one for Celtic, who won three out of a possible four trophies. Doyle had been injured in the early part of the season but was fully fit by the end of September (significantly, the three games that Celtic lost were all when Doyle was out) and he took part in the record 11-0 thrashing of Dundee in October, a 7-0 beating of Third Lanark in November and a 6-2 win over Rangers in December, by which time the League championship was virtually won.

Queen's Park had also been put to the sword 6-3 in the Glasgow Cup final, and would also bow the knee in the Charity Cup final at the end of the season, but the one discordant note of an otherwise fine campaign was when Queen's Park removed Celtic from the Scottish Cup at the first time of asking. Doyle did score that day on a difficult pitch at Parkhead in wintry conditions, but Celtic went down 4-2 to the amateurs.

It was the following season which saw the biggest mystery of Dan Doyle. It was 9 January 1897, the date of Celtic's infamous defeat at Arthurlie in the Scottish Cup – the biggest act of giant-killing in Scottish football history until the demise of Rangers at Berwick in 1967 – and one of the reasons was that Dan Doyle did not turn up. Why he didn't, no-one can say. Reports at the time mentioned a great deal of "stuff going on" before the turn of the year, with a players' strike – three men withdrew their labour because of heavy press criticism – and a bad run of form in December. One game in particular, against Rangers, seemed to indicate that certain players were simply not trying, but whether this was connected with Doyle's non-appearance is not clear.

It may be that Dan, sensing the vulnerability of the team and also aware that his own playing career was approaching its twilight, now that he was well into his thirties, chose this moment to turn petulant with a request for more money. If this was so, it reflects very badly on him, but there may have been other reasons. Perhaps Doyle was ill, he may have 'hit the bottle', perhaps he became lucky with a young lady; but for whatever reason, Doyle simply did not appear. Annoyingly, Willie Maley, who certainly would have known the reason, remained very reticent about Doyle's non-appearance.

That absence was crucial, and the team went down to a defeat which would haunt them for many decades. Even more surprising about this whole affair was his almost immediate restitution to favour. He was fined £5, but then played for Celtic for the rest of the season. And 1897 did see his return to international duty, and this time Dan was on the winning side. This was a famous occasion at the Crystal Palace, when Scotland beat England 2-1, their first win on English soil for eight years. "Lambie (of Queen's Park) captained the side, but Doyle bossed it," was the comment in one newspaper.

The Arthurlie disaster of 1897 was the catalyst for a seismic change in the structure of management at Celtic Park. The old committee system of picking a team was abolished and Willie Maley effectively became manager. Willie was, of course, an old teammate of Dan, holding him in great respect and friendship, but he was not blind to the left-back's faults. One presumes that there was a clear-the-air meeting between the two of them, because for a spell Doyle's form and attitude showed a marked improvement, and Dan was even made captain.

In 1897/98, Celtic regained the Scottish League crown, this time without losing a game! At international level that season, Doyle played twice. Once was against Ireland, in a 3-0 canter in Belfast, but then Dan suffered the personal disaster which brought his career to a close. Some 70,000 were at Celtic Park to see the Scotland v. England game, the ground having had to undergo several changes to accommodate the huge crowd. Scotland had gone two goals down, but pulled one back and looked as if they might go on to equalise, until Doyle made a gross mistake with a pass, which was directed into the path of the great Steve Bloomer, who put England 3-1 up.

Crowds can be fickle, and heroes can be fragile and prickly. Doyle never played again for Scotland and, indeed, played only sporadically for Celtic in the next season, 1898/99, before disappearing from the game altogether. In truth, Celtic had unearthed another fine full-back in Davie Storrier from Arbroath, and with John Welford and Barney Battles around, Celtic were not short of flank defenders. Noticeably, in the Scottish Cup triumph of 1899, Doyle does not feature.

Dan's later years, like those of many footballers, were far from happy. He now owned two drinking shops in Bellshill, but they both came to grief – "he was his own best customer", the cruel ones said – and he had to take a labouring job. Even that didn't last long. Towards the end of the First World War, Dan, having suffered serious ill-health for some time, contracted cancer and died on 8 April 1918 at the age of 53.

Chapter 2:

JAMES KELLY: "NO KELLY, NO KELTIC!"

No-one will ever know who it was who first said, "No Kelly, No Keltic." It has been attributed to John Glass, John H McLaughlin and several others, but the undeniable thing about it is that it is true. There might have been a Celtic club even if they had not persuaded James Kelly to play for them in their first-ever game on May 28 1888, and then to join them on a more permanent basis, but it is doubtful if Celtic would have reached the great heights that they did within a matter of years of their foundation. Kelly was the man, on the playing side, around whom it all revolved. Centre-halves were often called the pivot of the team. In a very real sense, this was true in other senses as well.

James Kelly was born in Renton in Dunbartonshire in 1865. He was of Irish stock, but of a different sort from the Irish who lived in the East End of Glasgow. He was wealthier, more middle-class, still very aware of his Irishness and very conscious of the fact that the Irish had a part to play in the developing Scottish nation as well. Not for Kelly was any feeling of self-pitying ghetto-mentality or mindless aggression. The Irish were now part of Scotland, and if there was any trouble in getting themselves accepted, then they simply had to work all the harder for it.

It was possibly for reasons like this that Kelly loved the idea of Celtic Football Club, whose very name gave a clue to the two-nation philosophy for Celtic (and there were still an awful lot of people who talked about the "Keltic", not least Michael Davitt as he planted the shamrocks that famous day in March 1892), for the word does hint at the fusion of two nations, in total contrast to the Hibernians of Edinburgh, for example whose name means 'the men of Ireland.'

There were, of course, other reasons why Kelly came to Celtic, than some vague philosophical notion about the unification of two cultures. The main one was economic. Football had grown enormously over the past 20 years, and, although Renton had won the Scottish Cup in 1885 and again in 1888, with Kelly well to the fore, it did not take a great deal of thought to work out that the days of the village clubs like Renton, Vale of Leven and Dumbarton, playing with the benign amateurs of Queen's Park, would soon yield to the clubs of the big city, particularly this new Celtic club, which could tap in to an enormous support from the ever-expanding city of Glasgow.

It was the way ahead, and, in addition, the new Celtic club could offer something else. Scottish football was, and would remain until 1893, amateur, but no-one was unaware that subtle inducements could be made, particularly in the shape of 'loans' which would help a player buy a public house, or at least give him a start as the licensee. Well-run public houses in the 1880s and 1890s were more or less blueprints for making money, and Celtic's hard-headed and shrewd founding fathers were totally aware of this. Inducements of such a kind would attract men like Kelly to the new club.

An ambitious player like Kelly might also have tried England. Professionalism had been legal there since the 1885/86 season, and the ambitious clubs all tended to be either in the Midlands, Lancashire or, increasingly in recent years, on Tyneside. They were, therefore, not all that far away from Scotland, and given the rapid travel now possible on the apparently ever-expanding railway system, communication was easy. In addition, the newspaper industry was also a potent factor in spreading the gospel of English football. Since the Education Act of 1872, most people in Scotland had at least a basis of literacy, and everyone knew all about Blackburn Rovers, West Bromwich Albion, Aston Villa, Sunderland and the other giants of English football.

On the other hand, Kelly was a home-loving boy, very happy to continue to live in Dunbartonshire, where he was hoping to expand his building business. He was aware that his football career had come along by leaps and bounds since he started playing for Renton, and he loved being with them, but the cry of the new club was a strong one, and after agreeing to play on a one-off basis in their first game, on May 28 1888, he stayed.

So, it was Celtic for Kelly. He soon became very impressed by the set-up and ambition of the club. He made friends with some of the other players, notable the Maley brothers, Tom and Willie, and the new club seemed the natural place for him to be. There was another, slightly more intimate, connection there as well, in that he was beginning to date a girl called Bridget McErlean, whose father Francis McErlean was already on the committee of the new club and had been very busy getting the club off the ground. In the early days of one's courtship, at least, it is always a good idea to keep on the friendliest of terms with one's potential father in law! They were married in 1891.

So that was why Kelly was attracted to Celtic. But why were Celtic attracted to him? He was quite simply a great centre half. He was already a Scotland Internationalist (admittedly in an awful 0-5 Scotland defeat to England in March 1888), and his Renton team had not only won the Scottish Cup but could also claim to be the Champions of the World, for they had defeated West Bromwich Albion, the English Cup-winners and Preston North End as well. This probably did make them the World Champions, and Kelly was their captain! He was, thus, already a Scottish personality player by the time that he arrived at Celtic. He looked like an ordinary man, and his landlady, when he came to live in Glasgow, insisted that he ate the same food as her other boarders, but he was one of the best known men in the country, and now he was playing for Celtic, the club with so many supporters!

Not only was Kelly playing for Celtic, he was actually their captain. Centre-half is always a good position for a captain – and one immediately thinks of men like Billy McNeill and Jock Stein – but Kelly in any case was a natural leader. People listened when he said something, but he could also play. He was not particularly tall for a centre-half, but this was not an age in which centre-halves needed to be tall. More emphasis was placed on build and agility. It was an age in which centre-forwards needed to know how to 'charge' the goalkeeper. The centre-half, therefore, had to be able to 'charge' as well, in order to protect his goalkeeper. In addition, centre-halves and centre-forwards changed rapidly – Quinn and Loney in the early 1900s could do this job to perfection - and this is the reason that we find Kelly's name on the scoresheet quite a lot in the early years. He soon found himself to be very popular at Celtic Park.

And what could Renton do about that? Well, not very much, for he was an 'amateur', as indeed was Neil McCallum, who had also made the same journey and who scored Celtic's first-ever goal in that game against Rangers on May 28 1888. Renton did, however, make a somewhat inflammatory statement, in that they might be less keen in future to use players of the Roman Catholic persuasion on the grounds that they might be attracted to Celtic or Hibernian!

In point of fact, Kelly had flirted with Hibernian as well as Renton but possibly had realised that Hibs were very badly run, hamstrung by their own sectarianism, and that in any case, the future crucible of Scottish football was more likely to be Glasgow rather than Edinburgh. Hibs, by winning the Scottish Cup of 1887, may have put an idea or two into the head of men like John Glass and Brother Walfrid, but from now on the focus of the Irish in Scotland would be Celtic rather than Hibernian.

The new club got off to a flying start. 1889 saw them reach the final of the Scottish Cup in the very first year of their existence. They were unlucky to lose the final to Third Lanark, the first attempt having to be played as a friendly because of a heavy fall of snow, and the replay lost the following week to a Third Lanark side who had just that wee bit more experience than Celtic at this stage. All this time, Kelly kept working for the club. He was a 'no nonsense' centre-half. He was not without footballing skills and trickery, but never disdained the powerful 'boot up the field' if necessary. He was never a dirty player, but he did not shirk tackles either and this meant, of course, the occasional picking up of injuries.

1890 saw major plans being drawn up by the ambitious founding fathers, but no major trophies for the club, something that the supporters craved. Season 1890/91 was the first of the Scottish League, and the new Celtic team were very much in the forefront of that idea, but the calendar year of 1891 brought home the Glasgow Cup not once but twice! They won the 1890/91 Glasgow Cup in February, by beating

Third Lanark, and then the 1891/92 Glasgow Cup in December, in the snow, by beating Clyde.

The Glasgow Cup was, of course, a major honour in the 1890s - and would continue to be so until the Second World War and even beyond - and these trophies were much celebrated by the Celtic support. Kelly, as captain, was to a large extent responsible for such success, although sadly, the idea of the Cup being presented to the captain at the end of the game in public is very much a modern one. The Cup was usually presented at the post-match dinner, often in the Alexandra Hotel in Bath Street, to the Chairman. The players would be there, however, and Kelly very much revelled in such occasions.

The Glasgow Cup triumphs of 1891 were good, but 1892 brought Celtic's first success in the most important trophy of them all, the Scottish Cup, sometimes called "the Blue Riband", the trophy which had been in existence since season 1873/74. Kelly, of course, had won it in 1888 with Renton, and 1892 brought his second Scottish Cup winner's medal. The opponents were Queen's Park, the final having to be played twice because of crowd encroachment the first time, but on April 9 1892, Celtic won the Scottish Cup to the great acclaim of their massive, impoverished but now optimistic support. Willie Maley talked about his joy at seeing the "urchins" of the East End with something to cheer about. James Kelly would have shared that happiness, and he was the man who led them on the field!

His career with Scotland continued, and in 1893 at Richmond, he had the honour of being presented, in his capacity as captain of Scotland, to Princess Mary of Teck. This lady was soon to be married to George, the Duke of York (she had previously been engaged to his elder brother Edward, who died in a flu pandemic) and she would in time become Queen Mary. Being introduced to royalty, even a fairly minor personage, as the Princess then was, was a great thing in Victorian society, and Willie Maley who tells us the story, is clearly not a little jealous of his captain! The story, however, did not end happily, for Scotland lost rather heavily.

But success continued for Celtic. There were a couple of Scottish Cup final defeats in 1893 and 1894 – the 1893 occasion was a particularly unlucky and unfortunate occasion – but there was ample compensation in the winning of the Scottish League in both of these years. The Scottish Cup was, and remains, more spectacular, but it is the winning of the League, where every team plays every other team home and away, which indicates the best and most consistent team in the country. Kelly was aware of this, and never failed to remind his men of this fact.

Season 1894/95 was a comparative disappointment, but it was all made up for in December 1895, when Celtic, by beating Rangers 6-2, actually won the 1895/96 League Championship. (The League tended to be finished by the New Year in those days). Kelly had, thus, led Celtic to three Scottish League titles in four years, a remarkable achievement.

He was ageing by the 1896/97 season, and perhaps ought to have retired before the horrors of the 1896/97 winter. But the 'strike' in November and the defeat by Arthurlie in January convinced Kelly that the club really needed to be run on a far more professional basis than it was. So, he was very happy to give up playing around about the time of the formation of the Limited Company, and to became one of the club's first Directors. He was Chairman for a while, from 1909-1914, but remained a Director until his death in Blantyre in 1932.

He was, of course, the start of the Kelly dynasty. History has been less kind (and with cause) to his son and grandsons, who ran the club in the 1960s and 1990s, but there is no need for anyone to denigrate the name of James Kelly.

He was, both as a player and administrator, a Celtic icon.

Chapter 3:

SANDY MCMAHON: THE ONE AND ONLY 'DUKE'

Celtic have always been famous for their goal-scoring heroes. Three super-heroes immediately spring to mind, in Jimmy Quinn, Jimmy McGrory and Henrik Larsson. There are others, like Jimmy 'Sniper' McColl, Joe Cassidy, the McPhail brothers, Dixie Deans and (possibly) Odsonne Edouard but the man who started it all was Sandy McMahon.

Born in the Borders in 1871, Sandy played his early football in the late 1880s in Edinburgh, for teams like Harp Juveniles, Woodburn, Leith Harp and the great Hibernian football club themselves. Sandy had been with Hibernian, then moved for a brief and unhappy time to a team called Darlington St. Augustine's, before returning to Edinburgh in September 1888. He played for Hibernian for two years but then, in December 1890 he joined Celtic. Hibs were at that time imploding, as a result of the rise of this new Irish team in Glasgow, and they also had major difficulties with their ground. Legally, there was no problem about McMahon jumping ship like this without any indication of a transfer fee because Scottish football, until 1893, was, at least in theory, amateur.

Sandy's competitive debut for Celtic was against Vale of Leven in Alexandria, near Dumbarton, on 24 January 1891. Sandy may or may not have been a professional, in theory or in practice, but the general amateurishness of Celtic's approach in the early days is evidenced by the fact that a player missed his train and Celtic had no reserves available. So, Sandy actually had to play left-back until the man arrived! The team lost 1-3, thereby losing what little chance they had of landing the League championship in 1891.

McMahon did not play in the club's big success that season, namely the winning of the prestigious Glasgow Cup, but he did play sporadically at first and later regularly for the team, hitting the highlights on 5 May with four goals in a spectacular 9-1 drubbing of Vale of Leven at Old Celtic Park. He was now settled at inside-left and could interchange brilliantly with Johnny Campbell on the left-wing. The passing game was, of course, the trademark of Scottish football, and he had an almost telepathic understanding with John Campbell. But he was also noted for his individual play, and the coming season of 1891/92 was to indicate the arrival of Celtic's first superstar.

Celtic won the Glasgow Cup in December 1891, and Sandy won a medal, scoring a goal in a 7-1 thrashing of Clyde at Cathkin, and, by the turn of the year, the team was going well in both the Scottish League and the Scottish Cup, with the crowd beginning to appreciate the inspired play of McMahon. In the Scottish Cup, Cowlairs fell in the quarter-final and Rangers in the semi, with McMahon's name on the scoresheet on both occasions. The Scottish Cup final was played at Ibrox on 12 March against Queen's Park, but although Celtic won 1-0, the game was declared a friendly, such were the chaotic conditions with the huge crowd. The cause? Principally, the widespread enthusiasm to see the now-famous left-wing combination of McMahon and Campbell.

Not only were the Celtic fans impressed by Sandy, so too were the Scotland selectors, and he found himself in his country's team on 2 April at Ibrox. It was a sad day, however, for both Scotland and McMahon, as they were engulfed 1-4 by a strong England team. Sandy never got going, but as he left Ibrox that night, he knew he would be back a week later for what he hoped would be a happier occasion. This would be the replay of the Scottish Cup final.

In this game, McMahon certainly scored two goals and possibly three (depending on how one reads certain newspaper reports) and the rejoicing in the East End of Glasgow that night was legendary. The Celtic had arrived. "Our Bhoys have won the Cup!" cried the urchins, the destitute and the ill-fed, as everyone swirled round the charabanc to the music of the bugles and the flutes, (Yes, flutes!) hoping to catch a glimpse of their heroes. Queen's Park, the team of the avowed amateurs, the middle-class, the rich, the privileged, had been beaten in a Scottish Cup final. The talk of Scotland was now of men like James Kelly, "Dan" (Doyle, but now simply referred to as "Dan") and, of course, "Sandy" or "The Duke," after the French President Duc de Mac-Mahon, although some say that Sandy was being compared to The Iron Duke, the Duke of Wellington.

But that same summer brought disturbing news of McMahon. He and Neil McCallum had, apparently, joined Nottingham Forest. Professionalism was, of course, legal in England, and McMahon was clearly neither the first nor the last to be "bought and sold for English gold." There then occurs one of the most famous stories in Celtic mythology, namely that a group of committee men, spearheaded by the energetic John Glass, hastened to the Midlands and persuaded Sandy to return home. Words like "kidnap" and "coup" have been used, and we are expected to believe that the still-amateur Celtic persuaded him back for no reason other than the love of the club.

Clearly, we will never establish the entire truth of this matter, but some suggestion that Celtic (illegally) offered more money than Nottingham Forest did to the homesick Sandy, and that he accepted, would not appear to be entirely wrong. Yet it is an indication of the reputation and prestige of the man that we hear stories of tables being knocked down as the raiding party rushed to the station, of someone detaining the Forest delegates while Sandy escaped, and a great reception organised by Willie Maley back in Glasgow.

Maley, who both played with and managed Sandy, said that "of speed he had little," but such were his other attributes that this was hardly noticed. There were, possibly, three aspects to McMahon's greatness. One was his goal-scoring ability with both feet and head, one was his dribbling (not for nothing was he called "The Prince of Dribblers") and the third was his telepathic understanding with left-wing partner Johnny Campbell.

Johnny was indeed lured away to England, to Aston Villa, for a couple of years (no adequate rescue operation having been arranged for him) and, in his absence, Sandy struggled for the want of an adequate partner, with 1897 proving a particularly low ebb in the club's short history. Campbell and McMahon, however, remained good friends to the extent that when McMahon married Annie Devine in May 1896, Campbell returned from England to do the honours as best man. But before the departure of Campbell, the club had won the Scottish League in 1892/93 and 1893/94, also losing the Scottish Cup final in both those years. Sandy scored 11 goals in 13 League games in 1892/93 and 10 in 15 in 1893/94. Twice he scored hat-tricks against Third Lanark and St Bernard's, and the fans of the green-and-white vertical stripes (which Celtic wore until 1903) talked about little other than Sandy McMahon.

Football was a rough game in those days and Sandy, like many forwards, was prone to receive more than a little hacking from none-too-gentle opponents. He was out for a long time on several occasions, notably in the bad season of 1896/97, when Celtic finished trophyless for the first time in that decade. He was injured on 21 November 1896, as Celtic went down to Rangers in the final of the Glasgow Cup, and never reappeared that term. His supporters must have wondered whether he was finished. They might well have asked the same question about Celtic themselves. Of course, 9 January 1897 was the day that Celtic shocked Victorian Scotland by going down to Arthurlie in the Scottish Cup. It would have been hard to imagine that happening if Sandy had been on board.

McMahon's value to the Celtic cause was underlined in the 1897/98 season. The team swept all before them in the Scottish League. They were undefeated, they drew on three occasions and won against everyone else. This included a spectacular defeat of Rangers at Ibrox on the Monday September holiday, competent victories against other challengers like Heart of Midlothian and Hibernian, and there was a particular relish for Clyde, who were put to the sword 6-1 and 9-1. In all of this, McMahon, playing at inside-left, was a goal-maker rather than a goal-scorer, supplying the ammunition for George Allan, a Celtic centre-forward whom history has curiously undervalued. Johnny Campbell, too, had returned, and was now playing at inside-right, to complete a prodigious inside trio.

But things came to a shuddering halt for Celtic in the Scottish Cup, when they went down to Third Lanark in late January 1898, the significant factor being the absence through injury of McMahon, and the consequent necessity to rejig the forward line. Even at this early stage of the club's history, the Scottish Cup was considered a vital tournament. Celtic had exited two years in a row in January. On both occasions, Sandy McMahon was not playing.

All this was made good in the Scottish Cup of 1899, when Celtic beat Rangers 2-0 to lift the trophy for the second time. League form had not been good. Rangers now had a great side and went through the 1898/99 League season with a 100% record, and on both occasions that they beat Celtic, they put four goals past them. They had also defeated Celtic in the Glasgow Cup final in October, so the green-and-whites had little reason to approach the Scottish Cup final on 22 April with any degree of sanguinity.

Half-time came with no score, then in the early part of the second period, the game swung decisively in favour of Celtic. Rangers had a goal chalked off, allowed themselves to be flustered about it, and Celtic took the initiative. They forced a corner, then for once McMahon eluded the eager attention of the two Rangers defenders detailed to mark him and rose "like a bird" to meet the dispatch and head home brilliantly. Celtic now took charge, with McMahon on song, winning balls, dribbling and "passing to a degree of excellence". It was no surprise when Hodge added a second, although Rangers claimed offside.

The game finished with Celtic 2-0 ahead, and Rangers were sporting enough to admit that, on this occasion, their Glasgow rivals were worthy winners. Thus, Celtic had won the Scottish Cup for the second time, and McMahon had earned himself another niche in the club's history for having scored a glorious header.

Another Scottish Cup would come Celtic and McMahon's way a season later. The year was 1900, and the new century was bringing in a new order to Scottish football. McMahon, however, defeated both Queen's Park and Rangers. The semi-final at Ibrox was drawn but then in the re-match, Celtic chose to turn on the style. They defeated Rangers 4-0, with McMahon "ubiquitous, ambitious and dominant," scoring two goals from the inside-left position. The Scottish Cup final against Queen's Park at Ibrox was a game played in a gale blowing in from the west. McMahon scored twice in the first half as Celtic went in at half-time 3-1 up, but that was with the benefit of the wind.

Realising the necessity of keeping the ball on the ground as much as possible against the wind, McMahon was instrumental in Celtic scoring early in the second half, releasing Divers to find the net. From then on, however, it was backs to the wall, with McMahon having to play his part in defence, as Queen's pressed and pressed. They did score twice, but too late in the game to have any effect, and when Mr Walker of Kilmarnock blew for up for time, the green-and-white vertical stripes had captured their third Scottish Cup, and Sandy McMahon and Johnny Campbell had participated in all three triumphs.

But the Celtic team were now ageing, McMahon as much as any of them. In addition, the Rangers teams of 1900/01 and 1901/02 were as good as had ever previously come from Ibrox, and Celtic also had the misfortune to lose two successive Scottish Cup finals to Hearts in 1901 and Hibernian in 1902. McMahon had also been the victim of injustice on New Year's Day 1902, when he was sent off by a referee suspected of being under the influence of drink.

It was now becoming clear to the energetic manager, Willie Maley, that changes were required. This involved the gathering of young talent, from which would emerge the mighty and virtually unchallengeable forward line of Bennett, McMenemy, Quinn, Somers and Hamilton. This meant that the old guard had to be gradually and gently pushed out the door. Sandy, in any case, missed a large part of the 1902/03 season through injury, and his last big game for Celtic was the dreadful Scottish Cup quarter-final against Rangers at Parkhead, when the team went down 0-3.

He finished his playing days with Partick Thistle, with whom he lasted barely a year. Then he did what so many other ex-footballers did in those days, he bought a pub. It was located at 209 Great Eastern Road, not far from Celtic Park, and became known as 'The Duke's Bar,' where he proved to be a genial host. McMahon had the advantage as well of being a well-read man, who recited Shakespeare and Burns at Celtic soirees. He lost his wife, Annie, in March 1908 in the most tragic of circumstances, in childbirth. She was only 33, and from then on Sandy's own life and health went downhill. Too old for war service in 1914, he found employment in the munitions industry as an iron-borer, a job he tried to combine with his interests in the licensing trade, but this did not last long. He suffered from nephritis, a chronic complaint of the kidneys, a condition which compelled his removal to the Glasgow Royal Infirmary, where he died on January 25 1916.

Chapter 4:

BARNEY BATTLES: CELTIC'S PRODIGAL SON

I suppose the very name might give you a superficial clue to his character. He was pugnacious, aggressive and a born fighter – at least on the field. He was well built, tackled hard (pardon the anachronism, but it could be said that he "went in like a tank") and liked to win. And yet, there was a great deal more to him than that.

He was occasionally called "gentle Barney" in the Press. That is, of course, sarcasm, but those who knew him well – his family and those who played alongside him with Hearts, Celtic, Liverpool, Dundee and Kilmarnock – are all unanimous that there was indeed a gentle side to him. He was a loving husband and father, and a very supportive colleague. He probably made one bad mistake in his footballing life – for which he suffered – but he remained loved by the Celtic family. He was indeed a cult hero and his tragic early death saw an outpouring of grief which was hard to parallel.

Bernard Battles was born in 1875 in Springburn, but early in his life he moved to Musselburgh, and spent his early footballing life in the east of Scotland. He was a big boy, and his very size and comparative lack of mobility restricted him to a full-back or possibly a half-back position, but one of his strengths was always that he could play on either side of the field.

He cut his footballing teeth with Linlithgow Juniors, Bathgate Rovers and Broxburn Shamrock, before joining Hearts in September 1894. This was a fine Hearts team, who indeed won the Scottish League in 1895 over a Celtic club, hamstrung by internal dissensions, which were a foretaste of what was to come. But Battles' success at Tynecastle did not go unnoticed at Celtic Park, and there is a certain indication that he was 'tapped and approached' by members of the Celtic committee before he joined up at Parkhead in summer 1895. He would claim himself that he did not always "fit in" at Tynecastle.

Battles then performed the unusual, unprecedented and possibly unparalleled achievement of winning the Scottish League in consecutive years for different clubs. It was Celtic who won the League title the next season, 1895/96. In fact, strictly speaking, he won the League twice in the SAME calendar year, for the League title was won comfortably by December 1895, and Barney was one of the stars and well-loved by the Celtic fans, with the half-back line of Maley, Kelly and Battles a very impressive one indeed.

An indication of the value of Battles came in January 1896, when he was suspended for the Scottish Cup game against Queen's Park, and Celtic lost. The circumstances of his suspension were controversial to say the least. Battles had been sent off in an insignificant friendly match and Queen's Park were widely believed to have exercised undue influence on the SFA committee to get Battles suspended. He might have made all the difference in the Scottish Cup game.

Barney's big mistake came in the 'strike' of November 1896, when he was foolishly prevailed upon to join Meehan and Divers in their refusal to play unless a journalist was removed from the Press Box before a game against Hibs. The journalist had come perilously close to libelling some Celtic players, saying that "they were always the aggressors" in the Glasgow Cup final against Rangers. In truth, the freedom of the Press being a very important Victorian concept, the 'strike' was foolish and ultimately self-defeating, with dire consequences for Battles himself and for Celtic. He did not play again for Celtic this year. Celtic's season imploded after their defeat at Arthurlie and Battles spent season 1897/98 with Liverpool and then Dundee. He never really settled in Liverpool – the truth was that he wanted back to Celtic – and his move to Dundee was a stepping-stone to that aim. His heart had never really left Celtic.

He had one great moment for Celtic while still playing for Dundee. On February 12 1898, he scored for Dundee against Rangers at Carolina Port, the home of Dundee. As Celtic beat St Mirren that day, Barney, even though playing with a broken wrist and being "a glutton for work," according to The Dundee Courier, scored the goal which won the League for Celtic! Sounds familiar? Yes, Albert Kidd did a similar thing in 1986, did he not? It was by no means an exact parallel, although the similarities lie in the rain, Celtic playing St Mirren and the crucial Dundee goal being scored by a man who wished he was playing for Celtic! In 1898, however, it made all of the Celtic family yearn for the return of the wayward and now repentant Battles, with The Glasgow Observer outspoken in its desire for the re-introduction of 'St Bernard Battles, the Patron of Parkhead.'

Willie Maley, the recently-appointed Secretary, was all in favour, but it needed a poor run of form in the early part of the 1898/99 season to convince the Directors that such an addition was necessary. Barney had, in the meantime, returned to Liverpool and more unhappiness, but was clearly pining for home, and eventually in early October, Maley went down to Liverpool and brought him back.

The return of exiles is always a dramatic and even romantic occasion. This one was no exception.

> Back to the Celtic again
> Let's join the happy refrain
> Bring out your rattles
> For Brave Barney Battles
> Is back with the Celtic again!

By supreme irony, his first game back was against St Bernard's on October 8 1898. It was a rather uninspiring 1-0 victory, but at least it was a start, and the rest of the 1898/99 season was a steady improvement, as Battles, all previous issues forgotten and forgiven, fitted in well with men like Doyle, McMahon and Campbell.

It was, however, the misfortune of Battles and Celtic that the next four years, when Battles was in his prime, coincided with Rangers at their best and most of the time a better team than Celtic, whose self-inflicted wounds of the mid 1890s were taking longer to heal than would have been wished, as the young Secretary/Manager, Willie Maley, took his time to learn the ropes.

This was a new Barney Battles. He still had his aggressive tendencies on the field, but he had also learned his lesson that he was basically a Celtic player. Not of the same temperament as the steady and shrewd Maley, the flamboyant Doyle or the more sophisticated and cerebral McMahon, he nevertheless worked hard to contribute to the team. He had learned his lesson about being a 'rebel.' It is often said that Celtic players are, by definition, 'rebels.' Maybe so, but they are far better when they are rebelling WITH the club and not AGAINST the green-and-whites. His private life would settle down as well, when he married Catherine Gecherin at Portobello in 1899.

Rangers may have dominated the Scottish League in 1899, 1900, 1901 and 1902, but Celtic were the team that was most associated with the Scottish Cup. Battles and Celtic would play in the next four Scottish Cup finals, winning the first two and losing the next two, one through a few goalkeeping errors in 1901, and the other by that old Celtic failing of underestimating the opposition in 1902.

Barney's strength in these years was his versatility as a full-back, or indeed as a half-back. In the 1899 Scottish Cup final, for example, he played at right-half in the half-back line of Battles, Marshall and King, whereas, in 1900, he was the left-back of McArthur, Storrier and Battles. Both games were great triumphs for Celtic and Battles. In 1899, he was singled out as "lion-hearted and ever-eager to join the fray," against the Rangers team which had a 100% record in the Scottish League and who were even having the word "invincible" linked with their name! Not on April 22 1899, however, for goals from McMahon and Hodge saw Celtic home, with Battles' name frequently mentioned favourably in newspaper reports.

If Battles was the "driving force" in that final, he had a different role in 1900. This final was played at a windy Ibrox against Queen's Park, with the gale so strong that the game is often called "the Hurricane Final." In this final, it was Battles' role to remain calm, to hold on to the ball as long as he could and to resist the temptation to batter it against the wind where it would surely come back again, especially if in the air! Battles played this role to perfection and won his second Scottish Cup medal, to match his two Scottish League medals of 1895 and 1896.

If 1900/01 was a disappointment for Battles, as far as Celtic were concerned, he certainly made up for it on the International front, for he was chosen to play for Scotland on all three occasions, thereby confounding the cynics who claimed either that he was not good enough, or that the Scotland selectors would never choose such a 'bad boy' as Battles. He did not let Scotland down either, for they thumped Ireland 11-0 at Celtic Park, and earned respectable draws against Wales and England. The game against England was at the Crystal Palace, and although some sources blame Barney for gifting England's equaliser to Steve Bloomer, other sources insist that he acquitted himself well.

Seasons 1902/03 and 1903/04 were seasons of transition at Parkhead, and Battles had to struggle to hold on to his place, not so much because he was being found wanting, but more because other men were now beginning to challenge – Donnie 'Slasher' McLeod at right-back, Willie Orr at left-back and, in season 1903/04, the mighty half-back line of Young, Loney and Hay began to come together.

Barney was not chosen for the 1904 Scottish Cup final, and began to ponder his future at places other than his beloved Celtic Park. In June 1904, Kilmarnock made an approach and Barney was on his way, preferring first-team football for Killie rather than being merely a fringe player at his still-beloved Celtic Park. He played well enough for Killie, earning a huge ovation as he ran out for them at Parkhead on Hogmanay 1904. No-one realised it at the time, but it was the last time that so many of them would see their much-loved Barney.

He played for Kilmarnock against Rangers, on January 21 1905. Kilmarnock lost 6-2, and it was generally agreed that he did not have a good game against Alec Smith. When he came home to his house in the Gallowgate, he complained of feeling unwell, but, being Barney, laughed it off and put it down to general exhaustion. It was several days later before he took to his bed with flu symptoms, from which he was slow to recover. Then, on Thursday February 9 1905, and without any real warning, he died suddenly, to the distress of the whole Celtic community. He had just turned 30, although, curiously, his gravestone states that he was 29.

Barney Battles was buried in Dalbeth Cemetery on Sunday, February

12 1905. The cortege was said to be 2,000 strong, and it was claimed that 40,000 lined the funeral route on both sides of London Road. His coffin was carried in turns by men like Dan Doyle, Sandy McMahon, Johnny Campbell, Alec Bennett, Jimmy McMenemy, Peter Meehan and Willie Orr. After the interment, the mourners were treated to tea and cake by Celtic FC in the old pavilion. Tribute was paid by Chairman John H McLaughlin and the vote of thanks was given by no less a person than William Wilton, the manager of Rangers FC! Celtic would donate the takings from the stand at the Scotland v Ireland game, to be held at Celtic Park, to his widow, Catherine, and her two daughters.

He was a man who possibly made enemies, but they did not stay enemies forever, and he was well-loved in Scottish footballing circles. Later that year, Catherine Battles, who had now moved back to Musselburgh to be near her relations, gave birth to Barney's posthumous son, also to be called Bernard or Barney, a man who would go on to star for Hearts.

Chapter 5:

WILLIE MALEY: THE MAN WHO MADE CELTIC

Willie Maley was, undeniably, the man who made Celtic. His career as a Manager, particularly in the years from his appointment in 1897 until the 1920's, was second to none. From 1920 until 1940, it is probably true that Celtic were second to Rangers in most things, but they were still a great side and not without their great moments and great players.

All this has meant that his career as a player has tended to be overshadowed. He was not, in all truth, a brilliant player – he had spent most of his early life as a runner rather than a football player - but he was steady, reliable and gave his all for Celtic on the field. His playing career can be likened to that of Jock Stein. Both were good, but not great players, but both learned from their experiences on the field to make them outstanding readers of the game and outstanding leaders of men.

He was born in Newry, County Down, on April 25 1868. He was, therefore, Irish, of a good Roman Catholic background, but he could never really be described as a "Fenian". Quite the opposite in fact. His father was a Sergeant in the 21st North British Royal Fusilier Regiment of Foot of the British Army! This tended to mean that, although Maley was a supporter of Irish Home Rule and possibly of Irish independence all his life, he distanced himself from the violent extreme. Indeed, there were times when he showed a disturbing respect for royalty.

Legend has it (Maley told the story himself) about how he joined the club by accident. His father had retired from the Army, a few years after Willie was born, and by December 1887, the family had moved to Cathcart. One night, Brother Walfrid and John Glass came to the house to ask his elder brother Tom to consider joining the new football club that was being formed. Tom, sadly, was out with a young lady, but Willie and his parents agreed to pass on the message, and then, just as an afterthought, one of the distinguished visitors turned as he was leaving the house and said to the 19-year-old Willie, who had earlier told them that he had played the game with Cathcart Hazelbank and had even had an outing or two with Third Lanark Reserves, "Why don't you come along as well?" It was from such a small acorn that a mighty oak grew.

It would be a shame if such a story were apocryphal. Both Maley brothers did, in fact, play in the first Celtic game in May 1888. Willie was a strong right-half, although The Scottish Sport magazine at one point described him as "too modest to shine on the field…where he always seemed to be holding himself in reserve." By this it would appear that he lacked the aggression of Sunny Jim, the silky passing ability of Peter Wilson or Pat Crerand and the determination of Bobby Murdoch. Yet he was not a bad right-half for all that.

Willie was an all-round sportsman, particularly involved in athletics (he won the Scottish Amateur Athletic Union 100 yard sprint at Hampden in 1896) and cycling, but very soon he discovered that not only was football the love of his life, but that the team he now played for was even more so. It was revealing that when he took part in athletic and cycling events, although he was sometimes happy to be described as "of the Cathcart Harriers," he increasingly came to be referred to as "W Maley, Celtic FC," or even as "W Maley of the Celtic".

It was not only as a player that he began to involve himself with Celtic. He was always willing to do a little secretarial and publicity work for nothing, something that would stand him in good stead when it came to the club appointing a professional secretary. His enthusiasm impressed important men like John Glass and John H McLaughlin, and endeared him to those he played with, in particular James Kelly and Sandy McMahon. But on the field, he won the Glasgow Cup twice in 1891, and then in 1892 he was fully involved in what was Celtic's greatest triumph to date, namely the winning of the Scottish Cup at Ibrox against Queen's Park. He was generally agreed to have had a good game, "his blocking and feeding was simply perfect...his checking, returning and general engineering was simply immense." This means that he kept up a continual supply of ammunition for Johnny Campbell and Sandy McMahon in the front line, as Celtic won 5-1.

It was this game that proved to the world that Celtic were here in Scotland to stay (if that hadn't been obvious by the impressively huge stadium that was being built in 1892), but what really impressed and influenced Maley on that day was the effect that the victory had on the support – an under privileged ethnic minority, who now had something to cheer about. The sight of the smiles on these dirty, ragamuffin faces convinced Maley, if he hadn't known it before, that this was where he wanted to stay. These people had little else going for them in their lives but Celtic could make then happy. He would have a few flirtations with clubs in the north of England, notably Manchester City, but none of them lasted and Celtic was the only club that he wanted to play for.

The year 1893 was an interesting one for Maley. Not only did he play an inspirational part in Celtic winning their first-ever League Championship, but he also won two Scottish Caps against Ireland and England. He had previously played in an unofficial international against Canada, and once for the Scottish League, but his selection against Ireland might have been a little contentious. He was, after all, an Irishman! His father was also an Irishman and his mother Canadian, so Scottish connections were scant. But the Scottish selectors chose to ignore these rather basic objections. He had lived in Scotland since he was a baby, and that was enough to qualify him. He played well as Scotland beat a weak Ireland team 6-1 at Celtic Park and won a place for himself in the big game against England at Richmond, on April 1 1893.

This was the game in which Scotland's captain, James Kelly, was invited to shake hands with Princess Mary of Teck, the current fiancé of Prince George and of course the future Queen Mary. Maley would have loved to have been able to shake her hand as well, but he had to be content to see his Celtic and Scotland captain having that honour! It was a sad day for Scotland, for they lost 2-5 after holding their own for a great part of the game. One Press report says that Maley was "...very good in the first half, but not so good in the second."

But the big disappointment of 1893 had come a little earlier, on March 11, when Celtic lost the Scottish Cup final to Queen's Park. Willie was badly injured, having sustained a kick in the face (accidentally, one hopes) and having had to leave the field for a while. He also had to visit the dentist to lose a few teeth on the Monday, and by that time, Celtic were no longer the Scottish Cup-holders, having lost to Queen's Park in a very rough game, and in which the Queen's Park players (who were praised in the Press for the "superiority of their charging") managed to convince an inexperienced referee that a corner-kick conceded by Dan Doyle had, in fact, gone between the posts. In many senses of the word, Maley was "sore" about that game.

1894 saw a repeat of 1893, in that the Scottish League was won (on 'the Maley-Kelly axis') but the Scottish Cup final was lost, this time to Rangers. Maley played in this game against medical advice, and under the influence of some strong medication. Although he scored a goal in a losing cause, he was hardly at his best, and for the second year in a row he had to be content with a loser's medal, although this time there was a lack of bitterness, and who could really be jealous of Rangers, who had at last won the Scottish Cup after 20 years of trying? In any case, Celtic got their own back a week later, when they beat Rangers to win the League.

Sometimes, supporters would be a little surprised to read in their newspapers that "Willie Montgomery" was playing for Celtic. When the team came out, it was immediately noticed that "Montgomery" bore a strong resemblance to Maley, and indeed, when the ball went out of play and "Montgomery" ran to pick it up from the crowd, it was confirmed that "Montgomery" was indeed Willie Maley. This was all because Maley was training as a chartered accountant, and he did not want his employers to know that he played professional football on a Saturday. They might not have approved! This could hardly be because he was playing for the 'Catholic' Celtic – they had after all employed him, whatever his religion – but there remained in Victorian Britain a strong horror of professional sport, even though it was now legalised.

He played another season for Celtic, 1895-96, winning another Scottish League medal (three in four years) but injuries, a general slowing down and a desire to do other things persuaded him that there were other things he wanted to do, other sports for example, and a desire to concentrate on the administrative and secretarial side of running the club, an area in which he clearly had some expertise. He was now married, happy to be on the Committee as Secretary, and he thought his football playing career was over.

But then something happened to change everything at Celtic. 28 November 1896 was the day of the strike when Peter Meehan, Barney Battles and John Divers refused to play, in protest at the presence of a certain journalist in the Press Box, who had written some unfair things about Celtic the previous week. Whatever the rights and wrongs of all this, Maley suddenly found himself having to play against Hibernian. There was a reserve handy, and another player was summoned from Hampden Park, where the 2nd XI were playing, as Maley, only recently retired, was pressed into service. He did well enough and the game against the Edinburgh side ended in a 1-1 draw.

That was, of course, far from the end of the matter. A direct result of all this was the Arthurlie disaster in January 1897, where Maley, like the rest of the Committee, had been overwhelmed by the amount of players who were 'injured,' suspended or simply failed to turn up. Maley did not himself have to play this time – albeit it might have been better if he had decided to do so – but the weakened reserve team went down to a desperately awful 2-4 defeat, something that might have imperilled the very existence of the club.

In fact, it was possibly one of these things that simply had to happen. The club had a fright, but these events proved that the club had to be better organised and the end result was the formation of a limited company and a more professional approach to the game, with the appointment of Willie Maley as the professional full-time Secretary as from April 1897. He was perfectly suited to the task. He was an accountant, a businessman (he had a Glover and Hatter's business in the Gallowgate) and a man with wide experience of football. He would now dedicate his life to Celtic, and would make his famous quote about how, without this club, "his existence would have been a very empty one indeed."

His great strength was his ability to spot a player. Most of the great side of 1905-10 had been cherry-picked by Maley, and they were undeniably the greatest show on earth. They were often reckoned to be as good as Jock Stein's team of 60 years later, in which case, they were very good indeed!

Chapter 6:

DAN MCARTHUR: SMALL IN SIZE WITH THE COURAGE OF A LION

Sarcasm is often difficult to take.

I recall an old Celt telling everyone about "Shaw, McNair and Dodds…," when a younger man, clearly not of the Celtic persuasion, curled his lip and said, "Can't you go back any further?" Without breaking stride, the old Celt turned, smiled sweetly and said "McArthur, Storrier and Battles…"

So, who was this Dan McArthur?

Celtic have always been famous for great goalkeepers – Davie Adams, Charlie Shaw, John Thomson, Joe Kennaway, Ronnie Simpson – but the earliest goalkeeping hero was this small man from Old Monkland, who joined the club in 1892 and played a glorious part in the history of the club for the next 10 years. He was born in 1867 and died in 1943.

Goalkeepers are often large, jovial sort of fellows, full of confidence and brashness. Not so, Dan McArthur. He was only 5 feet 5 inches, lacked any great bulk, but what he lacked in height, he made up for in pluck, agility and, particularly, courage. Like quite a lot of great Celts, he looked astonishingly like "an ordinary man."

It must be remembered that football in the 1890s was a brutal business. There was little, if any, protection afforded to the goalkeeper by the referee. Charging the goalkeeper was recognised as part of the game, and men like Jimmy Quinn and Sandy McMahon excelled at it. The goalkeeper had to be nimble enough to get out of the way, almost in the style of a Spanish bullfighter, or to rely on some of his defenders protecting him and, indeed, giving it out as well in retaliation. It perhaps explains why Victorian newspapers are sometimes reluctant to say who scored a goal when it is described as a "scrimmage". This possibly means that the goalkeeper has dropped the ball, someone has stuck out a foot and the ball has entered between the sticks. The abolition of charging is, one feels, one of the better changes in the laws over the years.

In addition, it seemed in order for a forward to attempt to kick a ball out of the goalkeeper's hands, even when the custodian was on the ground. Goalkeepers were often kicked unconscious, and concussion was a frequent occurrence. Dan died when he was 76. This would have been considered as old for a goalkeeper!

Dan made his Celtic debut on September 9 1892, against Abercorn, a now-defunct Paisley side, after first-team goalkeeper Joe Cullen had been badly injured in a friendly against Sunderland. He played well that day, but for the next two seasons found Cullen a difficult man to displace. These were very successful seasons for Celtic, who won the Scottish League on both occasions and came close enough to lifting the Scottish Cup as well.

Dan forced his way into the side for the Glasgow Charity Cup games at the end of the 1893/94 season. The tradition was that players were not paid in such games – it was all for charity – and McArthur was possibly still an amateur in any case, but he certainly took his opportunity. Celtic beat Third Lanark after a replay in the semi-final, and then at Ibrox before 18,000, he played with distinction as the team defeated Queen's Park 2-1 in the final. It was Celtic's third Charity Cup in a row, and they would make a habit of doing well in this tournament in the 1890s. The ever-gentlemanly and gracious Joe Cullen who was at Ibrox that night as a spectator, admitted that his friendly rival Dan McArthur had a good game.

As far as McArthur was concerned, he was the regular goalkeeper from now on. In 1894/95, he won both the Glasgow Cups, but the team lost the League to Hearts and went out to Dundee at Carolina Port. Significantly, perhaps, the Dundee game was one of the few games McArthur missed that season. Cullen was at fault for the only goal of the game, when he could only parry the shot of Maxwell, which rebounded to Sawers.

It takes time for supporters to fall in love with a goalkeeper, but the Parkhead crowd were very impressed by his litheness, his commitment and indeed his 'out' play. Goalkeepers, who in 1895 wore the same jersey as everyone else, needed to be good dribblers and kickers as well as acrobats, and McArthur had all these skills. He was, without any doubt, a brilliant goalkeeper whose courage, it was reckoned, would have put a lion-tamer to shame. Commenting on the game against Hibernian at Easter Road, on December 29 1894, Willie Maley remarked that "the match will long be remembered as McArthur's game, our popular custodian giving an exhibition between the sticks never equalled in our history."

But before that game, he had already earned his spurs in the Glasgow Cup final against Rangers. The 2-0 score line gives the impression of a comfortable win for the club, and so it was, eventually, but McArthur was largely responsible for keeping Rangers out, with the pressure significantly raised when Sandy McMahon had to leave the field at half-time with a bad injury. But Celtic, with the 'two Dans' – Doyle at left back and McArthur in the goal, were up to the demands of the situation, and McArthur earned the reluctant praise of Rangers at the end. The Scottish Sport summed things up characteristically well by saying, "McArthur had it all to do – and did it, rather!"

The performance of the 'two Dans' was enough to draw the attention of the Scotland selectors to their deeds, and they were chosen twice to play for Scotland in the spring of 1895. The first game was a routine 3-1 victory over Ireland at Celtic Park, but the other was a somewhat more controversial and difficult occasion, namely the 0-3 defeat to England at Goodison Park, Liverpool. It was "controversial and difficult" because, to the embarrassment of McArthur, presumably, the other Dan – Doyle – suddenly disappeared on the Friday night! Doyle was, of course, a loose cannon and his absence presumably had something to do with a Liverpool lady whom he had met a few years previously, when he played for Everton, but poor Dan McArthur was puzzled, bewildered and even a little apprehensive when he was naturally, as a teammate and colleague of the missing man, quizzed about his whereabouts. Doyle did, in fact, turn up – remarkably, he was allowed to play –

but the team was affected by all this, and McArthur was responsible for at least one of the three goals, a shot which he parried and the ball rebounded off Neil Gibson into the net. Apart from a 6-0 win in Wrexham, Wales, in 1899, this was the end of his international career.

McArthur played well the following season, in which the team won everything except the Scottish Cup, and he is one of the few Celts who comes out of the horrendous events of winter 1896/97 with his reputation intact. He was not playing against Arthurlie, genuinely injured, presumably (or was he? We can never be sure!), and the next four seasons at the club saw him at his best, with one notable and egregious exception.

1897/8 saw Celtic win the Scottish League once again, with McArthur a virtual ever-present in the goal, in spite of suffering multiple injuries with phrases like "kicked comatose" used several times to describe him. And yet how the crowd loved him for his courage, and his almost foolhardy diving at the feet of opposition forwards to grab the ball! But there was more to him than that. There were his cat-like reflexes, his fine positional sense, his ability to organise the rest of his defence and his dribbling skills, "the unbeatable little demon", he was called as well. His colleague, Tom Hynds, said, on one famous occasion, that if anyone were to kill McArthur, they would really have to shoot him!

Dan played in three consecutive Scottish Cup finals. The first one was in April 1899, against the Rangers team that had completed the entire League season with a 100% record. It was not expected that Celtic were likely to beat them, but in front of a large crowd of 25,000, which turned up at Second Hampden, some of them in different variations of the as yet incomprehensible 'horseless carriage' which startled and terrified douce Victorian Glasgow, Celtic won 2-0. Rangers had the edge on pressure in the first half, but then really piled it on in the second half, after Sandy 'The Duke' McMahon had headed Celtic ahead. Celtic looked in trouble when Jack Bell was injured, and remained little more than a passenger, but the Celtic defence of McArthur, Welford and Storrier were up to the task, and the victory was confirmed when Johnny Hodge added the second and clinching goal.

This was a great moment for Celtic and McArthur, the goalkeeper rightly considered one of the heroes of the hour, and another Scottish Cup was won the following year. This time the circumstances were totally different. The opponents were Queen's Park, and this final has gone down in history as the 'Hurricane final", for it was blowing an absolute gale at Ibrox. The game took place against the backdrop of the Boer War which was not at this time going all that well for the British, whose heavy casualties were not being hidden, even though sections of the Press tried to cover things up. The crowd at Ibrox that day contained one or two wounded soldiers and quite a few more anxious men awaiting their embarkation.

It was not a great day for football. Celtic played with the wind in the first half, and although Queen's Park surprised everyone by scoring early, by half-time Celtic were 3-1 up. And then immediately after the start of the 'second moiety', they scored again to make it 4-1. In normal circumstances, this would have been enough, but Celtic were now facing the wind. This was when the back three of McArthur, Storrier and Battles came into their own. Davie Storrier was a tough, crusty character from Arbroath, where he had learned a thing or two about winds and gales, and Barney Battles was broad and tough and on that day "the wind seldom got past him", whilst in between them, Dan was at his best, using on this occasion his skills of dribbling and passing as much as his shot saving ability.

Once again, the Celtic-supporting part of Scotland rejoiced in the greatness of Dan McArthur, with many members of the Press also puzzled as to why he was not being chosen again for Scotland. Season 1900/01 saw Rangers once again win the League but lose to Celtic in the Scottish Cup, in the early rounds, on a day in January when McArthur insisted on playing even though he was recovering from a broken wrist. Celtic won 1-0 with a goal from Willie McOustra, but on one occasion, McArthur sustained a severe kick on the head which required the attention of the doctors of both clubs and delayed the match for about five minutes. But Dan being Dan, he left the field with a smile on his face.

It was the 1901 Scottish Cup final which effectively marked the end of

Dan's great days with Celtic. The venue was Ibrox and the opponents were Hearts. 1901 was not, in all truth, one of Celtic's better years, but to reach three Cup finals in a row was no mean achievement. Indeed, it has to be said that they might have won the Cup if Dan had not had one of his rare bad days. But it was a bad day that would put all other bad days to shame. Celtic were 3-1 down late in the second half, and all three goals might have been laid at the door of McArthur, although there were other factors as well. But then Celtic fought back with a goal from McMahon and a wonderful solo effort from the young maestro, Jimmy Quinn. 3-3 and only minutes to go, it looked like at least a replay - but then Hearts scored again when Dan could not quite hold a powerful shot, and Hearts were able to score from the rebound.

It was a cruel end to the game, and particularly cruel on the man who was looked upon as one of Celtic's greatest-ever goalkeepers. He gave up the game in 1903, however, with more happy memories than sad ones.

Chapter 7:

JOHNNY CAMPBELL: TWO YEARS A VILLAIN BUT ALWAYS A CELT

Johnny Campbell was one of the best of the early Celts. He was a great friend and colleague of Sandy McMahon, forming the famous left-wing of McMahon and Campbell, but he was able to play all over the forward line, versatility being his strong point. He played for other teams as well – Aston Villa and Third Lanark - but he is one of those many players who will always have 'of Celtic' added to his name, whenever he is talked about.

Born in Glasgow in 1872 of Irish parents, Johnny grew up in the tough world of Victorian Glasgow and cut his teeth with teams like Possil Hawthorn and Benburb, until he joined the new but already famous Celtic club in 1890, playing his debut for them against Battlefield in a Glasgow Cup-tie in September of that year. Famously, Celtic then won the Glasgow Cup twice in 1891, beating Third Lanark in February in the final of the 1890/91 competition (their first major trophy of any substance), and then Clyde in December in the final of the 1891/92 season. Campbell played in - and scored a goal in – both finals.

By this time, it was appreciated that Johnny was a rather special player. He was bulky, but athletic, had a good turn of speed and, curiously for a man who found himself on the left wing quite a lot, was not a naturally left-sided player. It was often remarked that he moved the ball to his right foot to cross it – something that confused the opposition. But his strengths were in his ball-winning and his ability to score goals.

1892 was the first really great year in the history of the Celtic club, for it was the year that they won the Scottish Cup for the first time, beating Rangers in the semi-final and Queen's Park in the final, after the fiasco of the first game, which was held up repeatedly by crowd encroachment. The Scottish League had been in existence since 1890, but it was the Scottish Cup that was considered the more important competition. The Scottish Referee describes Campbell's contribution to the 5-3 victory over Rangers in the semi thus, "a good straight dribbler, a one screw kicker (sic!) and an accurate, quick, close passer."

The Scottish Cup final of that year is a story in itself. Campbell actually scored in the first game, which was subsequently declared a friendly. He would have been the hero of the hour and would obviously have been disappointed about that decision (which in truth, both at the time and with historical perspective, does look as if it had something to do with the desire to make more money!), but in the 'real' final of April 9, he scored two goals, and it was the more or less unanimous feeling of the Press that Celtic's left-wing of McMahon and Campbell had been immense. The celebrations among the now massive Celtic support have been well detailed in contemporary accounts, and there were no greater heroes than Johnny Campbell and his friend Sandy McMahon.

At the end of the 1891/92 season, Celtic won their third trophy, when they beat Rangers 2-0 in the Glasgow Charity Cup final, Campbell heading both goals. Celtic had won three trophies that year and Campbell had scored in each one of the three finals! He drew attention to himself by doing strange and unusual things. He scored 12 goals in one game (admittedly a reserve game) and then had the honour of scoring the first-ever goal at St James' Park, Newcastle, when Celtic were invited to play in the first game there. Strange to think that the Tyneside greats of Hughie Gallacher, Jackie Milburn and Alan Shearer are all following the tradition of Johnny Campbell! In 1897, Johnny also scored the first-ever goal at the present Villa Park.

It was clear that Celtic had unearthed a great player here, and this was confirmed both next year and the following year, when the team won the Scottish League Championship, although they narrowly missed out on the Scottish Cup on both occasions. Campbell was a virtual ever-present in season 1892/93, and his consistent form drew the attention of the Scottish selectors, who chose him for the games v Ireland and England. He and McMahon took Ireland apart, but England at Richmond were a different matter altogether. It was however a learning experience.

Johnny missed a chunk of the 1893/94 season through injury but still won a League medal, and then came season 1894/95, which was considered a failure, as Celtic lost out in both Scottish competitions although they did rather better in the Glasgow tournaments. There was a certain indication that things were far from happy behind the scenes, and this may be the reason for the departure of Johnny Campbell to Aston Villa. Willie Maley tells us that he left "through the stupid action of a very prominent committee man" – he declines to mention names or to go into any more details – but Johnny went to Birmingham and immediately became a great hero.

This was the heyday of Aston Villa. They had won the Football League in 1894 and the FA Cup in 1895. They were well led by an inspirational Scotsman called George Ramsay, who considered that Campbell was a great capture, even although he was joining an already fine club with excellent players like John Devey, Dennis Hodgetts, Charlie Arrowsmith, John Cowan and Stephen Smith.

1895/96 was a great season for Villa, as they won the English title with Campbell ending up top scorer with 26 goals. Back home in Scotland, it was a good season for Celtic as well, as they won the Scottish League (before the turn of the year!) and the two Glasgow competitions. Johnny may have had his argument with the "prominent Committee man", but he would have been delighted to hear of the success of his ex-teammates, particularly his good friend Sandy McMahon, for whom he acted as best man at his wedding. Indeed, there was a chance for Celtic supporters to see Johnny Campbell and Aston Villa on May 20 1896, in a friendly dubbed 'the championship of the world', because Celtic and Villa were the respective League Champions of both countries. The match was not well attended - it was out of season and no amount of embellishment could hide the fact that it was a friendly - but Celtic won 3-2. Campbell was given a great ovation, and the crowd, at least, gave him to understand that he would be welcomed back at any time.

1896 was good for both Celtic and Villa, but 1897 could not have seen a greater contrast in the fortunes of the two teams. Celtic had been nowhere in the Scottish League and had crashed ignominiously out of the Scottish Cup at Arthurlie, whilst Aston Villa won a League and FA Cup double to emulate Preston North End in 1889, and it would be a feat not repeated until Tottenham Hotspur in 1961. Villa's march to the final had been impressive, and Campbell had featured largely in their progress as they beat Newcastle, Notts County, Preston North End and Liverpool to set up a final against Everton at the Crystal Palace, on April 10 1897.

Before a crowd of 65,891, Campbell scored first in the 18th minute, then Everton hit back to go 2-1 up before Villa levelled through Wheldon and then scored a winner through Crabtree, with Campbell heavily involved in the build-up to both. This was good enough, but as they came off the field, they heard the even-better news that they were also champions because of the League results. They were, thus, the only team ever to win a Double on the same day!

For Johnny Campbell, it was a great moment, and he became one of the very few players to have won a Cup medal in both England and Scotland. And he was not finished yet.

Johnny was basically a Glasgow boy, and yearned for a return. The Arthurlie defeat in January 1897 had at least one beneficial side effect of seeing Willie Maley appointed as Celtic's Secretary/ Manager. One of the first things Maley did was secure the return of Campbell to the green-and-whites. When Willie's brother Tom Maley suggested the possibility to Campbell, Johnny accepted with alacrity. Barney Battles would return a year later, and as a result of all this, success returned to Celtic Park, with the League being won in 1898 and the Scottish Cup in 1899 and 1900. Aston Villa, on the other hand, missed him terribly as the following piece of doggerel verse might indicate;

> "Oh, one more sigh
> Is the Birmingham cry
> For oor braw Johnny Campbell!"

Campbell had enjoyed his time at Villa, but Celtic was his team. He described his feelings of his role in the 4-0 thrashing of Rangers in September 1897 as being "as proud as the day I won the Cup for Villa." It was a treat to see McMahon and Campbell back together again with their 'clockwork passing' and 'telegraphic understanding' of each other. His international career resumed as well and we had, for example, the phenomenon of two John Campbells playing for Scotland – one from Celtic and one from Rangers! – in the 11-0 defeat of Ireland at Celtic Park, on February 23 1901! In 1902, he captained the side against Wales at Cappielow in a 5-1 win, but his best international game was undeniably the 4-1 win over England at Celtic Park in what history has called the 'Rosebery International', for Lord Rosebery sponsored the Scotland side, gave them his racing colours and addressed the crowd, liberally using phrases like "michty me" and "och aye", to try to convince the sceptical Glaswegians that he really was Scottish! No doubt about Campbell, though. He didn't score, but he was the man of the match.

Johnnie continued to play for Celtic, heartbreakingly losing the Scottish Cup final of 1901 but winning the first Coronation Cup - or British League Cup, or Glasgow Exhibition Trophy - of 1902. He played with decreasing regularity in season 1902/03 and then he was offloaded. He was now into his 30s, and like most players of that age, prone to pick up injuries, and when he left Celtic to finish his career with Third Lanark, he did so with the best wishes of everyone. But there was a sting in the tail yet.

1903/04 was the one and only year that Third Lanark won the Scottish League. They had some fine players, were well-managed by a man with the unlikely name of Frank Heaven, and they now had the ageing but still able Johnny Campbell. Celtic too were fated to do well this season – it was to be the year of Jimmy Quinn's hat-trick in the Scottish Cup final and the year in which Young, Loney and Hay came together – but before that could happen, Third Lanark had beaten them three times in the autumn of 1903, and in each case, Campbell played a significant part. Celtic did get some revenge in the spring of 1904, when they beat them in the Scottish Cup semi-final, but Campbell's part in the triumph of the Cathkin men in the Scottish League was very important. It would be his sixth League medal - three for Celtic in 1893, 1894 and 1898, two for Aston Villa in 1896 and 1897, and now one for the gallant Thirds in 1904.

Johnny would have loved to have played for Third Lanark in their Scottish Cup triumph against Rangers in 1905, but he was struggling with old age and injuries by that time. He retired from the game in 1906 and does not seem to have taken any part in coaching, scouting or managing, as far as can be established. He died on December 2 1947, at the age of 75, and was duly buried among loads of other Celtic heroes at Dalbeth Cemetery.

Chapter 8:

JIMMY BLESSINGTON:
THE GROSSLY UNDERVALUED BLESSINGS OF BLESSINGTON

Jimmy Blessington is one of the lesser known Celtic players of the early years, but there are those who were of the opinion that he was one of the best. His comparative lack of renown is possibly because, unlike Campbell and McMahon, for example, he did not score very many high-profile goals in Scottish Cup finals, but the opinion of many supporters and commentators of that era was that he was an outstanding inside-right and, latterly, outside-right.

Jimmy was a smallish man, not particularly bulky but he was wiry and athletic, the build normally associated with inside-forwards. The role of the inside-forward was 'fetch and carry man' or the 'forager." He had to win the ball in midfield and bring it up to the centre-forward or supply the right-winger. That is, of course, a very simplistic way of describing what he did. Inside-forwards were also expected to score goals, and this Blessington could do as well.

He is one of the few Celtic players to have been born in Linlithgow. His father was a quarryman, and James was born in 1874. The natural place that he would turn to for football was Edinburgh, and we find him involved with Hibernian and Leith Athletic in the early 1890s, while he was an apprentice blacksmith. He was by no means the only player - Sandy McMahon and Willie Groves also spring to mind - whom Celtic pinched from underneath the nose of Hibs at this time, the word "badgered" was used to describe Celtic's efforts to get him. But then who, in summer 1892, could blame Blessington for wanting to join the new club with the huge support, ambitious Committee men and the winners of the Scottish Cup? Leith, on the other hand were going nowhere, and Hibernian were still ham-strung by incompetent management, dishonest officials (who kept disappearing with the money) and a foolish and self-defeating sectarian policy. It was hardly surprising that they were losing out to the far more progressive and forward-looking club of Irishmen in the west of Scotland.

The allegations of "poaching" made to the SFA, however, were enough to delay Jimmy's debut for Celtic. Leith Athletic, with whom he was still registered, were probably reconciled to the loss of Blessington, but were clearly wanting some money for him from Celtic. Celtic, however, were able to produce some evidence that it had been Blessington who had approached them on two separate occasions offering his services, and, of course, if he was an amateur, he could do that. The SFA, however, ruled that Jimmy was acting wrongly and suspended him for one week, but Celtic went unpunished. It may be that a sum of money surreptitiously changed hands to keep everyone quiet.

Be that as it may, when he did play his first game, against Pollokshaws Athletic on September 17 1892, a mighty Celtic career was launched. Jimmy was never dropped for the next few years, and was one of those players who seemed able to avoid being injured. He was never out of place in the distinguished company of Sandy McMahon, Johnny Campbell and Johnny Madden, and this Celtic team won their first Scottish League Championship in 1893, the title being confirmed on the late date of May 9, when they beat, of all people, Leith Athletic, one of the teams who had tried to stop Blessington joining Celtic.

He appears to have settled almost immediately, attracting headlines like "Blessington the Blessed" (something that went down well with Roman Catholic supporters!) and consistently, the newspapers praised his play. It was not all good news for Blessington in 1893, however, for the team lost the finals of the Glasgow Cup to Rangers and the Scottish Cup to Queen's Park, the Scottish Cup final leaving a nasty taste in the mouth because of the rough tactics and dubious practices of the amateurs. Blessington scored Celtic's only goal in the Scottish Cup final.

He had a tremendous game, however, in the Glasgow Charity Cup final of that year, when Celtic beat Rangers 5-0 in a game that was much commemorated by the supporters. It was the same in 1894, when the Scottish League was won once again, but the Scottish Cup narrowly lost. Blessington was fated never to win a Scottish Cup medal. This time the opponents were Rangers, who thus won the Scottish Cup for the first time in their 21-year history. Rangers were the better team on the day, Blessington frequently mentioned as being "always a threat," but it was not to be. It was a shame that he never won a Scottish Cup medal, for many players of lesser ability and application have done so. The following week, however, Celtic earned their revenge by beating Rangers 3-2 to win the Scottish League, and Blessington scored Celtic's second goal. The Glasgow Charity Cup was also lifted, when he fed both Johnny Madden and Joe Cassidy for their goals which beat Queen's Park.

By this time, Jimmy had caught the attention of the Scotland selectors, and he was chosen for two games in 1894. First there was a trip to Ireland to play at the Belfast ground with the lovely name of Solitude – a 2-1 win – and then he was chosen for the 'big' or 'real' international against England, held this year at Celtic Park. The new Celtic Park was, of course, built for such occasions, and 45,017 were there to see an exciting and dramatic 2-2 draw, with Scotland denied victory by a late goal after Sandy McMahon had put them ahead a few minutes earlier. It was generally agreed that Blessington was one of Scotland's better players that day, and he would have deserved his victory. He was singled out as "the finest forward on the field" and he "dribbled in a masterly and highly fascinating style."

Jimmy had one of his rare injuries in spring 1895, and both Celtic and Scotland suffered as a result, but he would not be denied his victory over England in 1896. The game was once again played at Celtic Park, this time before a crowd given as 56,000 but probably a great deal more than that, as even the luxurious, purpose-built Celtic Park struggled to cope with the huge crowd. Soldiers of the Gordon Highlanders from the Maryhill Barracks were kept in readiness – fortunately, they were never deployed – just in case the crowd got out of hand, (they had taken to pelting policemen with cinders before the game started when things got boring!) and everyone again saw Blessington at his best, as Scotland won 2-1. Some newspapers credit him with one of the goals, although the general consensus was that it was Lambie and Bell who had scored. All agree, however, that the left-wing (Jimmy proved his versatility by playing at inside-left) of Blessington and Bell was a superb combination. Jimmy had also played in the 3-3 draw in Ireland, the previous week.

He also won the Scottish League with Celtic that 1895/96 season and the two Glasgow trophies. The Glasgow Cup final was a fine game of football, won 6-3 over Queen's Park after being behind at half-time. The League was actually won before the New Year, on December 14, when Celtic beat Rangers 6-2 on a day of Biblical rain and Blessington scored twice. Another great game of that campaign was the 11-0 defeat of Dundee, in October. In fact, one can make excuses for Dundee with injuries and a slippery pitch, but Jimmy was superb. No-one will ever know for certain who scored all the goals for Celtic at Parkhead that day, but Blessington was reported to have scored "a few."

1896 was a great time for Jimmy. It was the acme of his footballing career with Celtic, as it was downhill after that. He got married to Madge McFarlane, in the Gorbals in 1897, but that was about all that went right in that year. It was of course the winter of the players' strike and the Arthurlie defeat. Jimmy was blameless in either of these two disgraceful affairs (he agreed that a protest should be made against the obnoxious journalist but thought that refusing to play was going a bit too far), but for all sorts of reasons, nothing was ever quite the same again. Nothing was won in 1897, and, like everyone else, Jimmy's form was affected by the events.

But there was more to it than that. The club were not happy with Jimmy's other job – he worked for a bookmaker. Bookmakers were technically illegal (although in practice tolerated) but they needed a 'runner', a man who collected the bets from the punters. Bets were taken for horseraces mainly, but also on football matches, and in the climate of 1897, when allegations of match-fixing were frequent, Celtic felt they had to ask Jimmy to give up that job. He was not really keen on that idea, and after a month or two of conflict, Jimmy was sent out to Preston North End on loan.

One wonders what Willie Maley's role in all this was. He was, by now, Secretary/ Manager. Technically, he had no say in all of this, but in practice he would have, one feels. He admired Blessington as a player – everyone did – but does not say much about the circumstances of Jimmy's departure.

Blessington then played for a variety of clubs, Derby County, Bristol City, Luton Town and Leicester Fosse (whom he also managed). He was also coach of Belfast Celtic, in season 1913/14, and was all set to take up an appointment in Germany, a part of the world where football was rapidly developing, but when war came in August 1914, he was prevented from taking up that job. He might have considered himself luckier than Steve Bloomer in this respect. The great England goal-scorer found himself on the wrong side of the border in 1914 and was detained at a civilian internment camp at Ruhleban for the duration of the war!

Now 40, Jimmy was too old to serve in the Army, but he enlisted in the scarcely less dangerous environment of the Merchant Navy, serving on the Atlantic Convoys. This involved him coming to Glasgow quite a lot, and he would always include a visit to Celtic Park. He had possibly fallen out with the Celtic establishment some 20 years ago, but his heart was still there.

After the war, Jimmy moved around England quite a bit. He was Manager of Abertillery Town for a spell, but then he resumed his career as an electrician in Luton, before running a hotel on Guernsey. He died in Newton Abbot, Devon in April 1939, probably the only Celtic player to be buried in that part of the world. It is a pity he is not better known nowadays, as he was a very fine player.

Chapter 9:

TOM MALEY: A CELT AT THE START AND AT THE END

Tom Maley is not as well-known as his brother Willie, but his contribution to Celtic is by no means minimal. It often comes across in a subtle way, through the influence that he had over his brother Willie, a man who for all his ability to run a football club, sometimes showed a surprising lack of confidence in dealing with the outside world. In such circumstances, he depended heavily on his elder brother Tom.

An example of this came in the mid-Atlantic in 1931, as Celtic were en route to America on the SS Caledonia for their famous tour of that year, taking the Scottish Cup with them. Willie Maley, a poor sailor apparently, confined himself to his cabin and threatened not to re-appear unless the Directors summoned his brother Tom to come on the next ship. One suspects that there may have been a disagreement on this issue between Willie Maley and the Directors before leaving Glasgow, and that Willie did not get his own way. Anyway, he sulked, threatened to go home on the next ship, and to take no part in the tour until the Directors yielded to his demands. He perked up immediately, when he heard that Tom was on his way, and became the life and soul of the tour. It was an excellent example of the way that Tom did a great deal for Celtic behind the scenes, in an unofficial sort of way.

Tom Maley, the son of a soldier also called Tom Maley, was born in Portsmouth in 1864 and is thus four years older than Willie. He became a great athlete and footballer once the family moved to Scotland, and had already played a few games for Partick Thistle, Third Lanark and Hibernian before that famous night in December 1887, when the two members of the nascent Celtic club came to ask for his services. He had trained as a teacher and would one day become Headmaster of

Slatefield Industrial Schools in Glasgow and St Mary's, Calton.

Both Maley boys played in the inaugural Celtic game on May 28 1888, Willie at right-half and Tom at inside-right. Reports of this game are not always clear or precise, but it may be that Tom scored a hat-trick that day. He was also reported as having been one of the entertainers at the post-match social soiree at St Mary's Hall, East Rose Street. Whether these stories are true or not, it is clear that Tom Maley was seen and, indeed, saw himself, as an integral part of Celtic FC from an early stage of its existence. Nor was he in any way modest about his achievements and attributes. "Speed, stamina and dash… all three were mine," he once said.

He was probably correct, but he was unlucky to lose out in Celtic's first-ever Scottish Cup final in February 1889, in spite of getting a good Press in most accounts of both the 'snow game' and the official game. He had scored goals against Cowlairs, Albion Rovers and St Bernard's then a hat-trick against Clyde on the way to the final, but in truth he was never a great player, in the way that some others were, and he was soon beginning to lose out to some of the new players that were coming to the club, in many cases from Hibernian.

The irony was that it was he himself who was playing his part in bringing the new players to the club, for he was now a Committee member, and an energetic one at that, doing all that he could to bring the very best of footballers to the Celtic club. Called "Handsome Tom" and now married to Elizabeth Mellon (in 1889, although he was willing to return early from honeymoon to deal with an SFA disciplinary matter pertaining to 'Darling Willie' Groves!), he also took part in a great many political activities, not least the matter of Irish Home Rule, the issue that exercised the minds of the Glasgow Irish community more than any other in the 1890s.

He was also involved in a less than savoury matter and was in fact very lucky not to be severely punished for his part. It was a Scottish Cup game against Larkhall Royal Albert at their ground Raploch Park in early December 1890. Larkhall was even then an 'Orange' area and the name Royal Albert tells us something about them as well, does it not?

Be that as it may, Celtic were coasting to a 4-0 victory, and although a few unpleasant things were being said by the less intelligent of the small and now dwindling Larkhall crowd, there was no indication that things were going to turn nasty, until a Larkhall player called Bobby Frame fouled Johnny Madden. A foul was awarded, but then Celtic's linesman (or Umpire as they were called in 1890) Tom Maley entered the field of play to remonstrate with Mr Frame. Frame argued back, a few "words of intemperance" were exchanged, and Tom either hit Mr Frame on the head with his flag or punched him, depending on what report one reads. The Larkhall 'thickos' suddenly saw a way of brightening up a really rather dull and depressing day and some of them ran on to attack Tom. Celtic right-back Jerry Reynolds came gallantly to his aid, as did the two local policemen, and the pitch was temporarily cleared. Later, Reynolds and a man called Cleland from Larkhall came to blows, more disorder ensued, and the game had to be abandoned with 12 minutes to go.

Tom should, of course, have let the matter go with Mr Frame, as the team were winning well. Incredibly, Larkhall - 0-4 down with just 12 minutes to go - claimed the tie and demanded, with rather more justification, that action should be taken against Celtic's Umpire, Maley. Some newspapers persisting in talking vaguely about an "incident" and an "accident", but The Hamilton Herald was more forthright: "A message to Tom Maley – Don't try yon again!" The SFA met on the Tuesday night. Astonishingly, they ordered a replay the next week – to take place at Ibrox! Equally astonishingly, they decided that no action was necessary against Maley!

A great deal more to Tom's credit was his involvement in the half-yearly meeting of the Celtic club in December 1894, when, according to James Handley in The Celtic Story, "TE Maley drew attention to the fact that, in the balance sheet, no donation to the Poor Children's Dinner Table appeared. The club had been originally formed to support east-end charities, and yet out of a princely income of nearly £7,000, not a penny had been devoted to the purpose for which the club had been instituted. His remarks, we are told, were received with cordial applause". Yes indeed, and the cordial applause should be echoed 125 years later in the 21st century!

Tom was made a Director in 1897, when the Limited Company was formed, and worked well with his brother in the re-building of a great team. He was particularly instrumental, we are told, in the bringing back of Johnny Campbell in summer 1897. Campbell had just won a League and Cup double with Aston Villa, but Tom took a train to Birmingham and persuaded him that there was a place for him "back home" with Celtic. The effects of this were electric.

In 1902, Tom decided that it was perhaps time to turn to management as well. The youngest brother of the family, Alec, would do likewise, becoming in time manager of Clyde and then Hibernian, but Tom, with his wide knowledge of English football gleaned from his many trips south of the Border to scout for Celtic, was invited to become the manager of Manchester City. City had been relegated in 1902, but Tom Maley, building a side around the legendary Welshman Billy Meredith and including a few Scotsmen like ex-Celtic men Tom Hynds and Willie McOustra, took them out of the Second Division in his first season, and then, in 1903/04, took them to the FA Cup final at the Crystal Palace against Bolton Wanderers.

The game was scheduled for April 23 1904. It so happened that the Scottish Cup final was the week before, April 16. Tom would have wished to have been in two places at once, for while Jimmy Quinn was scoring his famous hat-trick in the Scottish Cup final at Hampden, his own team were defeating Small Heath of Birmingham 4-0 at Hyde Road, to give themselves an outside chance of the English title, as Sheffield Wednesday lost heavily to Newcastle that day.

But the FA Cup final came first, and it would all be decided on the weekend of 23-25 April 1904. He invited brother Willie to Crystal Palace, and Willie felt able to leave Celtic for one week (Quinn scored five goals as they beat Kilmarnock 6-1) to come and see Manchester City beat Bolton Wanderers 1-0, and thus we had the rare phenomenon of the two Cup-winners in England and Scotland being managed by brothers! Sadly, City lost to Everton on the Monday and had to be content with second place in the Football League.

Sadly, that was about as good as it got for Tom at Manchester. Two years later, in June 1906, he was suspended sine die for offering illegal payments to players, over and above the regulation £4. This was hardly an unusual offence – indeed it was common practice – but it was high profile, involving Billy Meredith, and Tom paid the penalty. He protested, as indeed did the Press and public, but the draconian penalty remained until it was lifted in 1910.

During this time, Tom returned to Glasgow to resume his teaching career. He could not have any official capacity at Celtic, but he was always there in the background to help his brother and the players during the sustained success that Celtic enjoyed in that period. Then, in 1911, his suspension lifted, he returned to football management, this time with Bradford Park Avenue, where one of the first things he did was to change their colours to green-and-white hoops!

The Great War had an effect on Tom. In the family tradition, he was a great supporter of it, organising recruiting rallies and other things, and his whole-hearted support was in no way diminished by the loss of his son, Joseph, killed by shrapnel in the spring of 1915. He stayed at Bradford until 1924, then managed Southport for a while before he returned to Glasgow and his beloved Celtic.

Tom Maley died of pneumonia on August 23 1935, at the age of 70, at the house of his son-in-law in Giffnock, having suffered from indifferent health for a while. He had been several times to Lourdes but to no effect. He was much respected for his contribution to the game of football as a player, manager and administrator.

Chapter 10:

JOHNNY MADDEN: A FOOTBALLING PIONEER

Saturday, April 17 1948 was actually a good day for Celtic, at a time when good days did not come very often. At Dens Park, the team had saved itself from relegation, thanks to fine performances from Bobby Evans and Jock Weir, and a major embarrassment had been avoided. Newspapers, naturally, were full of this game, and indeed the Scottish Cup final at Hampden, where it was generally agreed that Rangers had been very lucky to earn a replay against Morton. One would, however, search in vain for any mention of a man called John Madden, who died that day in Prague, at the age of 83.

There were, of course, reasons for this. Prague had indeed been liberated in 1945 from the Nazis, but the 'liberators' had been the Soviet Union, and that was not really very much of a liberation at all. Prague and Johnny Madden were on the wrong side of the Iron Curtain, and news was one of the things that did not cross that barrier very often, particularly news about an obscure old Scotsman who once played and coached football teams.

And obscure was the word. If one had asked the Celtic fans, as they streamed out of Dens Park that day, delighted that their team had saved themselves, who Johnny Madden was, very few would have known. He had left Scotland in 1905, and although his contribution to the early years of Celtic FC was substantial and possibly even pivotal, very few supporters were old enough to have remembered him. Men like Willie Maley (who played with Madden and lived until 1958) would have remembered him, but there were very few of that generation still alive. A few supporters read about the history of the club now and again, and they would have known who he was, but there were not many of them in 1948.

John Madden was born in Dumbarton in 1865. That area is often referred to as "the cradle of Scottish football," and he was an excellent example of the many youngsters who were being reared to play the game in this part of the world. He was often referred to as Johnny, Jake or "the Rooter," the latter a nickname given to him because, according to his teammate Jerry Reynolds, it was believed that some of his ferocious shots could knock a goalpost out of the ground by the roots, as it were. On the other hand, some believe that it was because of his use of the backheel, root being an old-fashioned word in some parts of Scotland for a heel.

Johnny may well have seen Dumbarton win the Scottish Cup in 1883. He had already played for them at Boghead (as well as a few games in England for Gainsborough Trinity and Grimsby Town) when he was invited by the new Celtic team to turn out for them at centre-forward in their inaugural match in May 1888. It was an invitation that he accepted with some alacrity, it being a great honour. Madden was already working as a riveter in the shipyard near Whiteinch, and he had already heard stories about the ambition and enthusiasm of this new club.

Johnny played in the first game and would have played a few more games for Celtic, but found himself at the centre of a 'tug of love' battle, as Dumbarton tried to retain him. Scottish football was all-amateur at this time, but everyone knew (however much the authorities tried to deny it) that money and favours occasionally changed hands, and possibly at this stage, Dumbarton offered him more. It was not until September 1889 that he committed himself to the Celtic.

Stories abound about Madden (and a few others) being enticed away (words like "abduction" and even "kidnap" are used) by teams like Sheffield Wednesday and Nottingham Forest, for in England professionalism was legal, but in Madden's case, in spite of a few "flirtings with Saxon agents," he stayed with Celtic. He was a very talented player with the ability to entertain the crowd and, in particular, score goals. He also had the versatility to play all over the forward line, and a great feature of his play was his ability to dribble, a skill of the game which Victorian football crowds all loved. As important as anything, was his whole-hearted approach to the game.

Madden was very much involved in the two Glasgow Cup victories in the year 1891, but had the misfortune to be injured in the lead-up to the Scottish Cup final of 1892. He thus missed the first really important trophy of Celtic's history, and in fact this meant that he never did win a Scottish Cup medal. But he was a consistent star in seasons 1892/3 and 1893/4, when the Scottish League was won, albeit with the loss of the Scottish Cup on both occasions. He also won two international caps for Scotland, both against Wales and both, as it happened, at Wrexham, scoring four goals in 1893 and one in 1895. Many people thought that he would have been good enough to play in the 'big internationals' against England, but it never happened. Maybe it should have, for in the years that Madden scored against Wales, Scotland, without him, went down to heavy defeats against England.

His popularity with the Celtic crowd was indicated when the club experimented once or twice with some primitive form of floodlighting. This usually involved lights hanging from wires, and indeed they did brighten the place up, although the idea had to be abandoned because they ball kept hitting the wires. Celtic Park was christened "Madden's Shipyard" by the fans. This was, presumably, because Johnny was still a shipyard worker as well as a professional football player, and shipyards used electricity for their workers on the night shift or indeed the dark afternoons of December and January. This was the 1890s, and an awful lot of ships were being built on the Clyde. In fact, it might have been Madden who suggested the idea to the Celtic Park committee in the first place, but sadly, the idea of floodlights had to be shelved for the best part of 70 years.

Madden's last good season for Celtic was 1895/96. This was the year that the Scottish League was won before the New Year and the two Glasgow trophies were annexed as well, but as in the case of quite a lot of players, things were never quite the same again after 1897. Johnny was not involved in the Arthurlie fiasco – whether for reasons of injury or for something more sinister – but he had his wages reduced, and this was something that he would not stand for. Madden was, above all else, a professional football player, and he left Celtic Park in 1897. He played sporadically for Dundee and then Tottenham Hotspur, in season 1897/98, but seems to have decided that as he was now 33, it was time to call a halt on his professional football career.

He then returned to the shipyards, one presumes, but little is known about his life at this point. It may be that, like rather too many ex-footballers of this time, he hit a few problems in his life, but he certainly seems to have retained his interest in football, and the next that we hear of him is when he took up a post as manager of Slavia Prague, in February 1905. How this come about, we do not know. Possibly, the Prague team approached someone at Celtic Park, and Madden was duly recommended, but it does seem an extraordinary and indeed courageous step for a man from the West of Scotland to take in 1905, when Central Europe was virtually unknown and reputed to be the home of witches, vampires, gypsies and dictatorships.

It was not entirely unheard of for Scottish and English ex-players to go the continent to spread the word of football. It was sometimes given the somewhat patronising title of "missionary" activity. But, certainly, English and Scottish football were highly regarded and any man who had played for many years for the famous Celtic team in Scotland would be greatly respected. For whatever reason, Johnny went to Prague and very soon he made a difference.

The difference would be seen in two respects. One was tactics. The days of the 'passing' game as distinct from the 'dribbling' game had long gone, and good teams in both Scotland and England had perfected both aspects of the game. But there were other developments in team formations that had been perfected by teams like Celtic, not least the double centre-half/centre-forward ploy, to what extent the goalkeeper came out or stayed on his line, how he avoided shoulder charges and other things.

The other thing was discipline. It is notoriously hard to inculcate a sense of discipline with regular training, good diet, abstinence from alcohol and nicotine into men who are playing the game as part-time amateurs, or even part-time professionals. Professionalism was beginning to come into the game in Prague, but as the game was not yet in Central Europe the obsession that it was in Scotland, there would not have been the money to pay the salaries that players in Great Britain could have demanded.

Slavia Prague became one of the more successful teams of Central Europe, winning all sorts of local trophies before the Great War. What happened to football during the years between 1914 and 1918, we cannot tell, nor do we know what happened to Madden himself. Prague was part of the Austro-Hungarian Empire and Madden was British. Most likely he would have been interned, but after 1919, when the hybrid country of Czechoslovakia was formed, Slavia won the League title in 1925, 1929 and 1930.

In 1922, Celtic were the Champions of Scotland and arranged a tour of Central Europe. One of the teams that they met was Slavia Prague, so Madden had the opportunity to meet up with Willie Maley once again. Judging by Maley's reluctance to say a great deal about Madden in most of his memoirs, it is possible that they didn't always see eye to eye, and they certainly did not have a pleasant game on, of all days, May 25 1922. The game was described as a "kicking match," and Slavia won 3-2 in a game characterised by dreadful refereeing. Jock Gilchrist and Willie McStay were sent off for next to nothing, and the local team were allowed to kick and foul all they wanted. Five Celtic players were badly injured, notably the great Patsy Gallacher, whom the Czechs set out to crock. It would have been interesting to hear what Madden and Maley said to each other after the game!

Madden retired in 1930, but although now reduced to a wheelchair, he still attended Slavia games and even did a little coaching. When Czechoslovakia reached the final of the 1934 World Cup, against Mussolini's Italy, they fielded eight players who had learned their trade with Slavia Prague and Johnny Madden. He was now settled in Czechoslovakia and married to a lady called Francesca Chekhov, and even if he had wanted to come home to Scotland, the brutal Nazi invasion of his adopted country ensured that he spent the years from 1939 to 1945 in what was officially and euphemistically called the

Reich Protectorate of Bohemia.

His death in 1948 went unnoticed in Scotland by many people until years later, but in Czechoslovakia, he is still talked about in respectful tones for his work in the development of the game, sometimes even called the Father of Football. As with quite a few of the early Celts, there is quite a lot that we wish we knew more about.

Chapter 11:

JIMMY QUINN: THE BHOY FROM CROY

A hundred years and more have now passed since the floruit of the great Jimmy Quinn, but he still remains a potent legend in Celtic hagiography. Indeed, it is significant in the Willie Maley song that the first verse, referring to the early days of the club, states that "Gallacher and Quinn have left their mark." The Gallacher was, of course, Patsy Gallacher, and the Quinn was the miner boy from Croy.

Quinn joined Celtic in early January 1901. Maley was looking for youngsters. His spies scoured the country, and consistent reports reached his ears about this youngster called James Quinn of Smithstone Albion. Maley met him, was impressed by his earnestness, enthusiasm and build, took a chance and signed him on as a left-winger in the first instance.

Jimmy was unlucky to be on the losing side in Scottish Cup finals in 1901 and 1902, but he did have one great day at the Glasgow Exhibition Trophy final of 1902 (sometimes called the British League Cup or the first Coronation Cup) when his hat-trick beat Rangers.

Some say the Rangers are guid at fitba'
That Smith and Gibson and Speedie are braw,
But Jimmy Quinn, he diddled than a'
At the Glasgow Exhibition, oh!

Season 1903/04 was a pivotal one for Jimmy. It was the first in which Celtic wore the green-and-white horizontal stripes, as distinct from the vertical ones, and it was also the first season of the new Hampden Park, opened on 31 October 1903. The grand venue's first Scottish Cup final would be staged on 16 April 1904, and, appropriately, the teams taking part would be Celtic and Rangers.

Celtic were two goals down, but half-time had not even been reached. Quinn got the ball on the halfway line and kicked it forward. It held up in the wind and Jimmy charged forward, using his mighty bison-like shoulders to barge two Rangers defenders out of the way before drilling home a great goal. Minutes after that, fine work from Bobby Muir on the right enabled him to fire a ball into the goalmouth, where Quinn hammered home a second.

Thus, at half-time, things did not look all that bad. Two goals each. Indeed, looking at the large crowd of 65,000 in the new stadium, the managements of both teams might well have settled for a 2-2 draw, a replay and another big gate. But destiny called on Jimmy Quinn. Ten minutes remained, when a ball came to him from the left. He was about 30 yards from goal. He feinted to pass out to the right, but instead charged, head down, towards the Rangers goal. Using his weight, he once again shouldered the Rangers markers out of his path, reached the edge of the box, and drilled the ball past the advancing Watson.

But there was a sting in the tail of that 1903/04 season. In the Glasgow Charity Cup final, Quinn was the victim of a nasty challenge from Rangers' Nick Smith, was carried off to hospital and reduced to a cripple for the rest of the summer. This incident did little to make Quinn love Rangers and may have had something to do with another two incidents.

The first came on 25 March 1905, in the Scottish Cup semi-final at Parkhead (there were as yet no neutral venues for semi-finals). It was raining, and Celtic were having a bad day. They were 0-2 down. But Quinn had once before rescued Celtic from being 0-2 down and there was still hope.

A steepling ball came into the penalty area, but it was too high for anyone. Rangers full-back Alec Craig had jumped for it, but on landing slipped on the wet turf and, to break his fall, grabbed Jimmy, ending up holding his leg. Jimmy naturally shook his leg to rid it of such unwelcome, if accidental, attention, and in doing so, his foot came into contact with Craig's head.

Referee Tom Robertson of Queen's Park thought this was deliberate, and Quinn was ordered off for violent conduct. Craig, a decent and honest man, intervened on Quinn's behalf, but Robertson was adamant. The crowd, meanwhile, outraged by this decision, and perhaps seeing a little class prejudice in their hero being sent off by the referee who had such connections with the middle-class, snooty Queen's Park, invaded the field and the game had to be abandoned.

Jimmy was suspended for one month, but he still had one last laugh in 1904/05. Celtic and Rangers finished joint-top of the Scottish League, and instead of using goal average or goal difference (Rangers would have won on both methods), a deciding game was played at Hampden. In fact, a Glasgow League encounter had already been scheduled, and the Scottish League decreed that the winner would be the Scottish champions. Quinn did not score that day but was instrumental in both the Celtic goals as they won 2-1. Quinn had won the first of the six consecutive League titles that he and Celtic would collect between 1905 and 1910.

The other violent clash involving Quinn and Rangers came on New Year's Day 1907. This one concerned Rangers' Joe Hendry, who had just fouled Celtic's Jimmy McMenemy. Quinn came charging across to remonstrate and, in so doing, slipped on the wet turf, knocked Hendry to the ground and, accidentally, collided with his face. The referee, an Englishman called Kirkham from Burslem, thought that it was all deliberate, Quinn was sent off and eventually suspended for two months.

The merits of the case, however, paled into insignificance in comparison with the reaction of the Celtic support. They felt that this was all a deliberate ploy by the authorities to prevent Celtic from becoming the first team to win the Scottish League and the Scottish Cup in the same season, and Quinn, already a hero, now became a demigod in the eyes of the Celtic fans. A campaign was started to compensate him for loss of earnings, and a grand total of £277 was raised as money poured in from Scotland, Ireland and the United States. Concerts were held, and Jimmy was presented with money and a gold watch, with his wife Annie given a gold pendant.

His stock rose dramatically after his suspension in 1907. He was not picked for Scotland in any of their three games – to the absolute fury of his fans and to the puzzlement of many non-Celtic lovers of the game – but he did help Celtic to their first national double. In fact, the key game was Quinn's first back after suspension. It was a Scottish Cup-tie, as luck would have it, against Rangers at Ibrox.

"Masterly inactivity" would perhaps sum up Quinn's contribution that day to Celtic's 3-0 win. He was content to retain a low profile, carefully refusing to retaliate when his old enemy Joe Hendry 'accidentally' stood on his stomach and drawing Rangers defenders to himself while the rest of the forward line did the scoring. This was, of course, the heyday of the mighty half-back line of Young, Loney and Hay, but it was also clear to most spectators that Quinn's mere presence on the field was enough to spook Rangers.

Thus, Celtic won the double in 1906/07. The myth that this was not possible had been shattered. But if 1906/07 was good, 1907/08 was superb. It was the season in which Celtic won everything they had entered, a feat not paralleled until Jock Stein's team did the same in 1966/67. Basically, it was the year in which Maley's young team all matured at the same time. They got on wonderfully well, both on and off the field, and they played marvellous football

Quinn scored 24 goals that season, a fair amount considering that he was out for a long spell immediately after the New Year with a toe that turned septic and caused complications. Still, it was this year that revealed the other side of Quinn's play. Previously, it had been claimed by his detractors that he was simply a 'rumble-them-up' sort of centre-forward, relying on brute force and using a great deal of shoulder-charging. Now his admirers saw another side to Jimmy.

He was now a great passer of the ball, as he gave a masterclass in leading the line. He could distribute to his wingers Bennett and Hamilton, he could interplay with the prodigiously talented inside-forwards Somers and McMenemy, and he could be a partner for centre-half Willie Loney, who would frequently join the attack, particularly for set-pieces. In such cases, Quinn could hang back and help out the defence. He was a complete player, and totally deserving of the accolades that the Glasgow Herald, in particular, would hand out to him. "Quinn is a very master." "Quinn leads the Celtic forward line with panache and vigour." "Quinn is simply

Quinn – and that sums it up!"

1907/08 saw Jimmy also revisited the international scene. In particular, he returned to the land of his forefathers, to Dublin, on 14 March 1908, when Scotland beat Ireland 5-0. Jimmy scored four goals – a shot from the edge of the box, two tap-ins and a 'charge through' – and the Glasgow Herald praised his unselfishness and distribution. Not to the extent that the Dublin press did, though. Stressing that Jimmy's parents were Irish, they reported that the talk in the Dublin hostelries that night was "Quinn, Quinn and more Quinn," with one newspaper even declaring: "Not since the days of Charles Stuart Parnell was a man talked about so much in this city." Others shamelessly took over the description of Parnell and called Jimmy "the uncrowned King of Ireland."

All this meant that Quinn could hardly be passed over for the 'big international' against England, at Hampden on 4 April. But vast was the consternation among the Quinn faction when it was announced that Jimmy would switch to the left-wing to accommodate Andy Wilson of Sheffield Wednesday. Wilson was another fine centre-forward, but hardly in the Quinn class. To be fair, Quinn had experience of playing on the left flank – indeed, he had appeared there once or twice for Celtic that season when team circumstances demanded it – but it did seem strange to play the mighty man out of position in such an important game. It ended a 1-1 draw.

Quinn had no reason to be disappointed about that and the rest of 1907/08 saw Celtic mop up the Scottish League, the Scottish Cup (in a very one-sided final against an overawed St Mirren) and the Glasgow Charity Cup, to add to the Glasgow Cup that had been won in the autumn. Celtic had climbed Parnassus, and although the motivating forces included the mighty half-back line of Young, Loney and Hay, as well as the tricky inside-forwards Peter Somers and Jimmy 'Napoleon' McMenemy, the player who made it all happen for Celtic was the spearhead Jimmy Quinn, now quite clearly the most talked-about man in Great Britain.

Yet all this adulation sat ill with a profoundly shy man. He had the next campaign to think of. There was no time to rest on laurels. The 1908/09 season remains a dreadful one in the annals of Scottish football, for that was when the lovely new Hampden Park was ripped to shreds after the replayed Scottish Cup final.

What happened after the riot was significant, though. Celtic had to play eight games in 12 days to win the League. Jimmy played in all eight games and scored seven goals, never shrinking, never "wanting a break, Boss." He was determined that Celtic would win their fifth title in a row, which they duly did on the evening of Friday, April 30 1909, by beating Hamilton Accies 2-1 at Douglas Park, Hamilton.

Season 1909/10 saw Celtic win the League for a phenomenal sixth time in a row, although they would lose in the Scottish Cup semi-final to Clyde. Quinn scored two absolutely sensational goals that term. One was in the Glasgow Cup final at Hampden, when Jimmy, already limping from a slight knock, and three Rangers players (one of them the goalkeeper) went up for the same ball. No-one in the 55,000 crowd quite knew what happened but the ball ended up in the net and Jimmy finished with three Rangers men on top of him. It was the only goal of the game. The other was a brilliant individual goal at Rugby Park on Christmas Day.

There would be even more cause to laud Jimmy Quinn by the end of the season. Jimmy had long been a cult hero with Celtic fans, but now this hero-worship spread to all Scotland as well, after the international match on 2 April 1910. This game, against England, was widely recognised as the best ever. The score line was 2-0. The first goal arrived when Quinn hit the bar and Celtic colleague Jimmy McMenemy netted the rebound, then the man from Croy scored the second himself.

Quinn was 32 in 1910, and, inevitably, given the amount of injuries that he had suffered – many of them deliberately inflicted by despairing defenders – he began to slow down and miss games through fitness problems. The great Celtic team had reached its peak as well, although Quinn did manage another two successful Scottish Cup finals, in 1911 and 1912. In the latter season, as well, Quinn played for Scotland against Wales, scoring the late winner and rendering the 31,000 Tynecastle crowd "demented with joy." He also played his final international game, against England, in 1912, but the selectors once again put him on the left-wing, where he was not a failure but no great success in the mundane 1-1 draw.

Jimmy Quinn played his last game for Celtic in January 1915. He died on 21 November 1945, and he was buried in Kilsyth Cemetery. Not without cause is he called "the Mighty Quinn."

Chapter 12:

ALEC MCNAIR: ECK THE ICICLE

It was one of those annoying days when roadworks divert the bus off the main road to Celtic Park and compel you to take back roads, usually through villages and towns that one has heard of... but seldom visited. On this day, we passed a signpost to Stenhousemuir, well-known as the home of a brave but not really very successful team, and one of only three teams to have two u's in their name (the others being Dundee United and Queen of the South). And they play at a ground called Ochilview, are called The Warriors and play in maroon. But then a youngster asked if any great Celtic players had ever come from there. It was just the opening that Old Father Tim was waiting for, as he launched into an encomiastic eulogy of one of Celtic's best-ever players. He was still going strong as the bus pulled into the Emirates car park, even though some of his listeners had made excuses about "meeting a friend in a pub" and left the bus early!

Born in 1883, the young McNair had indeed started his career with Stenhousemuir, with whom he won the Scottish Qualifying Cup in 1901 and 1902. He played as a forward in those days and came to national attention when he scored the second goal in the Scottish Cup quarter final of 1903, as they beat Partick Thistle 3-0. This set up a semi-final against Rangers, in which Stenhousemuir, with McNair at centre-forward were well beaten, but the game at least did attract the attention of quite a few Scottish clubs, not least Celtic, for whom Maley was already on his mission of 'ingathering of talent.' He had a look at McNair, even gave him a trial (in a friendly at Airdrie), but decided that centre-forward was not McNair's best position. He did, however, have another look the next year, and decided that the Stenny boy, now playing in defence, was worth a go. In May 1904, not long after Jimmy Quinn had scored his famous hat-trick, it was reported that Alec McNair had been transferred to Celtic.

Never have Celtic been better served than they were for the 20 years between 1904 and 1924 by Alec McNair. Alec holds the record of appearances for the club, playing a total of 604 times in League and Cup matches and that does not include the Glasgow Cup, the Glasgow Charity Cup and the innumerable friendlies that Celtic played at home and abroad in the glorious days of the early 20th century. The otiose may argue that the man with record appearances for the club is Billy McNeill. It depends what games and competitions you count, but it us a matter of credit to each man that they can be mentioned in the same breath!

Alec's record number of appearances will seldom be broken, for it is hard to imagine anyone playing for so long at one club. He was rarely mentioned in newspaper reports - which is, of course, a great tribute to a right back - but he does score high in the memoirs of contemporary players and his Manager, Willie Maley, who sums him up as, "The coolest, most intelligent player I have ever seen." Even the referee, Jock Bell, said that, "It was a delight to see him wait for his man, pounce just when the moment was right and clear with such crispness and confidence."

Yet, perhaps curiously for someone who played such a distinguished part in the early years of the club, Eck was neither Irish nor Catholic. That, of course, only matters to the bigots, but Celtic's deployment of Eck McNair for so long shows two things about Willie Maley - one was that he himself was no bigot, and the other was that he could judge a football player. It was claimed that Eck was even a Rangers sympathiser before he joined Celtic. So? He was probably the first, but he certainly was not the last. He became a great Celt, and long after he retired, he was referred to as Alec McNair of Celtic, almost as if it were a hereditary title in the House of Lords.

Eck lived in Larbert or Stenhousemuir (the two villages adjoin each other) all his life and travelled on the train every day for his training, except when he was employed in the war years in the munitions Industry at Bo'ness, forging metal for horseshoes. He was a grate fitter to trade. The Great War was a tough time for Eck, because his wife Mary McNair (nee Niven) died in August 1915 of cardiac valve disease at the age of only 28. Eck had a young family of five children to bring up, but in the same way that he would never shirk a tackle on the field, McNair faced that problem with fortitude, determination and perseverance. His family grew up to be a credit for him, and his son Jimmy became a professional footballer with Stenhousemuir and Falkirk.

Eck was fortunate in several respects. Being a widower, and in any case a munitions industry worker, he was never likely to be called up for the carnage, and this meant that he could continue to play for Celtic, a club who in these days were very much a caring, family club. Not the least of Willie Maley's many talents was his ability, at this stage of his life at least, to comfort those with problems. Both McMenemy and Dodds had brothers who died in the dreadful Battle of Loos. They needed to be well handled, and it spoke volumes for the commitment of both manager Maley and captain Sunny Jim Young that the Celtic support network functioned well to sustain these players at their time of maximum need. It was why Celtic succeeded when others failed. Eck was also lucky in that his family and that of his wife were there to help out with the childminding.

Eck McNair was very much a defensive right back. His colleagues (Willie Orr, Jamie Weir or Joe Dodds) tended to be the attacking 'Tommy Gemmell' type of players and as centre-halves often went forward in those days as well, so it was vital that there was somebody dependable at the back. This was what McNair could do to perfection. His mistakes were so rare that they were mentioned as collectors' items. On New Year's Day 1916, for example, he fluffed a pass-back to give Rangers an undeserved draw. There were very few other times that McNair made a mistake.

The other thing that was observable in the unflappable Alec was that only as a last resort or 'in extremis' did he boot the ball up the field. That might clear the immediate danger, but the ball could come back very quickly. Far better to dribble the ball out of danger or pass the ball to a colleague. That could, of course, include a pass-back, something that the laws of football were far less strict upon in the time of McNair.

Indeed, passing back to Charlie Shaw became Eck's trademark, so that it became a Glasgow cliche to the question, "What will I do?" (about a job, a wife or any other problem). The answer was invariably, "Pass it back to Charlie!" One occasion, long after Alec retired from football, he was playing golf, and took a long time to work out what to do with a ball that had landed in a bunker. As he reflected, someone recognised him and shouted, "There's only one thing to do, Eck! Pass it back to Charlie!" Eck himself had to laugh at that.

Although he joined the club in 1904, it was not really until 1908 that he settled in as right-back. This was because Celtic had the admirable Donnie McLeod for this position, but also because McNair's versatility meant he could always be deployed as right-half, centre-half (particularly in 1906-7, when Willie Loney broke his arm) and even left-back. Just occasionally, he took the field as an inside-right, a position that he had played in occasionally for Stenhousemuir before he joined Celtic.

But from 1908 until 1923, Celtic's right back was Eck McNair. He won 12 Scottish League medals and Scottish Cup medals in 1907, 1908, 1911, 1912, 1914 and 1923. He won the respect of all who played with him, and that included really great players like Jimmy Quinn and Patsy Gallacher. His best season was that of 1913/14, when Shaw, McNair and Dodds went from October 4 until February 28 conceding only one goal! Small wonder that they won the League and Cup double that year! Eck won 15 caps for Scotland, his most famous game being the 3-1 win over England at Hampden in April 1914, in which Celtic colleague Jimmy McMenemy earned the plaudits, but it was the quiet confidence of McNair which won the day.

Curiously for a man of his temperament, Eck was only captain of Celtic for a short time (he also captained Scotland on three occasions), being quite happy to work for the likes of James Hay, James Young and Willie Cringan. He possibly lacked the 'devil' necessary for a captain, as he was more of a team man, and he preferred to concentrate exclusively on the task in hand.

He did have the ability to trouble-shoot. Not everyone was as calm as Eck, and now and again, men like Sunny Jim and Patsy Gallacher could 'lose it.' Often Eck was on the spot to encourage his more volatile colleagues that there was a certain value in simply walking away from trouble. He was seldom in trouble himself with referees, and it was also remarked that he had to ability to make a reasonable point to Maley without being blustered at in return, or without making the great man feel threatened.

His last big game was the Scottish Cup Final of 1923, in which Celtic beat Hibs 1-0. It was by all accounts a grim game, but newspapers are full of praise for the quiet veteran, now called "The Icicle" for his coolness and unflappability. Many times, in the long countdown to the final whistle, did McNair mop up and 'take the dog for a walk' to the corner flag to use up precious seconds. He was almost 40, and the Celtic crowd applauded him as he walked off at full time, knowing that they would seldom see his likes again.

Not least of his achievements was that he was a total gentlemen. He was so good a player that he did not need to foul, and was well regarded and respected by opponents, and that included great left-wingers like Alan Morton of Rangers and Alec Troup of Dundee. The friendship of Troup and McNair was deep and owed a great deal to the time in 1920 when Eck saved the life of the diminutive Troup from an angry crowd at Parkhead, who had invaded the pitch and were attacking some Dundee players and the referee.

Allowing Troup and other Dundee players to reach the sanctuary of the pavilion, McNair turned on Celtic's so-called supporters and gave them a verbal barrage, which was vitriolic but apparently, even in those extreme circumstances, devoid of foul language. For Alec McNair, foul language was as unnecessary as foul play.

After retirement, he was manager of Dundee from 1925 to 1927, but was not really cut out for the demands of that role and settled down as a stockbroker in Falkirk, a job for which his temperament was far more suited. But he retained his love and interest in football, being a referee supervisor for a spell, a short time before his death on November 18 1951, at the age of 68. Alec McNair died at 5 Rae Street, Stenhousemuir and is buried in Larbert Cemetery.

Chapter 13:

'SUNNY JIM' YOUNG: "FACE THE BALL, CELTS!"

"One fine big Celtic boy would play without the money
Parkhead's endless inspiration, the genial Sunny"

There could be no greater Celt than the legendary 'Sunny Jim' Young, who played for the team throughout the great days between 1903 and 1917. He was a remarkable footballer, who epitomised Celtic when they were good, when Maley's young side came to fruition and swept all before them.

The record speaks for itself – six League titles in a row, then a break for three years as the team re-invented itself, then another four titles in a row, in spite of the rude intervention of the Kaiser. A Celtic fan entering a hostelry in Edwardian Scotland would ask for a "Young, Loney and Hay." The barman would look at him quizzically, before the fan would say he was wanting three "halfs" of whiskey, for Young, Loney and Hay were "three halfs of the best!"

Yet Young's origins were not connected with Celtic. This may have been a problem with a few bigots on the committee or in the support, but it mattered not one iota to the visionary Willie Maley, who was pledged to build the greatest team in Great Britain, irrespective of religion or anything else.

In 1903, Jim Young was 20 and homesick. He played for Bristol Rovers but had not really made an impact in the past year, and he was missing his native Kilmarnock. Fate then decided that Celtic committee man Mick Dunbar came to Bristol to ask Bobby Muir to join Celtic. Muir was keen, and possibly mentioned that his friend Jimmy Young was interested in going back to Scotland as well. Young himself confirmed this and Dunbar, apparently acting on his own initiative but impressed by the strong athletic physique of the Kilmarnock man, signed both Young and Muir in the Black Swan Hotel at Eastville, then the home of Bristol Rovers, in early May 1903.

Success did not come instantly. The talent was there. Jim Young would note with approval the runs of Alec Bennett, the wiles of Jimmy McMenemy, the passing ability of Peter Somers and the strength of that shy and brooding introvert from the mining village of Croy, Jimmy Quinn. Young played well enough at centre-half, although he was never totally at home there, being frequently caught out of position and clearly stronger on his right side than he was on his left.

It was not until 27 February 1904, that Maley made a momentous decision before a difficult Scottish Cup replay at Dens Park, Dundee. Young would play at right-half, instead of centre-half. Thus Young, Loney and Hay came together, this time through the manager's choice rather than through compulsion forced by injuries, as had happened on one occasion previously, at Airdrie. Jimmy Quinn notched the hat-trick which won the Scottish Cup of 1904, but there is a danger that people might think that he was a one-man team. Not so. Behind Quinn, it was the mighty half-back line which supplied the ammunition, as Celtic came from behind to win 3-2.

This success fired the fans to great levels of enthusiasm, as the young team began to be spoken about in eulogistic terms. Celtic fans of all ages have always loved a trier, and this was what Jim Young always was. It was about this time that he earned the nickname 'Sunny Jim.' There were several reasons why he was so called. Some said it was because of his radiant smile. This was, of course, sarcastic, for on the field Jim was grim, determined and focused. Others said that it was given to him because of a song which was very popular in the Music Hall:

"Oh, Sunny, Sunny Jim,
Oh, how I envy him!"

But the most likely explanation was the contemporary advertisement for a breakfast cereal called Force, seen widely on billboards and in newspapers. The central character was strong and energetic, and underneath were pictures of him swimming rivers and climbing mountain, something that would strike a chord in those consumptive, undernourished Edwardian days.

The slogan ran:

"Vigor, Vim, Perfect Trim
Force made him – Sunny Jim."

Willie Maley, reminiscing in The Story of the Celtic, summed Young up:

"Celtic have never had a more whole-hearted player. He was a half-back of the rugged type, but there was class in his ruggedness, whilst for stamina, he stood in the first rank. His enthusiasm inclined him sometimes to excesses, but a kinder-hearted fellow never wore a Celtic jersey . . . In time he became captain of Celtic, and a splendid one he made. A player of dauntless courage, he served Celtic faithfully and ably for many seasons."

James Handley, the author of The Celtic Story, waxes poetic about the Celtic team of that period. Having talked about the forward line, he then goes on to affirm;

". . . and behind them, ready for the cut and thrust of the game stood the Porthos, Athos and Aramis of the football field – Young, Loney and Hay. The two lines drew equilateral triangles between them with the ball or moved forward with the smooth and forceful precision of piston rods, the diesel-powered Quinn in front thundering along the track to goal."

The record of that team speaks for itself. Under captain Jimmy Hay, six consecutive League championships were won, the Scottish Cup found its way to Celtic Park in 1904, 1907 and 1908, and might have done so as well in 1909, had it not been for the Hampden Riot. In 1907, Celtic became the first Scottish team to win the double of the Scottish League and the Scottish Cup in the same season, and in 1908, they became the first team in world history to win every competition that they entered, namely the Scottish League, the Scottish Cup, the Glasgow Cup and the Glasgow Charity Cup.

'Sunny Jim' was well to the fore in all that. His blond hair made him instantly recognisable and he was the icon of that Celtic side. He was out occasionally with injury or suspension, but never for very long and was always willing to do anything for the club. On one famous occasion, 'Sunny Jim' played in the goal.

It happened on 2 January 1909 at Kilmarnock. Young had been injured in the game against Clyde on Boxing Day and missed the New Year's Day game at Parkhead against Rangers. Without him, Celtic won 3-1, but goalkeeper Davie Adams was injured. The next game was the following day, and Maley had a problem. He dabbled with approaching a junior club for the loan of a goalkeeper, but 'Sunny Jim' offered his services, saying that he was still a bit stiff after his injury, but would be able to play in the goal as, "Ah widnae hae to run around sae much." It was not a success, but it showed the character of 'Sunny Jim' Young.

Following the Hampden Riot, even more remarkable, at least in footballing terms, was what happened next. The Scottish League insisted that their fixtures had to be completed by the end of April. Celtic, because of several replays and postponements, found that they had to play eight games within 12 days.

It is at such moments that mighty men like Jimmy Young stand up and are counted. He played in seven out of the eight games and performed magnificently in them all. Loney was out injured, so it was the young Joe Dodds who took the centre-half spot in those momentous days. Dundee were the other team who were likely to win the League but could do little other than stand in amazement and awe as Celtic completed this gruelling schedule, losing only one of these eight games, the second-last one to Hibernian. They drew another two and won the remaining five. It was a remarkable achievement, and the Sunny Jim breakfast cereal advertisement looked particularly apt as Celtic's man of the moment covered every blade of grass for the cause.

In 1911, captain James Hay went to Newcastle and 'Sunny Jim' was appointed captain. It was not easy. Rangers were on a high, and Celtic were in a period of transition. Loney, Quinn and McMenemy were out for a long time, and not all the youngsters brought into the side were instant successes. There were two who were, however, left-half Peter Johnstone - who was the replacement for Jimmy Hay - and a spindle-shanked youngster who looked as if a good plate of soup (or indeed the Sunny Jim Force cereal!) would not be a bad idea. The boy was called

Patrick Gallacher, but very soon he became known as Patsy.

Both these players needed careful handling, albeit for different reasons. Johnstone was big, strong and aggressive, and Young would need all his strong-mindedness to keep him in his place. Gallacher, on the other hand, looked as if he could be easily intimidated by coarse defenders, like the infamous 'Dirty Galt' of Rangers, and he might need a little protection. Fortunately, 'Sunny Jim' was up to both tasks, and at the end of his first year as captain, in 1912, Celtic had repeated the previous term's success by winning the Scottish Cup.

Season 1913/14 saw Celtic lift a League and Cup double with captain James Young well to the fore, the booming Ayrshire bark prominent and often heard clearly at the back of the stand. The half-back line was now Young, Johnstone and McMaster, only marginally less effective than Young, Loney and Hay. The back three of Shaw, McNair and Dodds were reaching legendary status, and up front, there were men like the cannonball shot Andy McAtee, the evergreen Jimmy McMenemy and, above all, the great Patsy Gallacher, now giving clear, visible and consistent indications of why he would become the "most talked about man in the trenches."

But no matter how great the team was, there still needed to be leadership. Clearly Maley provided that off the field, but on the pitch, there was no doubting the authority of 'Sunny Jim.' He went out to play convinced that he was going to win, and very seldom did his convictions let him down. His own crowd loved him and - always a sign of a great player - the opposition crowds hated him.

Celtic lost their first game in the initial wartime season to Hearts at Tynecastle, but only on another two occasions in the League that term were the green-and-white colours lowered. Young played in every game. By this time, his fair hair had turned a little darker, but he was still the same 'Sunny Jim', shouting at his men and dominating the game. "Face the ball, Celtic!" became his watchword. By the turn of the year, the Celtic team really turned on the style, and with Patsy Gallacher in his glory and a new centre-forward called Jimmy McColl ('the Sniper' as he was nicknamed) taking the place of Jimmy Quinn, nothing could stop them winning the Scottish League and the Glasgow Charity Cup. What a pity there was no Scottish Cup that season!

Further delight was provided for the supporters at home and abroad the following season, when Celtic, under Young's reliable, unspectacular, yet inspiring leadership, managed to win all three competitions they were entitled to enter, namely the Scottish League, the Glasgow Cup and the Glasgow Charity Cup. The Scottish League achievement included the famous occasion on 15 April, when Celtic played two games in one day and won them both, beating Raith Rovers at Parkhead, then getting into a charabanc to motor to Motherwell to defeat the home team! A rumour ran around Glasgow that Jim was looking for a third team to play that day!

Yet 1916 saw the beginning of the end of 'Sunny Jim.' The first day of the season saw Celtic at Love Street. Celtic won 5-1, but Young injured his knee and hobbled off near the end. He missed the next game, but after that there was a partial recovery. But the Saturday of 30 September 1916 saw the end of 'Sunny Jim' Young's career. A hard tackle on a Hearts player at Parkhead caused his knee to swell to a grotesque size and he was carried off to hospital. He would remain there until after the New Year, enduring several operations, but it was soon obvious that the great 'Sunny Jim' would never play again. This was made public in February 1917, and he officially retired at the end of the season. It was no accident that the first year of Young's retirement saw Rangers win the Scottish League championship, and from then on hegemony passed slowly, reluctantly yet inexorably to the Ibrox club.

'Sunny Jim' was not destined to live long, meeting his death in a motorcycle accident in 1922. It was Monday, 4 September, when the motorcycle on which he was a pillion passenger was in collision with a tram on the Wellington Bridge, between Hurlford and his native Kilmarnock. Jim sustained head injuries from which he never recovered. He died later that evening in hospital.

He had just reached his 40th birthday, and his death was a tragic loss of life. But they never die if they leave something immortal behind them. Nine League championship medals, six Scottish Cup medals, one Scottish cap (and there should have been a great deal more) and six Scottish League caps was enough for Eugene MacBride, in An Alphabet of the Celts, to claim that 'Sunny Jim' was the greatest Celt of them all.

Chapter 14:

PETER SOMERS: ALL SEASONS WERE SUMMERS WHEN PETER PLAYED

Peter Somers was born in 1878, in Strathaven, Lanarkshire. He cut his teeth playing for Mossend Celtic, Cadzow Oak and Hamilton Academical, to whom he would return in later life. Celtic, however, had heard of him through Maley's already impressive list of contacts, and in late November 1897, he joined the club. A week later, he made his debut, and an impressive one it was, scoring and playing well in a 4-0 defeat of Third Lanark in early December. He played this game on the left-wing, although his best position would be inside-left.

He was fortunate in that he came to Celtic Park when Sandy McMahon and Johnny Campbell were there. Not only were they great men to watch – one can always learn to play the game by watching the best – but they were also very supportive and encouraging of young players, being sufficiently secure of their own ability not to feel threatened by the appearance of talented youngsters.

But this was a good Celtic team – they had recovered from their Arthurlie disaster of early 1897 – and it was not easy for Peter to force his way into the side. In season 1899/1900, he was farmed out on loan to first Clyde and then, in 1900, to Blackburn Rovers. Rovers were generally reckoned to be a 'crack' English team and Peter learned a great deal in his two years there from 1900 until 1902. So impressed were Blackburn by Somers, that they offered Celtic £200 (a not inconsiderable amount in 1902) to upgrade the loan to a permanent transfer, but Celtic were equally impressed by reports they had heard of how well he was doing and recalled him.

He was given a good run in the Celtic team in season 1902/03, but it was not a great Celtic side and although Rangers' run of four Scottish League titles in a row was broken, it was broken by Hibernian rather than Celtic. Yet there was sting in the tail of better things to come at the end of the season, when Celtic won the Glasgow Charity Cup with new players Alec Bennett and James Young making their mark.

Somers began to really impress by his passing ability and his knack of taking a goal. He also benefitted by the sheer fact that he was playing alongside so many talented young players all developing at the same time. This was said about the Quality Street Kids in the late 1960s and early 1970s, and this was an earlier example of a good young side all coming together simultaneously and, as important as anything else, getting on with each other and taking a delight in each other's success. It is very easy to look upon the 1904 Scottish Cup final as an individual effort by Jimmy Quinn, but the modest Quinn himself would never have claimed as much, and he was very appreciative of the efforts of men like Peter Somers.

Very soon, Peter would earn the nickname of Celtic's 'powder monkey." It may even have been Maley himself who bestowed him with that name, and if so, it was a very apt analogy. The 'powder monkey' in the Navy in the time of the Napoleonic Wars and earlier was the small boy who would climb into the cannon and pack the ammunition in properly prior to firing. This was exactly what Peter did in the Celtic team. He was the supplier of the ammunition for Quinn and Bennett to fire. If Alec Thomson, a generation later, was 'McGrory's fetch and carry man,' Peter Somers could claim a similar role for himself vis-a-vis Jimmy Quinn.

This did not preclude him scoring goals himself – a skill that became more prominent as his career developed – and the great thing about this team was its interdependence. Somers had an excellent relationship with James Hay behind him, Davie Hamilton on his left and Jimmy Quinn and Jimmy McMenemy on his right. Celtic were a very difficult team to play against because of their enthusiasm and their ability to change position. There was nothing static about them, and of course they were well directed by Willie Maley, now at the height of his powers.

Somers was thus lucky to come into this team, but he created his own luck as well. It very soon became apparent that there was another side to him as well on the social scene. Maley was a great believer in taking his team away for intensive training sessions at Seamill Hydro and various places on Loch Lomond and in the Trossachs. The sessions were indeed hard work, but there was also the nice side of them – good food, hotel accommodation and entertainment soirees at which players were expected to do their 'turn' at performing for their team mates, the hotel staff and the other guests, often wealthy people who would then be prevailed upon to contribute to some Celtic charity. Somers was "as nimble of foot as he was nimble of tongue," according to Willie Maley, and was a past master in the art of repartee. He was also a great pianist and could do impersonations of men like King Edward VII and even Maley himself. His talents as a pianist also came to the fore in the series of concerts that were held for Jimmy Quinn, after he had been (unfairly) suspended in 1907.

He also had the benefit of a happy marriage, having married Jane Mitchell in 1900. A happy family life is often an asset to a football player, and very soon Scotland selectors began to notice him. He had already played once for the Scottish League, in 1899 (the first of three Caps for the Scottish League), when in March 1905 he was invited to play for the full Scotland team against Ireland. He played well enough to be chosen for the 'big international' on April 1 1905, at the Crystal Palace in London, against England. Sadly, it was not one of Scotland's better occasions, and they went down 0-1, but Somers received a good "Press" and it was still a great experience to play at the Crystal Palace. And it could have been so much different if Jimmy Quinn had been playing at centre-forward, but, sadly, Jimmy had been harshly sent off the week before and was not chosen as a result. Peter would also play against Ireland in 1907 and Wales in 1909.

In 1905/06, Somers won the Glasgow Cup and the Scottish League, and in 1906/07, he was a prolific and valued member of the first team ever to win a Scottish 'double' of the Scottish Cup and the Scottish League in the same year. It had been done previously in England by Preston North End and Aston Villa, but never before in Scotland. Peter also managed to score in the Glasgow Cup final of that year, and in the Scottish Cup final he scored twice as the team defeated Hearts. Both his goals were simple tap-ins from Alec Bennett crosses, but they all count, and Somers was given the match ball as a result.

It was a pity that the Glasgow Charity Cup was not won in 1907, but season 1907/08 saw Celtic, with Somers a virtual ever-present, win everything, with the forward line of Bennett, McMenemy, Quinn, Somers and Hamilton renowned throughout the British Isles, and James Handley, in The Celtic Story, talking about "a litany that made music for him (the average Celtic supporter) in five sweet symphonies." The facts are there for everyone to see. The team won every competition they entered, something that puts them in the same bracket as 1966/67, and that really says it all. Who was the weak link in 1967? There wasn't one! And who was the weak link in 1908? Similarly, none existed. Somers scored in the finals of both the Glasgow and the Scottish Cups, and life simply could not get any better.

1909 was, of course, the year of the Scottish Cup final riot, after extra-time was refused at the end of the replay. This was lamentable, but Celtic now had eight games to play in 12 days to win the Scottish League. Somers played in seven out of eight of them in those honourable and glorious 12 days of Celtic history, and he now had won five League medals in a row.

But then a minor mystery surrounds what went wrong after that. He was the first man of that great side (other than Alec Bennett, who committed his own form of suicide by jumping ship for Ibrox) to lose his place on a regular basis. People look for a hidden agenda here – perhaps he was just a bit too nimble-tongued with Willie Maley, perhaps he was blamed for the inexplicable Glasgow Cup final replay defeat to Third Lanark in October 1908 – but it may simply be that - Somers having lost his place temporarily through injury to the superbly talented Peter Johnstone - Johnstone simply played so well that he could not really be replaced. Somers was in any case now 32, and like many players in the rough game that Scottish football undeniably was in that era, he was beginning to slow down and suffer from the multiple injuries that he had sustained.

He was transferred to Hamilton Academical (a team that he had always had a soft spot for since playing for them more than a decade ago before joining Celtic) in January 1910, but he did not last any more than a season and a half before he gave up the playing side of the game. He did not, therefore, feature in either the 1911 Scottish Cup final or its replay against Celtic. He then became a Director of the club, a year later in 1912, having by then established himself (like so many ex-football players) in the wine and spirits business.

His death was sudden. In November 1914, Peter had been to Shotts with Hamilton Accies manager Alex Raisbeck to look at a player. It was wet and cold, and Somers complained about numbness in his left foot. The diagnosis was the dramatic one of suspected gangrene, and an immediate operation was necessary in the St Andrews Nursing Home in Glasgow for the amputation of his left foot and a bit of his left leg. The operation was a success, but Peter's heart never recovered from the trauma, and he died a few days later, on November 27. All of Scottish football was shocked, for he was only 36 years-old, and his funeral at the Wellhall New Cemetery was a very busy one indeed.

Peter Somers deserves a great deal more recognition. The fact that he died at the start of what would become a dreadful war, with scarcely believable casualties, possibly meant that his death was, as it were, buried under so many other tragedies, and he was quickly forgotten about. That is a shame, for he was a very fine player indeed and well worth his place in the Edwardian Celtic side which was deservedly called "the greatest show on earth."

Chapter 15:

WILLIE LONEY: "...THERE WERE DAYS WHEN THE WIND COULDNA GET BY HIM! NO ROAD THIS WAY!"

Willie Loney was a great centre-half. The fact that he was part of Young, Loney and Hay simply says it all. Unlike quite a few other centre-halves, Willie was quiet and determined. He was big and bustling, a 'no nonsense' defender with a grim determination that a ball must be cleared at all costs. Like the other defenders of this great side, Willie preferred to dribble the ball out of trouble if he could, but he did not disdain the undignified punt up the field, if he felt that this was necessary. The important thing was that the ball must be cleared. That is why he earned the four-word nickname, 'No Road This Way.'

He had more names than that. He was called 'the Obliterator,' 'the Destroyer,' and even 'the Lion Tamer.' He was reasonably good in the air, but his strong point was definitely on the ground, where he was able to get to the ball with devastating speed and accuracy and, crucially, without fouling anyone. He was emphatically not a dirty player, but neither was he any kind of shrinking violet. He knew how to tackle, and of course the same could be said of his colleagues, the two Jimmies, Young and Hay.

The role of centre-half was quite different in Loney's time, in comparison with today. Nowadays, a centre-half or 'central defender' does not tend to come forward very much at all. Not so, in the years that Loney played. He was expected to join the attack, and if he had a good understanding with the centre-forward, they could interchange positions. He and Quinn, both great players and good friends, could do just that. Loney, we will find, scored a surprising amount of goals for a defender – 29 over the years – but that is because he was not just a defender. He could attack as well.

Comparatively little (in comparison with other early Celts) is known about his early years. We know that he was born on May 31 1879, in Denny in Stirlingshire. His father, Tom Loney, was a coal miner. Willie played for Denny Athletic until he joined Celtic in 1900 at the age of 21. He was thus very much a child of the later years of the Scottish Industrial Revolution. In that, he had a great deal in common with the other talented Celts who joined up at that time.

One of the features of Maley's Celtic was the scouting network. Maley, at least in his early years, was a very sociable, genial sort of man, who made friends easily, remembering everyone's Christian name and giving them the impression that they were the most interesting person he had talked to for a long time. The sting however was always, "Any good players for me?" It was in such a way that he discovered the strapping centre-half of Denny Athletic called Willie Loney. Maley was also shrewd enough to know that the word 'Celtic' already meant an awful lot. He was very sincere in his belief that the club should be open to men who were not Roman Catholics… but he was no fool either. Like Jock Stein, he appreciated that for those of an Irish Catholic background, Celtic had a head start.

Willie Loney was a quiet, sensible youth. He cut the fine balance between being an extrovert show-off and a player who occasionally did not value himself enough. He was quietly confident in his own abilities, although he would be the first to realise that the expectations of Denny Athletic and those of Celtic were different things altogether. Even as early as 1900, the demands of filling one of those green-and-white vertical jerseys were very high indeed. There was already a huge support – potentially greater than any other team in the United Kingdom – waiting for more triumphs like the one they had just achieved a month or two before Loney had joined the club, the Scottish Cup of 1900.

Loney was given an early introduction. An injury to Tom Hynds led to a reshuffle of the half-back line, and Loney came in at centre-half on September 17 1900, for a game against Heart of Midlothian at Tynecastle. It could hardly have been tougher, for the rivalry between Hearts and Celtic was as keen in 1900 as it was one hundred years later, the difference being that Hearts were then almost as talented as Celtic were. But Loney was up to the challenge.

The game was the Edinburgh Monday holiday fixture, and it was played against a backdrop of recruiting drives for the Boer War and an imminent General Election. Loney did not allow any of this to upset or disturb him. A few timely tackles kept the Hearts forwards at bay, and then, to the delight of the travelling Celtic fans, he scored the second goal in the 2-0 win, "sending the ball past Philip with a long shot," just before the interval, according to The Scotsman. The second half saw him as "cool as a cucumber," as he dealt with Hearts increasingly-frantic efforts to get back into the game.

His Celtic career was thus well begun, but it was December before he could claim a regular place in the team. Season 1900/01 was not, in all truth, one of Celtic's best-ever seasons, but for Loney it was a valuable, learning experience. He would learn, for example, that the Celtic crowd did not always turn up in great numbers for the team's home games (often because, quite simply, they could not afford to do so), but that they were fiercely committed to the cause. He knew what it was like to lose to Rangers and to beat them, that a trip to Dundee meant a huge crowd at a very small ground, that St Mirren supporters had a particular hatred of Celtic and what they were supposed to stand for, and above all else, on April 6 1901, he discovered what a devastating thing it is to experience defeat in the Scottish Cup final.

He had now, however, established himself in the Celtic team, and barring injury (sadly he would suffer an awful lot of those, as we shall discover) he would be there or thereabouts until 1913. His position really was centre-half, but it was not unknown for him to appear at right-half, left-half, full-back and even on the right-wing. He was a versatile player, and this reflected his adaptability as a human being. He realised that there was great potential in this Celtic team under Willie Maley. No-one, however, yet realised just how much potential there really was.

1902 and 1903 were not great seasons for the club, but Loney kept learning and then suddenly, in 1904, it all came together. After a great deal of experimentation, Maley at last discovered that his best half-back line was Young, Loney and Hay. They came together in a Cup-tie at Dens Park in February, and from then on Celtic never looked back.

There was, of course, a great deal more to Celtic than Young, Loney and Hay. There was the goalscoring of Jimmy Quinn, the artistic magic of Jimmy 'Napoleon' McMenemy and Peter Somers, not to mention the goalkeeping of Davie Adams, but it was the half-back line which was the mainstay of the team, and they stayed together barring injuries and suspensions for the six successive Scottish League Championships which characterised those great years.

Barring injuries? Sadly, in Loney's case, there were an awful lot of serious ones. More or less every year, he was out for an extended period of time. There was a broken arm in 1907, various leg injuries in 1908 and 1909, a broken wrist in early 1911 and then, later in the same year, a bout of an illness called 'British cholera,' which might well have killed him. But Loney was still a strong young man and managed to bounce back in time to win his third Scottish Cup medal in 1912, to add to the ones he had lifted in 1904 and 1908.

It was his repeated injuries that delayed his international career until 1909 and 1910, when he played twice for Scotland and three times for the Scottish League, his best game being at Ewood Park, Blackburn, on February 26 1910, when he restricted the strong English side to two goals, while Jimmy Quinn himself scored two at the other end, as Scotland won 3-2. Loney's direct opponent that day was Jack Parkinson of Liverpool, and it was presumably he whom the anonymous poet had in mind when he wrote;

"We read his praises in the evening sheets,
His worth I'm not gainsaying,
But yet we seldom see such feats,
When Willie Loney's playing!"

Loney was a man who did not have many enemies – and he was always professional enough to deal with any animosity that might have developed within Celtic Park – and he was a great friend of Jimmy Quinn.

The story went that he and Jimmy were not averse to a little tipple. One day at the Celtic Sports (before the season started), the pair of them turned up a little the worse for wear after having met a few of their idolising fans. Maley, although he did not share Stein's obsession and paranoia about alcohol, was not best pleased and mildly rebuked Loney for having had rather too much. Loney said, "Aye, boss, but you should see Quinn!" Maley then approached Quinn to express his disappointment, but Quinn said, "Aye, boss, but you should see Loney!" No-one could vouch for the truth of this story, but it was one that circulated round the support and was an indication of the close friendship of these two quiet but, in their own way, brilliant men.

When Loney won the Scottish Cup in April 1912, he was now almost 33. He played another year in 1912/13, a rather unsuccessful season apart from the Glasgow Charity Cup, and then, in 1913, he was transferred to Motherwell, leaving the centre-half spot to Peter Johnstone. He later played for Partick Thistle and Clydebank, before retiring in 1917.

His career over after the First World War, he became a saddler, a most unusual business for ex-football players, who usually become publicans, if they were not to involve themselves in football. Willie correctly realised that he did not have the temperament to be a football manager, but he did not entirely cut himself off from the game, acting as a scout for Aston Villa officially, and for Celtic unofficially. He was a regular attender at Celtic Park, not least on the famous day in August 1953 when Willie Maley, who had fallen out badly with the club, was reconciled. Loney, McMenemy and Dodds, virtually the last survivors of the great days, escorted Maley to the centre of the field that day, and how the Celtic crowd rejoiced at the sight of these great old Celts!

Willie Loney, a widower, his beloved Roseann having predeceased him, died on March 6 1956, of a cerebral embolism. He was 76 and much grieved by the Celtic community, particularly those who had seen him play. Maley, writing in The Evening Times, describes him as a "treat to watch."

There were few who would be likely to disagree.

Chapter 16:

DAVIE ADAMS: THE MIGHTY CUSTODIAN

There will not be many Celtic supporters who know much about a place called Oathlaw, between Forfar and Brechin. It sounds as if it should belong in the Wild West, and although there may not be much else to boast about in that tiny village, it was apparently the birthplace of David Robertson Adams on May 14 1883. This man became as good a goalkeeper as Celtic ever had, even though there is strong competition for such a title.

His family does not appear to have lived there for very long. They moved to Dunipace, not far away from Willie Loney's Denny or Jimmy Quinn's Croy, for that matter. Central Scotland was a very fertile ground for Celtic players, and credit must, of course, be given for that to the ubiquitous and perpetually energetic Willie Maley, who left no stone unturned in his quest to find the greatest team on earth.

Maley would have been very impressed at his first sight of Davie Adams. He had had a great goalkeeper in Dan McArthur, but Dan had now aged and had never really recovered from his very bad game in the 1901 Scottish Cup final against Hearts. A new goalkeeper was a priority. Rob McFarlane and Andy McPherson had been tried, but neither of them had satisfied completely.

Adams had appeared for Avonbridge FC, Vale of Carron FC and Dunipace Juniors before he joined Celtic in December 1902. The first thing that Maley and others would have noticed in him was his size and bulk. He was 6 feet - and in 1902 there were very few men of that size - and he weighed 14 stone. Often in these days, goalkeepers were looked upon as a figure of fun, boys who were unathletic and too fat to play outfield were given a game in the goal on the grounds that they did not have to run about too much!

Not so David Adams! He realised that he had been given a break, when he was invited to join the great Celtic side, and he determined to take full advantage. It is not clear whether he was signed as a part-timer or a full-timer at this point – often in some teams a full-time goalkeeper was considered a luxury - but he certainly trained hard. He was also an easy man to get on with and very soon was part of the traditional dressing-room banter. His very size meant that no-one took any liberties with him.

He was given a game in the Inter City League (an insignificant tournament used to fill up free Saturdays in those days) at Easter Road against Hibernian on April 11 1903, then he played against Middlesbrough on a tour game in early September, and by the end of that month he had been given his League debut in a 1-0 win over Hibs at Celtic Park. The key part of the score line was, of course, "...Hibs 0," and from then on, Davie Adams would remain Celtic's goalkeeper for the next eight years. He was remarkably free from injury. There were a couple of spectacular ones, as we shall discover, but he tended not to get injured in the way that Dan McArthur, for example, suffered repeatedly from concussion. Adams' apparent invulnerability meant that for long periods of time, Celtic could get by without having a reserve goalkeeper!

Season 1903/04 was, ultimately, a great one in the history of the club, but it was also an unsettled season, as various team formations were tried out to deploy the clearly very impressive amount of talent that was present at Celtic Park. Adams was part of that talented group and was very proud of the fact that he was in the Celtic side that played in the first-ever game at the new Hampden Park on October 31 1903. He considered that to be a great honour.

Discerning spectators noticed his clean handling of the ball, his courage, his co-ordination with his other defenders and the general aura of command that radiated from his penalty area. In those days, goalkeepers wore the same strip as other players and, therefore, Davie was a proud wearer of the green-and-white horizontal stripes in their inaugural season. Goalkeepers were also expected to come out of their goal and take part in the general play. This Adams was reluctant to do, perhaps aware of how the game was changing, in that the goalkeeper was very soon to become a goalkeeper and nothing else, but also aware that dribbling the ball was not one of his strengths. Far better to pick the ball up in his huge hands and boot it up the field.

April 16 1904 was the day that all changed for Celtic. It was, of course, Jimmy Quinn's great day, but it was very nearly 'curtains' for the infant Celtic career of Davie Adams. Rangers were two goals up early in the first half, both scored by Finlay Speedie, and both might have been prevented by Davie Adams. But he had been understandably nervous and, as often happens, became so obsessed worrying about the loss of the first one that he immediately lost a second!

Fortunately, Jimmy Quinn had levelled things before half time, and any attempt to apologise to teammates at half-time was quickly silenced. There was still a job to be done, and Adams rallied to keep Rangers out in their attacks at the start of the second half, and then, after Jimmy Quinn had done the business at the other end, he was equally on song as Rangers tried a last, desperate push.

The next two seasons saw Adams on top form, as Celtic won the League in 1905 and 1906. He was not to blame for the unfortunate defeats in the Scottish Cup in those seasons, and, very often, newspapers pay him the greatest compliment of all, by not mentioning him. Sometimes he had very little to do – he did after all have in front of him men like Donnie McLeod, Willie Orr, 'Sunny Jim' Young, Willie Loney and Jimmy Hay. By any standards, that was quite a shield! And yet we do get the occasional mention of him "keeping out a forward dash," "being invincible between the sticks," or saving a penalty kick "which was heading into the top corner but was thwarted by Adams the claw."

Celtic never felt that they had to have a deputy goalkeeper when Adams was around, and thus we have the remarkable events of the start of the 1906/07 season. Davie was playing in a pre-season friendly at Ibrox for Finlay Speedie's benefit, when he caught his hand on a nail sticking out of a post, something that put him out of action for the first nine games of the season. And who deputised for him? Celtic, as we have said, had no reserve goalkeeper but Rangers did

– the worthy Tommy Sinclair. Tommy was duly loaned out to Celtic, kept eight straight clean sheets and then won a Glasgow Cup medal, before Davie came back to play an excellent part in the winning of the first-ever Scottish League and Cup double. Tommy Sinclair had, incidentally, then gone to Newcastle and helped them win the English League that season!

Things got even better for Davie Adams in 1907/08. He was an ever-present in the team that won everything. He was totally dependable, with 21 clean sheets out of 46 starts, and only on 10 occasions did the team concede two goals. Jamie Weir had now replaced Willie Orr at left-back and Alec McNair, who had played all over the defence, was beginning to oust Donnie McLeod at right-back, but it made no difference. Adams still enjoyed the confidence of everyone. The occasional goal that was lost was still a matter for self-reproach, however. Davie remained a perfectionist. His best game in that season was the final of the Glasgow Cup, a 2-1 victory in which, it was said, that Adams on his own kept Rangers out in the second half, after Peter Somers and Davie McLean had scored the goals for Celtic.

He never achieved any international honour, not even a game for the Scottish League. This was a shame, for he would have performed creditably at that level as well. But there were reasons for him not being selected. Nothing to do with any anti-Celtic feeling on the part of the Scottish selectors, but more because they never got a chance to see Davie under any kind of pressure. He was simply part of a team which was too good, and so the Scottish goalkeeping spot went to men like Peter McBride of Preston North End, Harry Rennie of Hibernian (and later Rangers) and Jimmy Brownlie of Third Lanark, a man who, ironically, had at one point shown an interest in joining Celtic but had been frightened off by a warning that he would never be able to displace Davie Adams!

New Year's Day 1909 saw Adams play a brilliant game in a 3-1 win over Rangers but, unfortunately, pick up an injury which ruled him out of the game at Kilmarnock the following day. As we have seen, Celtic did not have a reserve goalkeeper but someone rather surprising volunteered – one 'Sunny Jim' Young! Celtic then fixed up a specialist goalkeeper for the next game, a man called Jim Oliver. Davie Adams however, recovered, and then played a glorious part in the eight games in 12 days which won the Scottish League for Celtic at the end of the season, conceding only five goals and saving a tired Celtic team on many occasions.

His next absence was far more serious. This was in late February 1910, when he succumbed to a bad dose of pneumonia. It cost Celtic dear, for it was a factor in the defeat by Clyde in the Scottish Cup semi-final, but it was far worse for Adams, out for the rest of the season. He was replaced by a man called Willie Duncan, but Adams had still played enough games to win his sixth and last League medal.

Season 1910/11 was a disappointing one for Celtic, in that they lost the League. Davie Adams, however, played consistently well, and, in any case, there was a reward for a poor season when Celtic won the Scottish Cup again. They did so without losing a single goal in a Scottish Cup tie, with Adams outstanding throughout. It was his fourth Scottish Cup medal, and he was as good a player as any because there were several occasions, not least in the first game of the final against Hamilton Academical, when Adams saved Celtic's bacon. 1910/11 was also the season in which Davie became the first-ever Celtic goalkeeper to wear a yellow jersey, for this sensible idea was now recommended and gradually gained ground in this season.

Sadly, season 1911/12 was to be Davie's last. He had recovered from his pneumonia of 1910 but one of its lasting side-effects was rheumatism, a surprisingly common complaint in the 1910s, even among fit, strong, young men like Davie Adams. It was, of course, not helped by the awful, damp, cold houses that characterised Glasgow in those days, but there was also a problem with his eyesight, and this encouraged Celtic to engage another goalkeeper, John Mulrooney, to replace him. Davie's last game for Celtic took place on December 2 1911, by sheer coincidence the debut of the spindle-shanked Patsy Gallacher.

Davie Adams retired before the end of the season due to his various health problems. Although he remained proud of his glittering career with Celtic (137 shut-outs out of 333 appearances, 4 Scottish Cups, 6 Scottish Leagues, 4 Glasgow Cups and 2 Glasgow Charity Cups), he never seemed to show any desire to involve himself with football again, other than by watching it. His health issues presumably made it easy for him to avoid the carnage of the First World War, and he spent the rest of his life in the licensing trade in East Kilbride and Tranent. Not all his clientele realised just exactly who he was, although they might have guessed when they saw those huge goalkeeper hands holding a pint glass! He died in Edinburgh in November 1948, and those who saw him play were deeply saddened. He was a fine goalkeeper.

Chapter 17:

JAMES 'DUN' HAY: CAPTAIN COURAGEOUS AND CONFIDENT

No-one seems to know why Jimmy Hay earned the somewhat strange nickname of 'Dun.' Other nicknames of the time, like Napoleon, the Icicle and the Obliterator, are more easily explained, but why 'Dun?' It matters little, but what is in no doubt whatsoever is the contribution that this man James 'Dun' Hay made to the great Celtic team of this era.

For one thing, he was a member of Young, Loney and Hay, and that is, in itself, sufficient commendation. He was the left-half, and as he could play at left-back as well (as he did when injuries to other players demanded it), he tended to play a little behind the other two. 'Sunny Jim' could go forward – indeed it was difficult to contain his enthusiasm – and Willie Loney was, by nature and inclination not to mention the convention of the time, an attacking centre-half, so 'Dun' would tend to stay that wee bit behind them. But when the three of them moved forward together – "like a Russian troika pulling the Czar through the snow" – they were a sight to behold. Scottish football has never seen anything like it before or since. James Handley, in The Celtic Story, refers to them as the "Porthos, Athos and Aramis of the football field," and even today, more than one hundred years later, the average Celtic supporter can probably be relied upon "to complete the following.. Young, Loney and....?"

The other point about Hay was that he was the captain from 1906 onwards. No matter how great a team one has, they will always still need leadership. Maley provided that off the field, of course, but once the 11 men cross the touchline, the captain takes over. Therefore, when 'Sunny Jim' needed calming down, when Jimmy Quinn had just been injured yet again by a brutal defender, when Davie Hamilton was losing confidence or when young Jamie Weir was needing reassuring, captain Hay was always there.

His relationship with Maley was complex. Hay was the channel, the conduit between players and manager. Maley prided himself, at that time of his career at least, on his man-management skills. Nevertheless, there were times when relationships were not as good as they could have been, particularly after a defeat, when Maley's Edwardian version of what is now called 'the hairdryer treatment' could alienate and upset a few players. It was then the job of the diplomatic James Hay to pick everyone up. In this he excelled, and very few had a bad word to say about the Ayrshire maestro and mediator.

He was born on February 9 1881, in a mining village that now barely exists called Woodbank, near Ayr. He was the youngest of a family of nine and it would have been assumed that he was destined for a life underground as a miner, unless he made an effort to move. In Hay's case, it was a talent for playing football, and he found himself playing for Ayr FC in season 1902/03, when he came to the attention of Willie Maley of Celtic FC. Maley offered Ayr the huge sum of £50 for the services of this talented defender and midfielder, and a mighty career was launched.

Celtic, of course, were a huge club. It is not impossible that there may have been a few eyebrows raised about the young Hay joining the so called 'Catholic' or 'Irish' team. Fortunately, Hay himself did not bother. He was far too interested in football, and, in any case, he was not the only non-Catholic to play for Celtic. Indeed, another non-Catholic Ayrshireman had just arrived at Celtic Park, in his case via Bristol Rovers. This was 'Sunny Jim' Young.

The year 1903 was significant. Celtic had had a few poor seasons, but things now changed, not least in the strips, for, at the start of the season, green-and-white horizontal stripes replaced vertical ones, giving the teams a "faster, more youthful appearance." It was, indeed, a young team, and following the victory in the Scottish Cup final of 1904, Celtic really took off to become the best team that Scotland had yet seen.

Famously, that team got on well together. The captain until 1906 was

Willie Orr, and Hay, who would take over from him in that year, learned a great deal from Willie. Hay hardly missed a game in his early years, being lucky to avoid injury, and although he occasionally played at left-back when he had to, left-half was his position, especially when after 1904, the famous half-back line bedded in. Hay had also settled his private life, having married Susan Boyd in March 1905, and children soon came along. Although the wages that he received from Celtic would have been nothing in comparison to what professional football players earn today, it would, nevertheless, have been an adequate living, and a great deal more than what some of his family would have earned down the mines.

Hay was the obvious choice for captain in 1906, when Willie Orr showed signs of wanting to give it up. It was an orderly transition. A writer in The Scottish Referee claimed that the qualities of captaincy of a football team are "ability, tact and geniality," and captain James Hay had all three of these "in judicious measure." He was not like Dan Doyle before him nor 'Sunny Jim' after him, a shouter or a cajoler of players. Hay seldom lost his temper or raised his voice, believing that calmness was a great thing, and that if everything was well-planned and everyone acted according to the plan, then little could really go wrong for the team.

Certainly, nothing went too far wrong in his first season as captain, when Celtic became the first team to win a League and Cup double, in 1907. By this time, the team had gone to the continent together, unashamedly considering themselves as some sort of footballing missionaries, and it was a feature of the team that there were very few tantrums and fallings out. Even the players who were temporarily out of favour were always considered, and, indeed, considered themselves to be part of the club. This was a great tribute to manager Maley and captain Hay.

But serious trouble hit Hay in late 1907. Sometime round about Christmas, he had begun to experience abdominal pains and a slight fever. It was appendicitis, a condition that was normally considered a killer at that time, although there had been a few successes recently with an operation, not least with King Edward VII, whose Coronation in 1902 had to be delayed for this reason. But it was still a very risky business indeed. On New Year's Day 1908, 'Dun' was in the St Elizabeth's Nursing Home in Glasgow, undergoing the operation. Celtic supporters watching the 1-1 draw against Rangers at Celtic Park talked about their captain in hushed tones, and the worst was expected.

For a few days, his life was in danger, but eventually Maley was able to tell the Press that the operation had gone well, the effects of the anaesthetic had worn off, there was no other infection and that 'Dun' was recovering. He was out of the side, however, until March, but the bounce-back was then spectacular, for, by the end of April, he had led his team to another League and Cup double, and followed it up with the Glasgow Charity Cup in May. This meant that Hay's Celtic side had won every competition that they entered. Not without cause, were they called "The Greatest Show On Earth!"

Hay continued to play for and captain Celtic until summer 1911. It was then that he moved to Newcastle United. Much has been made about an argument with Maley over money, but it may well have been that Hay, now 30 years old, simply felt that he wanted a change. It was certainly an honour to be asked to replace 'Peter The Great' at St James' Park, Peter McWilliam, who had been injured playing for Scotland and has been hailed as the best left-half of all time. Newcastle United, under a Scottish manager called Frank Watt, had dominated English football in the same way that Celtic had dominated Scottish football in that era, and it seemed a good choice. Hay played for Newcastle until 1915, never winning any honour with the club but always maintaining their honoured and respectable place in English football. In 1915, when English football more or less ground to a halt in any meaningful sense, Hay returned to Scotland to work in the mines for a spell, and then, latterly, to serve in the Royal Field Artillery.

Hay's Scotland career was also illustrious. He played 11 times for his country between 1905 and 1914. Four of these games were against England, and he was never on the losing side against them, drawing in 1911 (he was captain in that 1-1 draw at Goodison Park) and in 1912, and beating them in the two glorious and victorious internationals of 1910 and 1914. In 1910, it was Quinn who was the hero, and in 1914, McMenemy earned most of the plaudits, but in each case, Hay played splendidly, and was delighted for the more spectacular heroics of his two Celtic comrades.

When the war was over, so too was Hay's playing career, although he coached a little with both Clydebank and Ayr United. He became the manager of Ayr United in summer 1924, but was (unbelievably) suspended sine die for blowing the whistle on one of his Directors, Tom Steen, who had offered referee Tom Dougray a bribe in 1925. Neither Hay nor Dougray would countenance anything like this, but Steen had connections in the SFA (he was the Treasurer!) and the authorities took his side. Hay refused to withdraw his allegations and was out of the game for a while, before he was eventually re-instated.

He probably had had enough of the game by now, and although he did some scouting for Newcastle United, he had little involvement in the game. This did not mean that he did not retain some interest in his former clubs, and if he had fallen out with Willie Maley in 1911, it was soon all made up. He was an honoured guest at the famous Celtic Golden Jubilee Dinner, a matter of days after the club had won the Empire Exhibition Trophy in 1938. Sadly, so many of the great team that he had played for, notably 'Sunny Jim,' Peter Somers and Peter Johnstone, were no longer there to meet him.

Jimmy was an insurance agent in Ayr during the 1930s. A war had effectively brought his stellar playing career to an end, and he died at the start of another, on April 4 1940. He was only 59, his funeral well-attended by men like Willie Loney, Jimmy Quinn, Alec McNair and Joe Dodds. In his excellent biography of 'Dun,' his grandson Roy Hay tells how in the funeral address, Willie Maley talks about him being an "honest man." This may have been the ritual thing that anyone says about a man from Ayr, or it might have been a comment on the business with Ayr United in 1925, from which he emerged with his integrity unimpeached.

He was certainly a great servant of the Celtic Football Club. He was not flamboyant, but he was whole-hearted, dedicated, professional and, above all else, he loved playing for the club. Like so many other men who were not, by birth, Celts, he very soon made it his business to become one. No-one wore the green-and-white with more passion, devotion, commitment and skill than James 'Dun' Hay.

Chapter 18:

JIMMY MCMENEMY: THE NAPOLEON WHO NEVER MET HIS WATERLOO

The problem with Jimmy McMenemy is that you don't know where to start, nor where to finish. His contribution to the Celtic cause is huge, and, indeed, there is a strong case for saying that, if one allows for his work as a trainer and tactician in the late 1930s, he was the greatest Celt of all time. Possibly, Jimmy was marginally less brilliant than Patsy Gallacher, and maybe lacked the strong personality of someone like Billy McNeill, but he is certainly in with a shout for the ultimate accolade.

He played for the team between 1902 and 1920, won 11 League titles, 6 Scottish Cups (plus another with Partick Thistle in 1921) and played 12 times for Scotland, at least twice being the hero of Scotland when they beat England, in 1910 and 1914, and was never on the losing side!

But even these statistics do not do anything like justice to this man, who was a prince among players for so long. He was blessed with longevity, dying in 1965 having been born in 1880. He attended Celtic games at Parkhead almost to the end, and it was difficult to reconcile his prolifically productive footballing career with the image of the smallish, well-dressed, dapper old man with a soft hat who talked to everyone who recognised him and greeted him with "Hello, Jimmy," or "Hello, Nap." In Homer's Odyssey, Odysseus at one point says, "I have heard it said that sometimes Gods walk among men." This was surely one such example.

Why was he called 'Napoleon?'

Some say that there was a slight facial resemblance (and certainly they were of similar build) to the little Corsican, but it was more because, even after Waterloo, the British remained in awe of Napoleon for his tactical knowledge and versatility. This was McMenemy's forte as well. Maley said that, to McMenemy, the football field was like a chess board, and that all moves were worked out well in advance. There was nothing casual or lucky about him.

Jimmy's early years were spent in Rutherglen, and he signed for Celtic, it was said, "up a close in Union Street," in May 1902. While the actual location is a matter of some doubt, the reason for his recruitment was obvious, not least his performance in the Scottish Junior Cup final, when Rutherglen Glencairn beat Maryhill.

He scored on his debut, against Port Glasgow Athletic in November 1902, and was in and out of the team for the rest of the 1902/03 season, but by the time the triumphant Scottish Cup campaign for 1904 began, Jimmy McMenemy was the regular Celtic inside-right. He had all that was necessary. He was a tricky dribbler, a visionary passer of a ball and the ability to 'read' a game, knowing who was having a good or a bad game and acting accordingly. He was not particularly fast, but he did have a great turn of speed and, for a small man, he had powerful shoulders and could not be easily be pushed off the ball. He also had a great shot. He could score goals, and how Celtic Park would reverberate to a McMenemy individual goal!

But he was also a success as a human being. The attitude was always right. He was, on occasion, rather too self-effacing and there was never any of the wrong type of arrogance. He was confident, however, in his own ability. He was never insecure enough to make any problems for a teammate. He knew that Quinn, for all his extraordinary and prodigious ability and achievements, occasionally needed to be picked up and encouraged. Somers, on the other hand, occasionally needed a gentle 'put down' now and again, and 'Sunny Jim' said a lot of things in the heat of the moment that weren't really all that well thought out.

Sadly, 'Napoleon' was not able to dissuade his old friend Alec Bennett from going to Rangers in 1908, but he did 'read' another situation very well in 1912, when he realised that Patsy Gallacher was at least as good an inside-right as he himself was, and in agreement with Maley, McMenemy agreed to move to inside-left to accommodate the diminutive but awesome Irishman. Thus, the forward line of McAtee,

Gallacher, McColl, McMenemy and Browning became almost as good a forward line as Bennett, McMenemy, Quinn, Somers and Hamilton had been, and that is saying something!

A feature of McMenemy's play was that he took every game seriously. He would approach and prepare for the visit of Port Glasgow Athletic or Morton to Celtic Park with the same calm determination as he would a Scottish Cup final at Hampden, or a visit to the difficult grounds of Ibrox, Brockville and Dens Park (Falkirk and Dundee were frequent thorns in Celtic's flesh in McMenemy's time), or indeed an international for Scotland. Every opposition was worthy of respect. It was a lesson that many people forgot.

McMenemy played in the 'double' season in 1907, the 'clean sweep' season of 1908 and the season of 1909 which was defamed by the Hampden riot at the Scottish Cup final but glorified by the eight games in 12 days which won Celtic the Scottish League. He played in seven of these eight games, and was very unhappy when an injury ruled him out of the other one, never complaining, always the consummate professional and always driven by the desire to win.

Jimmy was always known by his famous war cry, "Keep the Heid, Celtic." He was a man who was never likely to be bullied because he could hold his own, but he was also very seldom in any trouble with referees. He appreciated that football was an emotional, passionate sort of game, but he had also come to see that the game was usually won by those who remained calm, who did not rise to provocation (whether about religion, nationality or anything else) and who realised that, no matter how grim things could look, there were some ways in which the day could still be saved.

One occasion where he could not save Celtic, however, came in March 1910. He had played for Scotland against Wales, on March 5, and had been brutally targeted by the Welsh defenders, who quite rightly identified him as Scotland's key man. He was thus unable to play the next week in the Scottish Cup semi-final against Clyde, and as Celtic were also short of 'Sunny Jim' Young, who was suspended, and goalkeeper Davie Adams, who had pneumonia, they went down 3-1, the first Scottish Cup tie they had lost since 1906. 'Napoleon' was back, however, to lead them to their sixth successive Scottish League title in April, and that was after he had become one of the goalscoring heroes of Scotland for his part in the 1910 international against England. The other hero, we are not surprised to discover, was Jimmy Quinn!

A surprising thing about McMenemy was that he matured with age. A strong case could be made for saying that his best year was 1914, when he was 34! He opened it with a great goal against Rangers at Parkhead on New Year's Day, beating five men before hammering home. He scored for Scotland against England in April, and was the star of the Celtic side which won a League and Cup double later on that month. Later that spring, he played his part in dazzling them all in Europe as well.

Although the dark war days descended, they were not completely dark for McMenemy, for Celtic won the League in 1915, 1916 and 1917, and one particular occasion in October 1915, McMenemy revealed his courage. It was the Glasgow Cup final, played at the same time as the horrendous Battle of Loos. Both McMenemy and Joe Dodds had lost a brother in this engagement, and Maley put it to them that if they wanted to miss this game, they could. To Maley's delight, both insisted on playing, and Celtic beat Rangers 2-0. It didn't bring his brother back, but it eased the family pain.

Jimmy worked in the shipyards in the war years (full time football was not allowed), and took part in the 'two games in a day' in 1916 which won the Scottish League that year. He won the League in 1917 as well, but not in 1918, when a bad knee injury began to cause trouble. He also had reason to believe that he was about to be 'combed out,' and compelled to enlist as a soldier, a job that would never have suited the peaceful and kindly Jimmy. He therefore announced that he was retiring from football. He was 38, and it would have been no great surprise. But there was still a little bit to go yet!

For some reason, the call-up papers never came. McMenemy had been working in the shipyards in Belfast for a spell, and more or less as the war fizzled out in November, announced that he was now returning to Celtic Park. Except, he did not, and there was a sinister reason for that. Jimmy was one of the victims of the 'Spanish flu.' He had a particularly virulent dose of it and for a while it was "touch and go," according to The Glasgow Observer but the 'Parkhead Foch,' (a change from Napoleon! Foch was the current French General who had dictated the Armistice terms!) pulled through. On December 14 1918, the Parkhead crowd rose as a man, some of them with unashamed tears in their eyes, to greet the return of Jimmy McMenemy redivivus (returned to life) as he ran out of the Parkhead pavilion. Willie McStay arrived back from the forces the same day and Andy McAtee returned early in the New Year (required for his work as a miner). These were the first steps to the recapture of the Scottish League in May 1919.

Jimmy played for Celtic until 1920. He earned his last Scottish cap at the age of 39 years 154 days in March 1920, something that stood as a record for 90 years, but to the disappointment of many, he parted company with Celtic that summer. It was felt that he still had quite a lot to offer, and he proved that point quite conclusively by going to Partick Thistle and winning their only Scottish Cup for them in 1921, beating, of all people, Rangers at, of all places, Celtic Park! It was an extraordinary achievement enjoyed by Thistle and Celtic fans alike.

His playing career now fizzled out, but he still had a glorious sunset to come, and that was in the years of the late 1930s, when he became the Celtic trainer. The other Napoleon returned from Elba, now this one was back as well. It was a rare brainwave from those who ran Celtic in those days. Maley was now depressive, frequently ill and not always easy to deal with, prone to talk about his great "Celts of old," when he should have been paying more attention to the Celts of today. But what a great idea to get one of his "Celts of old," arguably even the best of them, to run the Celts of today. Technically the 'trainer,' 'Napoleon,' in fact, was in charge of the team.

And could there have been a better man?

Friendly, knowledgeable, sympathetic, understanding, kindly, hard-working, modest, a tactical genius, and a man whom Maley and the Board could trust, Jimmy McMenemy was successful in at least one particular area. Delaney, MacDonald, Crum, Divers and Murphy were famous for their ability to interchange position at will and at speed with almost telepathic understanding of each other, and to make it very difficult for the opposition to mark them. And why could they do that so slickly? Why, for no other reason than that Bennett, McMenemy, Quinn, Somers and Hamilton could do the same!

So, perhaps he was the greatest Celt of them all!

Years after he retired, Jimmy and his old friend Dave McLean went to the famous 7-1 game in October 1957. After the game was over, and the Scottish League Cup presented, the two warriors went down to the Celtic dressing-room to congratulate them. They were immediately recognised and admitted, and great men like Peacock, Evans, Tully, Fernie and Collins, at the greatest moment of their lives, listened in respectful silence to the sincere congratulations of, yes, the greatest Celt of them all!